UNDERSTANDING AFGHANISTAN

This book delves into the history of Afghanistan, its people, and its relationship with its neighbors, to unravel the intricate politics and ethnolinguistic diversity of the country.

It discusses the history of innumerable invasions which left imprints over the country and its people and created a complex fabric of different ethnic, linguistic, religious, and cultural groups. The volume looks at the various empires which warred over the land including the Persian, Greek, Mongol, and Sassanid dynasties, as well as the later interferences by the British and the Russians and the emergence of the Taliban. It examines the correlations between war, power politics, religion, local governance, and the opium trade and economy in Afghanistan. The author, through personal stories and anecdotes of his visits and journeys in Afghanistan, provides a very rich and extensive view of Afghan politics, culture, and history. The relationship between Afghanistan and Pakistan and Afghanistan's unique position in the politics of the region is also a thread which runs through the entire book.

This book will be a great resource (and of interest) to researchers and students of politics, history, Central and South Asian Studies, war and international relations, political economy, and peace and reconciliation studies. It will also interest journalists, diplomats, and international development organizations.

Abdul Qayyum Khan earned his PhD in Agricultural Economics from Colorado State University and received his Master's in Economics from Quaid-i-Azam University in Pakistan. He has worked as a Project Director at the University of Illinois at Urbana-Champaign (UIUC) and New Mexico State University. He has also worked with the United States Agency for International Development (USAID) and Food and Agriculture Organization (FAO) of the United Nations.

UNDERSTANDING AFGHANISTAN

History, Politics, and the Economy

Abdul Qayyum Khan

LONDON AND NEW YORK

First published 2022
by Routledge
2 Park Square, Milton Park, Abingdon, Oxon OX14 4RN

and by Routledge
605 Third Avenue, New York, NY 10158

Routledge is an imprint of the Taylor & Francis Group, an informa business

© 2022 Abdul Qayyum Khan

The right of Abdul Qayyum Khan to be identified as authors of this
work has been asserted by him in accordance with sections 77 and 78 of
the Copyright, Designs and Patents Act 1988.

All rights reserved. No part of this book may be reprinted or reproduced
or utilised in any form or by any electronic, mechanical, or other
means, now known or hereafter invented, including photocopying and
recording, or in any information storage or retrieval system, without
permission in writing from the publishers.

Trademark notice: Product or corporate names may be trademarks
or registered trademarks, and are used only for identification and
explanation without intent to infringe.

British Library Cataloguing-in-Publication Data
A catalogue record for this book is available from the British Library

Library of Congress Cataloging-in-Publication Data
A catalog record has been requested for this book

ISBN: 978-0-367-72273-9 (hbk)
ISBN: 978-1-032-05447-6 (pbk)
ISBN: 978-1-003-19837-6 (ebk)

DOI: 10.4324/9781003198376

Typeset in Bembo
by Deanta Global Publishing Services, Chennai, India

Dedicated to the men, women, and children of Afghanistan and to the memories of late Oval Myers of Southern Illinois University, Carbondale, and late Mohammad Yasin Mohsini, former Dean, Faculty of Agriculture, Kabul University

CONTENTS

List of figures	*ix*
Preface	*x*
Acknowledgments	*xiii*
Glossary	*xiv*
Select Chronology	*xv*

1	Ancient history of Afghanistan	1
2	Genghis Khan and his dynasty	34
3	Amir Temur and his dynasty	51
4	Rise and Fall of Durrani Dynasty	69
5	The British Interference in Afghanistan	79
6	Struggle for Independence of Afghanistan	99
7	Rise and Fall of the Communist Regime in Afghanistan	122
8	Rise and fall of Taliban	135
9	Land and people	145
10	The gorges crossed by the foreign invaders	160

viii Contents

11 Wedding ring tossed in the Oxus River   165

12 The Crossing of the Oxus River   170

13 The trio   174

14 Nauroz   179

15 The opiates economy of Afghanistan   181

Index   *197*

FIGURES

I.1	Gorges crossed by the foreign invaders	xviii
1.1	Rivers of Pakistan	8
9.1	Agricultural Market in Mazar Sharif, Balkh	150
10.1	Salang Pass	163
15.1	Poppy Crop in Afghanistan	194

PREFACE

After the fall of Taliban in 2001, the United States and other international donors started assisting Afghanistan in its rehabilitation and economic development. One such activity was implemented by the University of Illinois at Urbana-Champaign, which I led as the Director, Field Operations. The activity related to the capacity building of agriculture sector in Afghanistan. This activity provided me with an opportunity to work with ministry officials; departments, faculties and students of universities; vocational schools; farmers; and the private sector. I engaged with them, worked with them, broke bread with them, and traveled throughout Afghanistan. I noticed that the devastation of the war and the destruction of their yard did not nudge their morale. They endured their suffering with courage and dignity. They had lost their families, houses, and possessions and were left only with body and soul, but did not compromise on their faith, independence, and pride. They did not lose hope and were determined for quick recovery of their homeland. They were hungry for the knowledge to transform their condition, to become the consummate professionals to play their role in the economic development of Afghanistan. I became curious about these people who had stood against the many superpowers and empires and protected the independence of their yard and pride. It spun my mind to know about them, who they are, where they came from, and whose remnants they were. I knew that this would involve a lot of research and my mind continued spinning to find answers to these questions.

My mind overwhelmed me to sacrifice my developmental work in the field and to embark on a research project to find answers to these questions. After my extensive experience of nine years in Kabul, Afghanistan, and having read numerous books on the country, I felt many of these resources were unable to fill the void with regard to understanding the people of Afghanistan, because they just paid a lip service to their predecessors. This prompted me to use my first-hand

Preface **xi**

experience of working with the people of Afghanistan and further research about them to author a book that would give a holistic history of Afghanistan and its people from the key perspective of invaders, people, Islam, and drugs.

The invasions of the foreigners in the past two thousand and five hundred years have created a complex fabric of the different ethnic, linguistic, religious, and cultural groups with their different attitudes, behavior, culture, and temperaments. To understand Afghanistan, it becomes necessary to know their predecessors who came as invaders. Equally, it becomes important to understand the Afghans who acquired different attributes being subject to the foreign invaders.

This book covers the traces of the imprints of all those invaders who committed a trespass in the yard of Afghanistan over a period of more than two thousand five hundred years of established history. To know those invaders would help to understand the Afghans. This book is organized into fifteen chapters which are related to different aspects of the history of Afghanistan. Chapter 1 discusses the ancient times or prehistory of Afghanistan being the subject of the Persian empire, the Greek empire, the Sakas from Central Asia, the Parthians, the Kushan dynasty, the Sassanid dynasty, and the Arab Muslims, who transformed the lives of the people of the region of Central Asia, Persia, Afghanistan, and modern-day Pakistan by bringing them into the fold of Islam with which they are attached to this day as a way of their life.

Chapters 2 and 3 relate to the Mongol invaders in 13th century AD. Chapter 2 discusses how Genghis Khan damaged the infrastructure of Afghanistan by mass killing and razing to the ground the big cities of Herat, Nishapur, Balkh, Bamian, and other places which were not able to recover and be restored in a period of hundred years. Chapter 3 discusses how after hundred years of Genghis Khan, Tatar Amir Temur or Tamerlane or the Temurid dynasty, which landed on the territories of Persia, Afghanistan, and modern-day Pakistan, was different from Genghis Khan and why it was considered a period of glorious history. The Moghul dynasty (1526–1857) that was founded by Zahir-ud-din Babur, a descendant of Genghis Khan and Amir Temur, who ruled the Indian subcontinent, has been briefly discussed. After the Moghul dynasty, Afghanistan became the subject of the Safavid dynasty of Persia ruled by Nadir Quli Beg, also known as Nadir Shah. In 1747, how the assassination of Nadir Shah by his Qizilbash military officers led to the circumstances that helped another military officer, Ahmad Shah Abdali, to disassociate and create an independent country in the name of Afghanistan from the Safavid dynasty has also been discussed.

Chapters 4 through 8 discuss how Afghanistan emerged as an independent country under the Durrani dynasty of the Saddozai tribe.The chapters also discuss why and how Afghanistan remained an unstable country under the Mohammadzais of the Barakzai tribe after the Durrani dynasty. The causes of patricide and fratricide among Mohammadzais have been discussed. The circumstances under which Afghanistan was subjugated by the British and the factors that compelled the British to grant sovereignty to Afghanistan in 1919 have been briefly discussed. A detailed discussion has been provided on how the

xii Preface

communist regime was installed in Afghanistan by Russia that culminated in the occupation of Afghanistan by Russia, how the Mujahidin fought the Russians and compelled them to withdraw, and finally how the Taliban managed to hijack power and how they were quashed.

Chapter 9 discusses the land and the people of Afghanistan. The main dominant ethnic groups and political parties have been identified and discussed. Chapter 10 discusses and identifies what gorges were used by the foreign invaders to get in and out of Afghanistan. Chapters 11 through 14 discuss the nature of the gender relations and other socioeconomic concerns in Afghanistan.

Chapter 15 discusses the correlation between the Afghan–Russian war and opium production and the importance of narcotics in the economy of Afghanistan. This chapter discusses and identifies Afghanistan as a trendsetter for the global production of opium and heroin.

An attempt has been made to learn about the invaders and their remnant indifferent ethnic groups with their attitudes, behavior, attributes, culture, and temperaments. The Afghans have been identified as very independent people who cannot compromise on their independence, faith, and culture. In truth, it is easy to invade Afghanistan but it is difficult to actually conquer it. The main purpose is to know the history of the Afghani predecessors to understand the Afghans and their country. That's what this whole book is about.

ACKNOWLEDGMENTS

I am thankful to Shahab and Naureen for the encouragement they gave for embarking on the project of authoring a book on Afghanistan. I am deeply thankful to Shahab, who has helped me in preparation of the maps and figures.

I thankfully acknowledge the help and assistance from my numerous Afghan friends, just a few to mention here: the late Mohammad Yasin Mohsini, former Dean, Faculty of Agriculture, Kabul University; Abdul Qayyum Ansari, Dean, Faculty of Agriculture, Balkh University; Agha Mohammad Jabarkhel; Hazrat Hussain Khaurin; Sadruddin; Mohammad Asif; Mohammad Kabeer Sharifi; Rabbani; Mohammad Rauf Yaqubi; Mohammad Ibrahim; Saida Jan; Afzal Anwari; Khalid Osmani; Akram Anwari; and many students and faculty members of Kabul, Nangarhar, Kandahar, Balkh, and Herat universities.

Specially, I am beholden to my trusted and loyal driver, Babrak, escorted by his brother Ahmad Shah, who drove me safely throughout the country during my stay of nine years in Afghanistan. Mohammad Agha Jabarkhel was my guide in Afghanistan.

GLOSSARY

anda	Sworn brothers
Diyat	Blood money, which is the payment in the form of money if one faithful kills another faithful unlawfully
ger	Felt tents
Gur Khan	Title in the Mongol steppe, meaning supreme khan
Hissar	Citadel
Jihad	Holy physical or nonphysical struggle to defend Islam
khuriltai	Official council for making decisions
Kotal	Hill
Loya Jirga	Traditional governing council
Mujahidin	Warriors of Islam
Mullah	Religious leader
Nauroz	Iranian/Persian New Year's Day
Naurozi	A gift that a boy gives to his fiancée on the day of Nauroz
Oxus	Greek name for the Amu River
Pul	Bridge
Pushtunwali	Pushtun's code of conduct that sets obligation of revenge (badal), hospitality (melmastia), and sanctuary (nanawati)
Qisas	Law of equality in Islam as life for life, eye for eye, tooth for tooth, and wounds equal for equal
Ramadhan	Ninth month of Islamic calendar when the Muslims fast throughout the month
Satrap	Governor or viceroy to the ancient Persian empire
Surah	One of the chapters of Holy Quran
Surkh	Red
Taliban	Religious students
tumen	Army unit of ten thousand
ulus	Domain such as Chaghatai ulus

SELECT CHRONOLOGY

BC

550–330   Afghanistan subject to the Achaemenid empire founded by Cyrus the Great.

330   Bessos overthrows and kills the last king, Darius-III, of the Achaemenid empire and becomes the king.

329   Alexander pursues and executes Bessos and conquers the Achaemenid empire.

327   Alexander defeats Oxyartes, the satrap of Bactria (Balkh), and marries his beautiful daughter Rhoxane. Alexander conquers the whole of Afghanistan. Afghanistan becomes subject to the Macedonian empire.

326   Alexander defeats King Poros of Jhelum and the Mallian tribes of Multan, Pakistan.

323   Alexander dies in Babylon (Iraq).

135   Afghanistan becomes subject to the Kushan dynasty.

AD

226   Ardsheer establishes the Sassanid dynasty by overthrowing the Kushan dynasty. Afghanistan becomes subject to the Sassanid dynasty.

634   Twenty-one-year-old Yazdjurd ascends to the throne as the last Sassanian king.

644   The Muslim warrior Ahnaf bin Qeis captures Herat and Afghanistan falls under the Muslim rule. The Muslims eliminate the mighty Persian empire.

xvi Select Chronology

1189	Temujin after beating the Kereyid, Jurkin, Taycichiud, and Jadaran tribes of the steppe becomes the khan of his own tribe.
1206	Temujin becomes Genghis Khan, a title which he himself chose and was approved by the khuriltai of his tribe.
1219	Genghis Khan captures Bokhara, Samarkand, and Khwarizm Shah's empire.
1221	Genghis Khan captures Azerbaijan, Georgia, Urgench, Termez, Uzbekistan, Balkh, Herat, Nishapur, Bamian, Ghazni, and Peshawar. Afghanistan becomes subject to Genghis Khan's empire.
1222	Genghis Khan crosses the Indus River and reaches Multan. Due to the hot weather, he returns to Afghanistan.
1227	Genghis Khan dies. Before his death, he distributes his territories among his four sons. Jochi gets the territory in the west of the Irtish river known as the Golden Horde. Chaghatai gets Central Asia. Ogodei gets western Mongolia. Tolui gets the seat of his father in Mongolia.
1258	Hulegu, the grandson of Genghis Khan, captures Baghdad and destroys it. He also captures Damascus without any resistance.
1260	September: The sultan of Egypt, Baybars, defeats Hulegu at the battle of Ain-al-Jalut known as the Spring of Goliath in modern-day Israel. This defeat of the Mongols stops the expansion of their empire.
1370	Tatar Amir Temur defeats Amir Hussain of Balkh and captures Balkh. Hussain is killed and his wife Saray Mulk Khanum becomes the senior wife of Amir Temur. At Balkh, Amir Temur crowns himself as the imperial ruler. Afghanistan is now subject to Temur's empire.
1393	Temur takes over Baghdad and Egypt.
1398	Temur takes over Multan in Punjab of modern-day Pakistan and then conquers Delhi after defeating Sultan Mahmud. After plundering the city, Temur leaves Delhi without any ruler.
1401	Temur takes over Damascus and ruins the ancient Umayyad Mosque.
1504	Temur and Genghis Khan's descendant, Mohammad Zahir-ud-din Babur, capture Kabul, Ghazni, and Kandahar. Afghanistan becomes a subject of the Mughal dynasty.
1526	Babur attacks and captures Delhi by defeating Ibrahim Lodi of the Lodi dynasty. He becomes the ruler of Delhi and lays the foundation of the Moghul dynasty.
1709	Mir Wais is released by the Safavids. He organizes his forces and kills the Safavid governor of Kandahar, Gurgin Khan. At the same time, the Abdali Pushtuns take Herat from the Safavids.
1739	Nadir Shah of the Safavid dynasty forays into India and defeats the Moghuls and captures Delhi. Nadir Shah gets hold of the famous Koh-i-Noor diamond and brings back a lot of booty from India.
1747	Qazilbash officers of his army kill Nadir Shah. The death of Nadir Shah provides an opportunity to Ahmad Shah Durrani to proclaim an independent Afghanistan. Ahmad Shah becomes the first king and lays the

Select Chronology **xvii**

foundation of the Durrani dynasty in Afghanistan which ruled for ninety years until Dost Mohammad became the Amir-ul-Mominin in 1837.

1863 Dost Mohammad dies and is succeeded by his son Sher Ali Khan. Dost is buried at Herat.

1880 The British install Abdur Rahman as the Amir.

1893 Abdur Rahman signs the Durand Line Agreement with the British Foreign Secretary, Mortimer Durand, on November 12, at Rawalpindi. Abdur Rahman rules for twenty-one years and is succeeded by his son Habibullah, who ratifies the Durand Line Agreement.

1978 Nur Mohammad Taraki, with the support of Russia, overthrows Daud and kills him and his family and takes over the government as the communist president and the prime minister.

1979 The seven major **Mujahidin** groups, with the help of the American CIA and the Pakistani ISI, fight the Russians. Whatever US contributes, Saudi Arabia matches it.

1988 Russian President Gorbochov announces the withdrawal of the Red Army that will be complete within a period of ten months starting on May 15, 1988.

1996 Taliban enter Kabul and kill Najibullah and hang Najibullah and his brother's bodies in the square.

1997 Pakistan, Saudi Arabia, and the UAE recognize the Taliban government.

1999 The UN Security Council demands Afghanistan to handover Osama bin Laden within one month. The Taliban consider it against their traditions and don't yield. The UN imposes sanctions and freezes their assets.

2001 August: The Taliban capture the eight Christian aid workers of Shelter Now International on the charges of proselytizing Afghans, which carries the death penalty. The Supreme Court indicts them.

September 11: The terrorists attack the World Trade Center in New York and the Pentagon in Washington.

October 7: The US attacks Afghanistan through air bombardment and the ground operations were left for the Northern Alliance.

November 13: The Taliban leave Kabul.

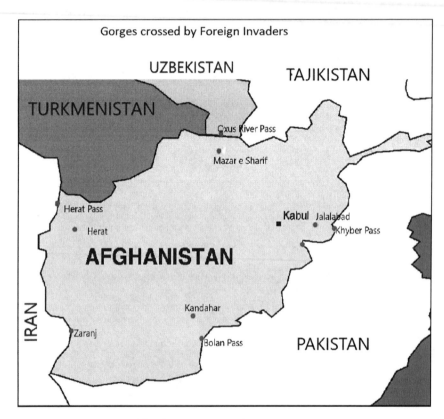

MAP I.1 Gorges Crossed by the Foreign Invaders.

1

ANCIENT HISTORY OF AFGHANISTAN

The great Persian Empire, according to Omrani and Leeming, was established by King Cyrus[1] (550–529 BC) stretched from the parts of the Balkan states to Uzbekistan, Turkmenistan, Turkey, Babylon (Iraq), Syria, Palestine, Egypt, Libya, Iran, Afghanistan, and modern-day Pakistan. After the death of Cyrus, Darius I became king in 521 BC and ruled until his death in 486 BC. According to Ewans, Darius consolidated and expanded the Persian Empire from Central Asia to the Indus Valley in the south – Iran, Afghanistan, and modern-day Pakistan – and established the governorships at Herat (Aria), Sistani (Drangiana), Balkh (Bactria), Merv, Khiva, Ghazni, Kandahar, and Peshawar Valley (Gandhara).[2]

The Persians were the first of the invaders who hit the road of conquest into the land of Afghanistan. The Persians established their authority in the plains of Balkh which were very fertile for agriculture and the place became a center for international trade of lapis lazuli. Balkh and Mundigak near Kandahar were the international trade centers that served the areas from Mesopotamia, an area between Tigris and Euphrates rivers in modern-day Iraq, to the Indus Valley (now in Pakistan). While moving southward, the Persians directed their expeditions on two sides – one leading to the Iranian plateau and the other leading toward Bolan Pass through Mundigak, Kandahar, to the Indus Valley. After Darius I, many Persian rulers ruled until the last king of the Persian Empire, Darius III, who started ruling in 336 BC. Darius ruled until his death at the hands of his second-in-command General Bessos in 330 BC. Darius was having difficulty in governing the tribes of Afghanistan. The tribes of Balkh were in continuous war with Darius until the arrival of Alexander the Great of Macedonia.

King Philip-II of Macedonia wanted to invade the Persian Empire as an act of revenge for the Persian king Xerxes' unsuccessful invasion of Greece in 480 BC.[3] According to Romm and Strassler, Alexander alleged that his father King Philip-II was assassinated by the anti-Macedonian Athenians and one suspect,

DOI: 10.4324/9781003198376-1

2 Ancient history of Afghanistan

Kharidemos, fled to Asia and joined Darius' army. Later, his twenty-year-old son and student of Aristotle, Alexander the Great, took the task of completing his father's unfinished business.

After controlling and consolidating Macedonia and the Greek Empire, Alexander started his conquest of Asia in 334 BC. Alexander traveled through the Edirne city of Edirne Province of northwest Turkey, which borders Greece and Bulgaria and falls within Europe. Edirne is in the north of the Sea of Marmara, which is within the borders of Turkey and which separates the European and the Asian territories of Turkey. Alexander then crossed the Dardanelles Strait, also known as the Hellespont Strait, into the Canakkale city and the sea port of Canakkale Province of Turkey on the South Asian coast of the Dardanelles Strait. Edirne was the capital of the eastern branch of the Roman Empire before the present capital of modern-day Istanbul, previously known as Byzantium and then Constantinople.

Alexander, on his way, conquered the small cities and towns of the Asia Minor region, also known as Anatolia, and established his satrapies in these areas. When Alexander reached the Granicus River in Canakkale Province of Turkey, he got the information that the Persian armies had already assembled at Zeleia across the river to meet Alexander's army.[4] The Persian army had 20,000 horsemen and some Greek mercenaries. The two armies stood against each other across the Granicus,[5] now the Biga Cayl river, near modern-day Ergili, Turkey. The Persians were attacked from all sides and were cut into pieces with the exception of the Greek mercenaries.

This was the first battle, known as the Battle of Granicus, between Alexander the Great and the great Persian Empire in which the Persians were defeated.[6] All the Persian generals were killed in this battle.[7] About 1,000 Persian horsemen died. Alexander captured about 2,000 Greek mercenaries who were made slaves and were sent back to Macedonia to work as laborers. On the other hand, Alexander's twenty-five companions, sixty horsemen, and thirty infantry men died. Alexander buried the dead the next day with their arms.

After the Battle of Granicus, Alexander captured the northwest, the central west, and the southwest of the Anatolia region. The areas that were subjected by Alexander included the city of Daskyleion in the northwest of Turkey, Sardis, now called Sartmustafa in Manisa Province, Ephesus in Izmir Province, Aydin Province, western Anatolia and Halicarnassus, and the port city known as Bodrum. Alexander appointed his own men as the satraps of the conquered areas to collect the taxes as were being paid to Darius before.

Alexander left for Ankara and heard that Darius had camped in the east of the Gulf of Iskenderun. Alexander and his general, Parmenion, moved southward to reach Iskenderun. Darius on the other hand moved northward to attack Alexander from behind. When Alexander reached Issus (Iskenderun), he left the wounded and the sick soldiers at Issus and continued advancing southward to get hold of Darius' army, unaware of the fact that Darius was behind his forces. Darius with his army arrived at Issus and captured Alexander's soldiers that he

Ancient history of Afghanistan **3**

had left behind and cut off their hands and also cut the supply line of Alexander.[8] This was the first victory of Darius at Issus.

In autumn 333 BC, Darius directed 30,000 horsemen and 20,000 army troops, who crossed Pinaros River[9] that falls into the Gulf of Issus and the battle was fought in the south of Issus. The exact name of the place of battle is unknown. The battle was called the second Battle of Issus. The army of Darius comprised 600,000 fighters in total.[10] The two armies were positioned at the right and the left flanks against each other. Alexander ordered his army to attack the left flank of the Persian army. Although the Persians at the left flank bolted, the Greek mercenaries found a gap in Alexander's two units and attacked his forces to drive them back to the river and a fierce battle ensued in which 120 Macedonians died.[11] To relieve the pressure on the struggling Macedonians, Alexander attacked the central unit of the Persian army. The Persians did their best to withstand the Macedonians but failed. When the Persian army heard that Darius had fled and the Greek mercenaries had been cut, those who survived became confused, panicky, and were in disarray. The Persians started their retreat desperately. The Persian generals were killed. Only 4,000 Persians survived,[12] who later joined Darius and then crossed the Euphrates River. Darius took the treasures to Damascus. In Darius' camp lived his family including his mother (Sisygambis),[13] wife (Stateira), and daughters Barsine, also known as Stateira II, and Drypetis. Alexander took Darius' family in his protective custody.

Darius then sent a letter to Alexander negotiating a peace treaty and requesting an order for the release of his family members. According to Romm and Strassler, Alexander wrote back to Darius, stating,

> your ancestors came to Macedonia and the rest of Greece and did us a great harm, though you had suffered no harm before then. I, having been made leader of the Greeks and wishing to take revenge on the Persians, made the crossing into Asia, but it was you who began the quarrel. When my father died at the hands of conspirators whom you had organized and sent the Greeks unfriendly letters about me inciting them to war against me. When you did all this, I marched against you. Now I have prevailed in battle and the gods have given me possession of the country. Approach me and ask for your mother, wife, children and anything else you like. And in future address me as the king of Asia. I will get you wherever you go.[14]

In 332 BC, Alexander moved toward the south along the Mediterranean coastal region of Syria, Lebanon, and Israel known as the Phoenician region. Alexander captured the Syrian ports of Byblos, now called Jubail, Sidon, and Tyre. Darius once again requested Alexander to renegotiate a peace deal. Alexander again rejected Darius' request for peace. When Darius saw no hope of peace with the Macedonians, he started preparing for another war.

Now, Alexander started to march toward Egypt. On his way, he was resisted by the people of Gaza in Palestine. The Gaza Strip was very important for

4 Ancient history of Afghanistan

Alexander to be able to enter Egypt. Alexander made three assaults on the fortress but could not succeed. On the fourth assault, Alexander's forces were able to break the gates and walls of the fortress and capture it. Although the city was captured by Alexander, Gaza's residents decided to fight till their death. All the fighters were killed and Alexander enslaved the women and children and resettled the city with his followers.

After Gaza, Alexander reached Pelusium,[15] a city near the site of modern-day Tell el-Farama, located in the south of Port Said in Sena Peninsula with the Gulf of Aqaba in the southeast, the Gulf of Suez in the southwest, and the Red Sea in the south. The Persian satrap of Pelusium did not resist Alexander and surrendered his city. Alexander established his garrison here and crossed the Nile River and reached Memphis, known in Arabic as Menf, about 20 kilometers south of Cairo on the west bank of the Nile. The city of Pelusium does not exist now but its ruins can still be found near the modern-day town of Mit Rahina. After this, Alexander marched along the Mediterranean coast and found a site where he founded a new city after his name as Alexandria, which exists even today in Egypt[16] and where he is buried.

Alexander now planned to return back to Asia. He wanted to cross the Euphrates River to reach Mesopotamia.[17] Both these rivers originate in Turkey. The Euphrates flows through Syria into Iraq and the Tigris flows from Turkey into Iraq. These two rivers meet at a place in the north of modern-day Basra in Iraq and then fall into the Persian Gulf. Darius had appointed Mazaios with 3,000 horsemen including 2,000 Greek mercenaries to guard the Euphrates River. On hearing of the arrival of Alexander, Mazaios fled. Alexander crossed the Euphrates River without any resistance. Alexander now marched through the countryside of the Mesopotamian region to reach Babylon. Babylon, a Greek name, was the capital of Mesopotamia, and its ruins can be found about 85 kilometers south of Baghdad of modern-day Iraq.

Darius had assembled a big force of 40,000 cavalry and a million infantry units accompanied by 200 chariots and a good number of Indian elephants. Darius set up his camp at Gaugamela, which was reported to be roughly 75 miles from the city of Arbil, or near Mosul in modern-day Iraq. Both the Persian and Macedonian armies stood opposite each other at a distance of 4 miles.[18] Darius took his position at the center; Bactrians and Syrians were at the left and right flanks. Alexander took control of the right flank, Parmenion was in charge of the left flank, and other Macedonian forces took their position at the center.[19] The Persians in the left and right flanks fled and Alexander lost about sixty of his companions. Alexander pursued Darius but could not apprehend him, though he got hold of his treasures. Alexander lost about 100 of his men and about 1,000 horses; the Persians lost about 300,000 fighting men and more than that number were captured alive by Alexander's forces. Alexander scored a decisive victory over the Persian Empire and captured a substantial segment of Darius' army, which included the Arians, Persians (Parthians), Afghans, Indians, and also the elephants and other supplies of army materiel.

Ancient history of Afghanistan **5**

That was the end of the third battle at Gaugamela between the Persian and Macedonian forces.

From Babylon, Alexander reached Susa, at which site now the modern-day Iranian town of Shush in Khuzestan Province is located. Alexander entered Susa and seized a lot of treasury and artifacts that he sent to Athens. Alexander advanced further and captured Persepolis, seized the treasury, and burned the royal palace of the Persian Empire in revenge for the burning of Athens by the Persians.[20] Persepolis is the Greek name of the ancient Iranian city of Parsa, now Takht-e-Jamshid, located about 50 kilometers to the northeast of Shiraz in the southern Fars region of modern-day Iran. Persepolis was the ruling center with the royal palace of the Persian king Darius I, whose son Xerxes had invaded and destroyed Athens in 490 BC. After burning down the royal palace of Persepolis, Alexander declared that he had paid back the Persians in the same coin.

After the capture of Persepolis, Alexander followed Darius III. During his flight, his soldiers deserted him and went back to the countries where they had come from. While moving eastward, in the spring of 330 BC, Alexander heard that Darius had been arrested by his second-in-command, Bessos, who proclaimed himself as the soi-disant successor of Darius and was assembling a large army in Bactria.[21] Bessos took the captive Darius along with him. When Alexander reached near Bessos in Damghan city in Semnan Province of modern-day Iran,[22] his two men, Satibarzanes and Barsaentes, stabbed Darius to death.[23] Thus, the last king of the Achaemenid Empire, Darius III, was killed by the men of his deputy. Bessos left the dead body of Darius and moved toward Bactria. When Alexander heard this, he was saddened to know that his adversary had met death in such a way. He found Darius' dead body in modern-day Damghan city[24] and ordered that his body be carried to Persepolis, the former ceremonial capital of the Persian Empire, and arranged a royal burial for him.

After conquering the Persian Empire, Alexander moved toward the east and, according to Ewans, entered Afghanistan in 330 BC[25] in pursuit of Bessos. Alexander captured cities and established new ones such as Aria, modern-day Herat, Sistan (Iran), Kandahar (Arachosia), Bagram Fort (now Bagram base is being used by the NATO forces and was also used by the Russian forces during the Russian occupation of Afghanistan), and Kapisa north of Kabul. To stabilize his control over this region, Alexander appointed his own satraps who controlled the conquered areas and collected the taxes.

Alexander then pursued Bessos who was fleeing to Bactria. Alexander chased Bessos. Bessos was expecting that Alexander would take the easy route to Balkh through the Ghorband valley and Bamian. Bessos gathered his army in this area to confront Alexander. In spring 329, contrary to Bessos' expectations, Alexander took the difficult route through the Indian Caucasus, the modern-day Hindu Kush mountain range, and passed through the Panjshir Valley and reached Kunduz via Khawak Pass.[26] Bessos was surprised to see Alexander's army at his rear position. Alexander fought and defeated Bessos and seized Balkh. Bessos fled to the north of modern-day Uzbekistan by crossing the Oxus River,

6 Ancient history of Afghanistan

which forms the boundary between modern-day Afghanistan and Uzbekistan. Alexander's men pursued Bessos and captured him. After cutting his nose and ears, he was brought before Alexander who sent him to Balkh for execution.[27]

Alexander now moved to the north and captured Samarkand (Marakanda) and built a new city in the name of Alexandria-Eschate on the Syr Darya. Now Oxyartes (satrap of Bactria) rebelled against Alexander. Alexander crushed his forces and took him captive and married Oxyartes' most beautiful daughter, Rhoxane,[28] in 327 BC. With the death of Darius and his successor Bessos, Alexander got complete control of the huge Persian Empire in the north.

Next Alexander eyed the conquest of Afghanistan and the Indian subcontinent in that it was important for Alexander to be the king of the whole of Asia. According to Dupree, Alexander crossed the Hindu Kush mountains again and reached Charikar[29] in modern-day Parwan Province of Afghanistan. Alexander moved to the south, which is now Pakistan, by taking two routes. At Jalalabad, Alexander divided his army into two units and sent the bigger unit under the command of Hephaiston to cross the Khyber Pass and capture the area east of the Indus River and then prepare to cross the river. Alexander himself took a different route by taking the small army via Nuristan, the Kunar Valley, through Bajaur and Swat.[30]

While Hephaistion was on his way to the Khyber Pass, Alexander himself marched through modern-day Nuristan in Afghanistan. Here the local people tried to resist him and Alexander was appreciative of their courage to face him. Alexander took the young people into his army that was heading to India.[31] In autumn 327 BC, Alexander's army subdued the Kunar Valley and crossed into Bajaur and passed through Arigaion, the modern-day main city of Nawagai in Bajaur[32] Valley. Alexander now led his forces to Massaka,[33] located near modern-day Wuch near Chakdara in lower Swat Valley. Alexander's forces fought with the local tribes who were later defeated. About 200 locals were killed in the fight and Alexander himself was wounded. The locals who survived became a part of Alexander's army as a result of a peace deal. Alexander passed through Bazira, modern-day Barikot, and Ora, modern-day Ude Gram in lower Swat Valley. After subduing the inhabitants of Shangla and Pir Sar, or Pir Sarai, Alexander reached modern-day Hund where he camped and waited for Hephaistion to join him.

Hephaistion crossed the Khyber Pass and reached Peukelaotis,[34] modern-day Charsada. Astis, the governor of Charsada, resisted, but Hephaistion seized the city for about thirty days and Governor Astis was defeated and put to death. After capturing Peukelaotis (Charsada), Hephaistion's army joined Alexander's army at Hund for crossing the Indus River on their way to India. At Hund Alexander received submission from the ruler of Taxila, reportedly named Mophis, with gifts in the form of elephants.

At Hund, the two components of the Macedonian army combined and then crossed the Indus River through a bridge of boats and reached Taxila. Alexander set up a garrison and left the sick soldiers who were unfit for a fight at the Taxila base camp. In the spring of 326, Alexander's forces marched toward the Hydaspes River, now called the Jhelum River.[35] Alexander reached the west bank of the Jhelum River and took his position against Poros. Alexander was very careful of the potential problems that his horses could face against Poros' elephants.

The Macedonian forces were spotted by Poros' riders who immediately reported to Poros about the arrival of Alexander on the east bank of the Jhelum River. Poros sent his son with a small army. Alexander attacked the forces of Poros and made them run away. About 400 of Poros' horsemen including his son died and the remainder of his army fled. Now Poros advanced with the big army to face Alexander at a place known as Nikaia, which was established by Alexander after his victory at the Hydaspes River in Punjab Province of modern-day Pakistan.[36] Poros considered his elephants as the big bulwark against Alexander's horses and thus placed them at the center while placing infantry and cavalry at the flanks. Alexander positioned himself on the left flank and sent Krateros to the right flank on the west bank of the river. When Alexander attacked the army of Poros from the left flank and destroyed it, Poros ordered his right flank to go to the aid of the left flank. Poros' weak left flank, unable to withstand Alexander and his army, bolted. At that point in time, Alexander ordered Krateros on the right flank to ford the river and attack Poros' elephants and forces engaged in the left flank. Poros' elephants became confused and panicky.

Poros' forces could not withstand Alexander's attack and about 20,000 foot soldiers and 3,000 horsemen, including two sons of Poros, were killed.[37] A few hundred Macedonians were killed. But the brave Poros stood steadfast and decided to fight until his death. Alexander ordered his men not to kill this brave king as he wanted to see him alive. Alexander sent a messenger from Taxila to talk to Poros about his plan. On seeing the messenger from Taxila who was his old enemy, Poros attacked him. He fled back and informed Alexander about Poros' attack. Alexander sent another messenger who met Poros and Poros asked him to take him to Alexander. When Poros was presented before Alexander, he asked Poros what he expected to be done to him. Poros, according to Romm and Strassler, replied, "treat me like a king, Alexander".[38] Alexander appreciated this brave answer. He asked Poros what else he wanted. Poros replied that his wishes are included in the same statement, "treat me like a king". Alexander granted the request and made Poros his vassal of the Macedonian Empire to rule the area the way he was ruling before. Poros remained loyal to the Macedonians for the rest of his life.

Alexander crossed Akesinos, modern-day Chenab River, and ordered Ptolemy to seize Sangala (or Sankala, modern-day Sialkot), which he did. Alexander razed Sangala to the ground. Now Alexander wanted to advance further by crossing Hyphasis, the modern-day Sutlej River, which flows through Indian Punjab into Pakistan and joins the Chenab River that finally falls into the mighty Indus River. On reading Alexander's intentions, one of his companions, Koinos, took the courage to speak to Alexander. Koinos stood up, and using his age, experience, and contributions to the Macedonian victories, advised Alexander not to go further in the best interests of the Macedonian army. Koinos continued to argue that a lot of the army members had been killed and that the past victories were no guarantees to future victories, and that the Macedonian army needed refreshment. Koinos advised Alexander to go back home and revive the Macedonian army with new recruits and to limit his kingdom in Asia up to modern-day Pakistan. Alexander then decided to return home from Pakistan in Asia and did not go further to India.

In autumn 326, Alexander returned to the Jhelum River and reached Nikaia and Boukephala, the two cities that he had established at the site of the war with Poros. Alexander now divided his army into three parts for their homeward journey through different routes but destined to unite in Kirman, Iran. After crossing the confluences of the rivers Jhelum and Chenab, and Ravi and Chenab (Jhelum and Ravi both fall into the Chenab River), Alexander reached the plains of Punjab. Alexander's forces now met the confederation of the tribes of the Malloi (Mallians, Malva) and the Oxydrakai (Ksudraka), who inhabited Multan, Jhang, and Sahiwal areas, and defeated them (Figure 1.1).

On his homeward journey, Alexander entered the kingdom of the Mousikanos, whose capital was Alor, modern-day upper Sind. The ruler of the Mousikanos

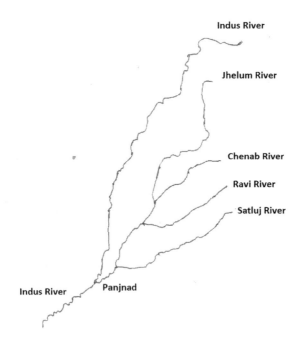

FIGURE 1.1 Rivers of Pakistan.

surrendered. After subduing the Mousikanos, Alexander entered the kingdom of Sambos, a local ruler, whose capital was Sindimana,[39] modern-day Sehwan Sharif in the Jamshoro District, Sind, Pakistan. Sambos too surrendered. Alexander arrived in Hyderabad, whose inhabitants had already fled. Alexander granted them amnesty to return and settle themselves in Hyderabad. As usual, Alexander built the garrison and the citadel. Here again Alexander divided his forces into three segments. Krateros was to travel by road through the Helmand Valley and Sistan to Kirman (Iran), where all Macedonian forces would be united. Nearkhos was to sail along the Makran coast (Gawdar or Gedrosia) in modern-day Baluchistan in Pakistan. Alexander himself took the elite force and decided to take the difficult route by road through the Gedrosia (Makran) coast, which was once taken by Cyrus who had lost his entire army on this route. The route was difficult in that it was barren, sandy, and had rugged rocky hills, with no food, water, and guide to lead the route. The army became so hungry that not only did they attack the food meant for Nearkhos' regiment but ate the animals they were carrying along.[40]

After crossing the semi-desert coastal strip of Makran, Alexander, in the winter of 325 BC, arrived in Kirman in Iran, where he was joined by his forces led by Krateros and Nearkhos. Alexander then moved to the ancient Persian capital Pasargadae, called Pasargad in Persian, which was built by Cyrus the Great and is also the location of Cyrus' sepulcher. Pasargadae is located near modern-day Shiraz city in Fars Province. Alexander was saddened to see the desecration of the sepulcher of Cyrus and ordered its reconstruction to present itself as a royal tomb. On Cyrus' tomb it was written in Persian, "You there! I am Cyrus, son of Cambyses, who founded the Persian Empire and reigned as the King of Asia. Do not begrudge me my monument".[41] Later, Darius shifted the Persian capital to Persepolis. Alexander revisited the burned capital of Persepolis and regretted its burning by the Macedonian forces.

In the spring of 324 BC, Alexander held a mass wedding ceremony at Susa in Iran, which was the capital of the Persian Empire during the reign of Cyrus' son Cambyses II. Alexander took the elder daughter of Darius known with two names, Barsine and Stateira II (after her mother's name), as his second wife, as he was already married to Rhoxane, daughter of Oxyartes, the Bactrian satrap who was Darius' brother. Alexander gave Darius' younger daughter Drypetis, his wife's sister, to his companion Hephaistion. Amastrine, another daughter of Oxyrates, was given to Krateros. In all, more than 10,000 Macedonians married Asian women[42] at a mass wedding ceremony held at Susa. Alexander gave dowry to the brides and gifts to all those who married Persian women. Interestingly, Alexander followed the marriage practices of the Persians. He ordered all the grooms to register their names for their wedding.

In summer 323, Alexander held a drinking party that continued through the night at the residence of his companion. Alexander became ill with fever but he continued to plan his campaign of Arabia. He remained ill for eleven days and his health worsened day by day. He became flaccid, felt pain in his abdomen, and lost

10 Ancient history of Afghanistan

his voice. Whenever his companions, bodyguards, and soldiers visited him and passed by his bed, Alexander did not say anything as he was voiceless but greeted them all silently. Alexander died young at the age of thirty-three, in Babylon, after ruling for a period of thirteen years, ever since he became the king in 336 BC after the assassination of his father, King Philip II. His conquests included Asia Minor, the entire Persian Empire, and modern–day Pakistan. Now the question to be answered by historians was as to what caused his death. Was it the fever, the wine, or poisoning?

Many historians have considered this issue and ruled out the possibility of the wine and poisoning in that Alexander could not have survived as long as eleven days had he been poisoned. Similarly, the wine could not be linked to the fever that Alexander experienced. However, the report of the Maryland clinicopatho-logical conference on Alexander's cause of death[43] rules out poison and malaria and points out that the cause of his death could be an infectious disease like typhoid fever, complicated by other factors.

After the death of Alexander, the question of a successor from among his blood relations arose. After a heated discussion, it was decided that Arrhidaios, his half-brother who was mentally sick, was to be renamed as Philip III and the unborn son of Rhoxane would share the throne with the support of the regents acting on behalf of the king. Perdikkas and Meleagros agreed on the issue of regency. Rhoxane gave birth to a child who was named Alexander IV. Later the child king was deposed from the kingship.

Another group of Scythian nomads known as Sakas from Central Asia, who ruled from Hungary to Mongolia, crossed the Oxus River. The Sakas reached Balkh where they were confronted by the Parthians who had occupied Iran and established their kingdom which stretched their empire to modern–day Pakistan. The Parthians (Persians) compelled the Sakas to move toward the east where they occupied Sistan and then extended their control southward to Gandhara and northern India. The Sakas ruled for one century and were finally defeated by the Parthians.

The Parthians' rule was brief as they were routed out by another group from Central Asia known as Yueh-Chi, in 135 BC. This group captured Gandhara and Punjab from the Parthians. This group belonged to the Gui-shang tribe and established its rule as the Kushan dynasty. Their king, Kanishka, who ruled during the 2nd century AD, had established the capitals at Kapisa, in the north of Kabul, and the winter capital at Peshawar[44] in Pakistan. The Kushans exploited their position of being located on the Silk Road through trade. The Silk Road took its name from the finest-quality silk transported along this route. Kapisa was the major trading center of the empire. The cities of Dilbarjin in the north-west of Balkh and Kandahar prospered during the Kushan period. Trading routes were established for the Middle East and China.

The Kushans were reported to be fire worshipers as a fire temple dedicated to Kanishka had been found at Surkh Kotal near Pulikhumeri in Baghlan Province of Afghanistan.[45] During their rule, Buddhism also spread in central Afghanistan,

Ancient history of Afghanistan   **11**

where images of Buddha have been found carved into the cliffs of the Bamian Valley. These images were later destroyed by the Taliban and thereafter were rehabilitated by the UNICEF and the Agha Khan Foundation. Bamian was a large Buddhist center, which was visited by Buddhists from all around the world. The Kushan dynasty ruled for about five centuries until they were ousted by the Sassanids in AD 226.

Ardsheer, son of Babak of Fars, who a vassal king under the Parthians, rose against his masters and defeated and killed the Parthian king Ardawan in the Battle of Hormuz in AD 226. Ardsheer became the founder of the Sassanid dynasty. The Sassanian Empire became very powerful and ruled over many parts of the current Middle East, from Syria to Iran, Afghanistan, and Pakistan. When the Sassanid dynasty came into power, their religion was Zoroastrian. Ardsheer invaded the east and captured India, in the north took over Balkh and Khurasan, and conquered Makran and Central Asia. In the west, Ardsheer defeated the Roman army and captured Armenia. Shahpur II, who was declared the king even before he was not born, ruled for seventy-five years. Shahpur was followed by Behram Gor.

During the sway of Behram, the Hephthalites or White Huns crossed the Oxus River from Turkmenistan and captured Bactria and Khurasan from the Persians. The White Huns then crossed the Hindu Kush to the northwest of the Indian subcontinent. They destroyed cities and slaughtered their people. Behram was unable to defend against the Hephthalites. Finally, the Persians, with the help of Turkish forces, fought the Hephthalites and defeated them and got control of all those areas that were under them. The remains of the tombs of the Hephthalites have been found near Kunduz in the plains of Shakh Tapa[46] in Afghanistan.

Behram was followed by Anushirwan, who defeated the Romans and captured Syria and Egypt from them. He also defeated the Turks and extended his empire beyond Balkh, Farghana, Bukhara, and Samarkand. He invaded Abyssinia and also captured Yemen. Anushirwan organized his empire into four satrapies under four governors. The northeast satrapy with its capital at Khurasan included the provinces of Khurasan, Sistan, Kirman, and Herat, including the territories of Balkh, Bukhara, and Samarkand. The satrapy of the southeast with its capital at Persepolis included the provinces of Fars, Khuzistan, and Baluchistan. The satrapy of the southwest with its capital at Ctesiphon comprised the entirety of Iraq. The satrapy of the northwest included Isfahan, Rayy (now Tehran), Azerbaijan, and Armenia. Parts of Armenia were under both the Persians and the Romans. The Persian Empire, with its capital at Ctesiphon, was at the height of its glory and prosperity under Anushirwan.

Anushirwan ruled for forty-eight years and died in 579. After Anushirwan, the Persian Empire started dwindling. Khusro Perwez, the grandson of Anushirwan, became the emperor. Khusro Perwez recaptured Syria, Asia Minor, and Egypt from the Romans. However, in 628, Heraclius, the Roman king, retook these territories from Perwez. Khusro Perwez ruled from 591

12 Ancient history of Afghanistan

until 628 when he was deposed by his own son Sheeruya. Sheeruya prisoned, blinded, and killed his father. He also killed about fifteen of his brothers and half-brothers just to eliminate all the male members of the family with the exception of his son Ardsheer to do away with competition for the right to the throne.

However, in addition to Ardsheer, Yazdjurd bin Shahryar escaped the slaughter of Sheeruya miraculously. Sheeruya died within a short period of time, and after his death, his seven-year-old son, Ardsheer, ascended the throne in September 628. After one year, the young emperor was dethroned by General Shahrbaraz. People did not like him and killed him within forty days of his coming to power and dragged him through the streets of Ctesiphon.

After Shahrbaraz, one of Khusro Perwez's two daughters, Borandokht, ascended the throne and ruled for about a year after which she was dethroned by the Persian nobles and was replaced by Shahpuri-Shahrbaraz, who also ruled for a short period. Shahpuri was rebelled against by another Persian faction led by Feroz Khusro, who dethroned and replaced him with Khusro Perwez's other daughter, Azarmidokht.

Azarmidokht was a very beautiful Persian woman.[47] According to Akram, Farrukh Hormuz, the satrap of Khurasan, wrote to Empress Azarmidokht, "Today, I am the hero of the nation and the pillar of the Persian empire. Marry me".[48] The Queen wrote back, "It is not permissible for a queen to marry, but should you wish to satisfy your desire for me come to me at night".[49] Actually, Azarmidokht did not like this and had a plan in her mind for Farrukh Hormuz. She informed one of her personal guards to kill him as soon as he enters the palace. Farrukh Hormuz left Khurasan for Ctesiphon. At night, he entered the palace and was killed instantly. His dead body lied in the palace yard. In the morning, the news of Farrukh Hormuz's death had spread throughout the empire.

When Farrukh Hormuz's son, Rustam Farrukhzad, heard the sad news, he became infuriated and swore to avenge his father's death. After the death of Farrukh Hormuz, Rustam became the governor of Khurasan. Rustam took his army and marched toward Ctesiphon. The royal forces could not resist him and he took Ctesiphon and captured Azarmidokht. Rustam blinded and killed her. For about one month, Rustam ruled the empire. Later, Rustam restored Borandokht to rule for the second time. Boran was killed by Feroz, who was killed by the people within one month.

Now the throne became vacant again and the Persian nobles looked for Yazdjurd, son of Shahryar, who was hiding in Istakhr (Persepolis). Twenty-one-year-old Yazdjurd was brought to Ctesiphon and was enthroned as the thirty-eighth and the last king of the Sassanian Empire in 634. After one year of Yazdjurd's succession to the throne, the Muslims invaded the Persian Empire.

In Zul Qada, 6 Hijri, the Holy Prophet had written a letter to Khusro Perwez, the king of Persia, which was hand-carried by Abdullah bin Hudhafa. According to Tabari, Akram quoted extract of the letter read as follows:

In the name of Allah, the Beneficent, the Merciful. From Muhammad, Messenger of Allah, to Chosroes, the Lord of Persia. Peace be upon whoever follows the Guidance and believes in Allah and His Prophet, and whoever bears witness that there is none worthy of worship except Allah and that I am the Apostle of Allah to all mankind, sent to warn all who live. Accept Islam and be at peace. And if you refuse, then upon you will die the sin of the Zoroastrians.

An interpreter translated the letter for Khusro. As soon as the interpreter stopped, Khusro Perwez took the letter and tore it up into the pieces. Abdullah bin Hudhafa returned to Madina and explained to the Holy Prophet how his letter had been torn up by Khusro, the king of Persia, whereupon the Holy Prophet remarked "His empire will also be torn up".[50]

Islam spread throughout the world at an unbelievable speed because it had enlightened the faithful Muslims with the spirit of Jihad. Iraq in those days was under the mighty Persian Empire. The Christian Arabs migrated from Yemen to Iraq and under their chief Malik bin Fahm of the Lakhm tribe established the Lakhm dynasty in western Iraq. The Christian Arabs ruled Iraq for two generations as the vassal of the Persian king.

The Arabs knew that the Persians had plenty of resources and strength. Iraq was the land of the two mighty rivers named Tigris and Euphrates, north of the Nile. The ancient cities of Iraq were Baghdad on the west bank of Tigris and still exists in modern-day Iraq and Ctesiphon on the east bank of Tigris, which was the capital of the Persian Empire. Hira on the west bank of Euphrates was the capital of the Lakhmid dynasty. Both the cities – Ctesiphon and Hira – are non-existent in modern-day Iraq. The site of Hira was 12 miles to the northeast of Najaf.[51] Uballa was the main port city engaged in international trade, which stood at the site where modern-day Basra known as Ashar stands.

Khalid bin al-Walid at the age of forty-eight was all set to invade Iraq. Khalid raised an army of 18,000 warriors.[52] Khalid in the third week of March, 633, wrote a letter to Hormuz, the Persian military governor of Dast Meisan District with its capital at Uballa. The letter said, "Submit to Islam and be safe, or pay jizya and be under our protection, otherwise get ready for the war". Hormuz was very proud and despised the Arabs, considering them poor, low-level, desert people, and boasted to the Persian king that the Persians will teach the Arabs a lesson that will be remembered by them for life and will never dare to challenge the Persian Empire again.

The first point of entry into Iraq was the Uballa port. Hormuz's forces arrived in Kazima (modern-day Kuwait) and were led by his generals, Qubaz and Anushjan, at the flanks. According to their normal practice, the Persians got their soldiers in the order of 3, 5, 7, or 10 men in chains[53] so that they stayed steadfast against the enemy and were unable to run away from the battlefield. That's why the Battle of Kazima is also known as the Battle of Chains. In the first week of April 633, the Battle of Chains started. When Khalid

14 Ancient history of Afghanistan

killed Hormuz, the Persian commanders at the flanks, Qubaz and Anushjan, ordered a withdrawal and fled. The Persians in the chains were killed. The Muslims also conquered Uballa, and its population on agreeing to pay jizya enjoyed protection from the Muslims. The spoils of the war were collected. According to the system for spoils distribution that was determined during the time of the Holy Prophet, Khalid sent one-fifth of the spoils to the Caliph as the state's share and the rest, four-fifth of the spoils, was distributed among the warriors, strictly in accordance with the revelation of the Surah Al-Anfal[54] of Holy Quran.

General Qarin crossed the Maqil river and finalized the battle formation at the south bank of the river. The battle started and both the Persian generals, Qarin and Qubaz, were killed. About[55] 30,000 Persians were killed in the Battle of the River, and the Muslims collected the spoils more than what they got at the Battle of Kazima. The local population agreed to pay jizya.

After the battles of Kazima and River, Khalid continued his movement to the north. In early May 633, the Persian and the Muslim armies stood against each other at Walaja, which according to Yaqut was on the east of Kufa-Mecca road. The Muslim mounted warriors attacked the Persian army led by General Andarzghar and completely destroyed it at the Battle of Walaja. Andarzghar fled and died of thirst in the desert.

After the Battle of Walaja, Khalid's eyes were on conquering Hira, the task that Abu Bakr had given him. The Persian forces led by General Jaban arrived in Ullais. Now General Jaban took command of the armies of the Persian and local Christian Arabs. In the middle of May 633, Khalid left Walaja with an army of 18,000[56] and reached Ullais. The battle took place in the southeast of Ullais between the Khaseef and Euphrates rivers. The battle was fiercer than Walaja. The Persian army was destroyed and thousands were killed, and the Persians and Christian Arabs who tried to escape were captured and brought back alive to the river bank where their slaughtering continued for three days and their blood mixed with the water of the river, turning it red.[57] That's why this battle is also known as the Battle of Blood River. According to Tabari, 70,000 Persians and Christian Arabs were killed. However, the commander of the Persian army, Jaban, managed to escape.

After the battle of Ullais, Khalid, in the middle of May 633, marched for Hira via Amgheeshiya. Khalid seized Amgheeshiya and destroyed the city.[58] Azazbeh, the governor of Hira and the commander of the garrison, decided to defend Hira against the Muslims. Azazbeh's son was killed in the battle and at the same time he heard that the Persian king Ardsheer had died. He did not see any ray of hope after this and decided to move to Ctesiphon and leave Hira for Khalid. Khalid entered Hira from the rear and there was no resistance from the residents. But the matter did not end there. There were four citadels in the city under the control of the four commanders of the four garrisons. First, they rejected the offer and decided to defend. Soon they realized the intensity of the attack and then agreed to pay 90,000 dirhams every year and act as sleuths and guides for the Muslims.

Khalid left Hira for Anbar at the end of June 633, with his half army of about 9,000 men.[59] When Khalid arrived in Anbar, he found that the city was protected by a wall which was further protected by a deep and wide moat around the walls of the fort. On arrival of the Muslims, the Persians had destroyed the bridges over the moat. Thus, there was no direct access to the wall without crossing the moat and crossing the deep and wide moat was not possible without boats. Neither boats nor materials necessary for making the boats were available. Khalid gave orders to his 1,000 archers to zero in on the eyes of the guards. In a short while, about 1,000 eyes of the people of Anbar were lost. That's why the Battle of Anbar is also known as the battle of eyes.[60]

Khalid ordered that the jaded camels of the Muslim army be brought to the ridge of the moat, and while archers engaged the guards through shooting arrows, the camels were slaughtered and thrown in the moat. After a while their carcasses appeared on the surface of water which were used by Khalid's 1,000 archers as bridges to cross the moat, and these bridges were called the bridges of bone and flesh. Just when Khalid was about to order his men to scale the wall, Khalid received a message from Sheerzad which said that he would surrender if the Persians were allowed to leave the city without their possession which Khalid accepted. In the second week of July 633, Sheerzad, along with the Persians and their families, left Anbar for Ctesiphon. The Christian Arabs of Anbar surrendered their arms and agreed to pay jizya. By the end of July 633, the Christian Arabs who had occupied the fort of Ein-ut-Tamr also surrendered to Khalid.

In the first week of November 633, Khalid took over Muzayyah. From Muzayyah, he turned to Saniyy and Zumeil and captured those as well. Khalid now relaxed. He had destroyed the major Persian army in less than a month in the four battles which covered an area of 100 miles. In early June or July 634, Muthana led a force of 8,000 men and defeated the Persian army at Babylon, a city which does not exist now but its remains can be found about 85 kilometers to the south of Baghdad, Iraq.

After the death of Abu Bakar, Umar became the Caliph. Umar announced Abu Ubayd bin Masud as the commander of the Muslim army in Iraq and Muthana was placed under his command. Abu Ubayd was not an experienced soldier but he was appointed the commander as a reward for his courage and bravery. However, Umar had instructed Abu Ubayd to consult the companions of the Holy Prophet in the war matters and obey their advice.

Rustam ordered his generals Jaban and Narsa to win back Suwad from the Muslims. Suwad was a very rich and prosperous land between the two rivers of Euphrates and Tigris, stretching from Basra to Ctesiphon and in the north to Mosul and Hulwan. Jaban crossed the Euphrates River and reached Namariq. Abu Ubayd with his army of 12,000 warriors left for Namariq. At Namariq, in the second week of October, Abu Ubayd's army confronted Jaban's army and defeated it. Jaban was captured by a Muslim soldier who did not recognize him. The Muslim soldier released him on a ransom.

16 Ancient history of Afghanistan

After the Battle of Namariq, the Muslim army met the Persian army led by Narsa at Saqatia near Kaskar, in which Narsa'a army was defeated. The Muslims returned to Hira. When the Muslims reached Euphrates on their way to Hira, they were confronted by the third army of Rustam led by General Jalinus. Both the forces met at Baqsiasa in the district of Barusma and Jalinus' forces were defeated. Jalinus along with some of his army fled the battlefield. Abu Ubayd had thus defeated three armies of Rustam and felt confident.

Rustam had not expected that three of his armies would be so easily defeated by the Muslims. Rustam now gave the standard of the Persian Empire known as "Dirafsh-e-Kavian" to Bahman and ordered him to advance toward Hira, fight with the Muslims, and destroy them and drive them out of Iraq. Bahman advanced toward Hira and camped at Quss Natif on the east bank of the Euphrates River, below the site of Kufa in the north of Hira. On the other side, Abu Ubayd marched from Hira on the west bank of Euphrates and camped at a small village called Marauha. Abu Ubayd ignored the counsels of the advisors and against their advice decided to cross the river over to the Persian side because his passion for martyrdom overwhelmed him.

In the morning of November 28, 634, the Muslim army crossed the river. The Battle of Quss, also known as the Battle of the Bridge, was ready to start. Bahman had deployed on the front a cohort of elephants including the monstrous white elephant. These elephants were decked on their back with howdahs carrying Persian soldiers well equipped with javelins and bows and arrows. The animals were also wearing bells around their necks and trunks. As the Muslims got close to the Persians, their horses became frightened by the noise of the elephants' bells and darted off. It became very difficult for the Muslim riders to control their agitated horses and soon the army fell into disarray.

The Muslims abandoned their horses and pulled out their swords. Seeing the situation, Bahman ordered the Persian army to attack the Muslims. The Muslim warriors' spirit and courage worked well to prevent their collapse.

The Muslim soldiers managed to cut the girth of the elephants and brought several Persian soldiers down from the howdah and killed them. Abu Ubayd was having a duel with the white beast, and he struck the beast with his javelin, blinding its one eye. He then got under the elephant and cut its girth and brought the howdah and its occupants down. Some of the occupants of howdah managed to escape Abu Ubayd's blows and fled. Abu Ubayd then launched his attack on the one-eyed white beast by attempting to cut its trunk. The infuriated beast pushed Abu Ubayd down with its leg and stepped on his chest and soon his body collapsed under the heavy weight of the white beast.

After the death of Abu Ubayd, Muthana took command of the rest of the army and ordered the repair of the bridge and, when ready, asked them to cross it peacefully. At last, only Muthana and Saleet were left behind. Saleet also collapsed and Muthana received injuries at the hands of the Persians. Muthana was the last man to cross the river, and after crossing the bridge, Muthana dismantled it so that it could not be readily used by the Persians. Bahman returned

Ancient history of Afghanistan **17**

to Ctesiphon. Of the 9,000 fighting men of the Muslim army, 4,000 died or drowned and 2,000 fled the battlefield. Only 3,000 Muslim fighters were left. Six thousand Persians died. This was the most shocking defeat for the Muslim army in history.

Muthana bin Harisa with an army of 8,000 fighters arrived on the west bank and encamped at Nakheila near Kufa. The Persians had prepared another army of 12,000 fighters under the command of General Mihran. From Euphrates, a small river called Buweib ran southward by Nakheila joining the Ateeq river. The two armies met at a place called Shumia about half a mile from the river. Muthana and his brother Masud attacked the Persians. Masud fell through. When the Muslims found that the Persians were exhausted, Muthana ordered his reserve force, which was led by his brother Mu'anna, to attack the Persians. The Persians started retreating toward the bridge. Seeing this situation and to encourage his forces, Mihran, the Persian general himself, proceeded forward and was killed by a Muslim warrior. The Persian soldiers fled to the bridge but were captured and killed. The Muslims got the victory at the Battle of Buweib. Muthana led his army to Anbar and then further to Baghdad and Tikreet.

The four Persian districts that were important for the Persian war machinery from resource-generation point of view included: Furat, Abarqubaz, Dast Meisan, and Meisar. The seizure of these four districts would cut the supply line of the Persian Empire coming from Furat and make their war machinery inconsequential and ineffective. The governor of the district of Furat, with an army of 4,000 men, was defeated at the present-day Zubeir, 12 miles from the modern-day Basra. The governor was captured. The district of Furat and Ubella fell to the Muslims in August–September 635.

After Furat and Ubella, Utba then marched toward the district of Dast Meisan and defeated the Persian force. After Dast Meisan, Utba marched toward the district of Abarqubaz which also welcomed them without any resistance. Now all the eastern districts of Tigris were under the control of the Muslims. By November 635, all the four districts which were rich resource bases for the Persian war machinery had come under the control of the Muslims.

In order to solve the problem of revolt after occupation, the Muslims needed a big army to handle. For this purpose, Umar appointed Sa'd bin Abi Waqqas as the commander of Iraq. In April–May 636, Sa'd left Madina and encamped at Zaud with an army of 29,500. Before the arrival of Sa'd at Sharaf in July 636, Muthana had died of the wounds that he had suffered during the Battle of the Bridge. Sa'd married Muthana's widow named Salma bint Khasfa, after completion of her four-month widowhood period.

The Muslim forces captured Uzeib and Qadisiyya and Sa'd encamped at Qadisiyya. The Muslims captured the western edge of the bank of the Ateeq river and captured Qudeis in the south. Sa'd sent a delegation of Muslims to offer Islam to the Persian emperor Yazdjurd. The delegation offered the options of Islam, jizya, or sword to the infidel Yazdjurd. Yazdjurd flushed with anger and said that he had not seen such despicable people on earth before. Yazdjurd

18 Ancient history of Afghanistan

ridiculed and insulted the delegation. In return for jizya, Yazdjurd gave them a bucket of dust, which the delegation received happily anyway and crossed the Ateeq river.

Yazdjurd collected the army of the Persians, Turks, Kurds, Armenians, and Christian Arabs, and this group marched from Khurasan and Azerbaijan toward Ctesiphon and joined the Persian army led by Rustam. Yazdjurd ordered Rustam to attack and destroy the Muslims and cast them out of the land. Rustam, however, procrastinated as he was not interested in fighting a war with the Muslims.

Rustam ordered General Jalinus to march toward Qadisiyya as an advance army. General Jalinus crossed the Euphrates and encamped at Najaf. The total strength of the Persian army was 60,000 fighters and 33 war elephants. On the east bank of the Ateeq river, the Persian army got itself settled. On the west bank of the river, opposite of Khaffan, Rustam found a Muslim camp, where the Muslim soldiers were standing. Rustam sent an envoy across the river to bring the Muslims' commander to the bridge for a talk.

Sa'd had selected seven persons to talk to Rustam and sent them one by one. After meeting with the persons individually, Rustam was not satisfied and brought the discussion to a head, "will you cross the river to our side, or shall we cross over to you?" The group responded that the Persians should cross to the Muslims' side and having said that left the court. The Persians crossed the river with their troops, horses, elephants, and baggage. After establishing his camp, Rustam immediately deployed the Persian forces in five corps.

Fifteen thousand Persian soldiers were concatenated with a chain length of 3, 5, 7, 9, and 10,[61] which was a normal practice in the Persian army to ensure suicidal commitment rather than fleeing from the battlefield. The army was aided by 33 elephants, each mounted by men with javelins and bows. The white beast was the leader of the elephants' group. At the camp, Rustam arranged for a raised platform to monitor the war. Then all of a sudden, Rustam was perturbed by the recollection of a dream about Umar's sealing of the Persians' weapons. Then Rustam shouted that "Umar has eaten his heart. May God burn him".[62] On the other hand, Sa'd had deployed the Muslim army in five corps as well. The Muslim army strength was 30,000 men. Sa'd had set up his headquarters at Uzeib and had appointed as his deputy Khalid bin Urfula, who would relay his orders to the army.

On November 15, 636, all of a sudden, Rustam launched an attack with the elephants on the Muslims' flanks. The Muslim soldiers severed the girth of the howdahs, and the mounted Persian archers fell and were cut to pieces by the Muslims, while only some managed to retreat. Now all the elephants were without howdahs. Abu Ubaida sent additional reinforcements from Syria led by Sa'd's nephew Hashim and another force of 700 men led by Qa'qa. A major problem for the Muslims was the two elephants, the white beast and the scabby; these two were the trained leaders among the Persian elephants. Now the two brothers, Qa'qa and Asim, shot their arrows and javelins at the white elephant, piercing its eyes and striking at its head. The elephant screamed in pain and shook itself so violently that all the occupants of howdah fell down. Qa'qa first cut the trunk of the white elephant, making the beast an ineffective operator. Then both the brothers slaughtered all the men who fell from the howdah. Meanwhile, across the Muslim center, Hammal and Rabeel did likewise and blinded the scabby elephant and cut his trunk. The blinded and wounded elephants screamed in pain and were no longer useful as a part of the Persian battle strategy. The impaired elephants became violent and ran wildly and, crashing through the Persian ranks, made their way to the Ateeq river, where they plunged and swam to the west bank.

On the fourth day, the battle turned out to be the deadliest one. Rustam realized the pressure on the Persian army and could hear the noise of the battle from his throne. He also realized that the Battle of Qadisiyya was over. He saw a standing mule loaded with two saddle boxes of his possessions. He mounted on the mule and left for the Ateeq river. Qa'qa reached the empty throne of Rustam. Qa'qa sat on the throne and sent his men to look for Rustam. One Muslim, Hilal bin Ullafa,[63] saw a mule and chased it near the river. Hilal reached the mule and cut the rope of the saddle and the boxes fell and one box fell on the head of Rustam. Rustam got up and ran toward the river and then jumped into the river. Hilal followed him into the river and got him back on the bank. Hilal got his sword and struck Rustam at his head and face, rendering him beyond recognition. Rustam was killed. Hilal went back to Qa'qa seated on the throne and said, "By the Lord of Kaba, I have killed Rustam".[64] Hilal brought back Rustam's body, which had one hundred wounds on it.[65] Hilal got all the possessions of Rustam and sent to Sa'd, who returned them back. Rustam's cap embedded with jewels and diamonds was worth 100,000 dirhams. Hilal sold other possessions of Rustam for 70,000 dirhams.

About 6,000 Muslims were martyred and buried in the valley of Musharraq. About 40,000 Persians, including 15,000 chained soldiers, were killed. The top Persian generals who died in this battle included famous Rustam, Bahman, Beerzan, Jalinus, and some not-so-famous ones. Those who survived included Hormuzan, Qarin, and Khusro Shanum. The Muslims' victory at the Battle of Qadisiyya was a harbinger of the tearing up of the Persian Empire. Sa'd's victory over the Persian army, one of the most mighty, well–trained, and well-equipped armies of the world, opened the gates for Islam into the land of Zoroastrianism. After this victory, Sa'd's next mission was Ctesiphon, the capital of the Persian Empire, known to the Arabs as Madain.

Zuhra moved to the north of Najaf and captured it. When Zuhra arrived in Burs, the district mayor of Burs, named Bastam, approached Zhura and offered peace which was accepted. In the third week of March 636, the final battle of Babylon was fought between the Muslims and the Persians in which the Persians were defeated and Hormuzan fled toward the southeast to Ahwaz and the remaining Persians fled northward. When Zuhra arrived in Sura, his forces pushed the Persians toward Deir Kab. Zuhra arrived in Deir Kab and confronted the Persians led by Nakheer Jan. Nakheer Jan was killed and the Persians retreated toward Kusa.

20   Ancient history of Afghanistan

Sa'd spent a few days in Kusa and visited the place where the Prophet Ibrahim was imprisoned by the cruel Nimrod. Sa'd prayed at this site and solicited Allah's blessing upon the Prophet Ibrahim and the Prophet Muhammad, peace be upon him. After Kusa, in early January 637, Zuhra arrived in Sabat, four miles south of Ctesiphon, where he was met by Sheerzad, mayor of the town, who surrendered the city to the Muslims. Sabat was the last blocking point for the Muslims before Ctesiphon.

As soon as Sa'd landed on the east bank, he ordered Asim to move to the city of Ctesiphon. Asim arrived at the white palace where he received a little resistance by a small contingent of the Persians army, which was defeated. Here, Salman Farsi played an important role in negotiating with the Persian army. Salman told the Persians, "I am actually one of you and I feel for you".[66] Salman offered them the usual three options of Islam, jizya, or the sword. The Persians accepted jizya and surrendered the white palace to the Muslims, and thereby Ctesiphon came into the hands of the Muslims'.

Ctesiphon was one of the greatest cities of the Persian Empire and was also its capital. Sa'd entered the white palace of Khusro in Ctesiphon which had seven palaces. He established his headquarters at the white palace. Sa'd took his residence in the Great Hall, Taq-i-Kasra. In the yard of the white palace, he built a mosque with a pulpit for the imam, who was Sa'd himself. He led an eight rakat victory prayer which was attended by the whole army present in the white palace premises. Next day Sa'd kept a fast. The mass conversion of the Persians to Islam followed thereafter.

Sa'd was interested in taking over Suwad which was not possible without taking control of Jalaula and Khaniqeen. In March 637, Hashim bin Utba left Ctesiphon for Jalaula with an army of 12,000 men. The Muslim army arrived in Jalaula and found it fortified with ditch and the obstacle of wooden caltrops. Neither of the armies could do anything. Tactically, Hashim withdrew his forces to allow the Persians to come forward beyond the ditch. Mihran's forces crossed the caltrops belt and got ready for the battle with the Muslims. On one morning in late November 637, the Battle of Jalaula was fought.

When Qa'qa and his men, taking advantage of the darkness caused by the dust storm, managed to get behind the Persians, Qa'qa beckoned the announcer to make the announcement. The announcer in a loud voice said, "O Muslims, here is your commander who has got to the ditch and captured it. Advance to him and let none stand between you and him".[67] On hearing the announcement, Qa'qa attacked the Persians from behind. Hashim attacked the Persians from the front. The Persians were sandwiched between the Muslims. After a severe fight, some Persian units broke and the soldiers of the broken units fled and fell into the ditch and died. The Persians who were trying to flee were caught by Qa'qa and were killed. The Muslims captured Jalaula without any resistance. In the Battle of Jalaula, half of the Persian army of 30,000 was killed. Mihran himself fled safely toward Khaniqeen. After Jalaula, while Mihran was organizing the Persian forces, he was approached by Qaqa who killed Mihran and captured Khaniqeen.

Ancient history of Afghanistan **21**

After hearing the news of the death of the Persian general Mihran at Khaniqeen, Yazdjurd left Hulwan for Qum and left behind General Khusro Shanam to take care of Hulwan. When Qa'qa arrived in Qasr Shirin, Khusro Shanam fled to the hills and Qa'qa occupied Hulwan. The inhabitants of Hulwan surrendered to the Muslims and agreed to pay jizya. Hulwan then was a big city but now it is a small city known as Pul-e-Zohab. Qa'qa returned to Ctesiphon. By February 638, all the three approaches to Suwad − along the Tigris valley, along the Euphrates valley, and the Kermanshah road − were under the control of the Muslim Persian army led by Muslim Persian officers.

When Yazdjurd left Jalaula, Princess Shahr Bano was left behind because she was ill. Later on, she, as a part of the Persian convoy, left for Hulwan and that convoy was apprehended by Hashim bin Utba, who killed most of the escorts of the convoy and got hold of Shahr Bano. Hashim sent Shahr Bano to Madina as spoils of the war. In Madina, while Princess Shahr Bano was being sold in the marketplace as a slave, the Caliph was among the people sitting there. Umar said that the princess was looking at Hussain ibn Ali and immediately she was given to Hussain in marriage.[68]

While the Muslim raids continued in the region, all of a sudden, a Persian force led by Azeen, son of Hormuzan, emerged from the Kirmanshah mountains. Sa'd sent Zarrar bin Al Khetab (not the relative of Umar) to deal with Azeen. The two armies met and fought probably at Bahandaf. Zarrar captured the Persian commander Azeen and killed him. Zarrar pursued the fleeing forces and reached Seerwan, a town in the district of Masabzan in the Kirmanshah mountain region. Zarrar told the fleeing people of the village that they can live in peace in return for payment of jizya. The people accepted the terms and came back to their town and agreed to pay jizya. Thus, the district of Masabzan came under the control of the Muslims. Zarrar returned to Sa'd. By the end of January 638, the whole of Suwad, with the exception of Ahwaz, was under the Muslims' control. This was the end of Sa'd's campaign in Iraq against the Persians.

With the help of Amr bin Abdul Maseeh bin Buqueila, an old Iraqi prince, Sa'd had found a place like a mound of sand, which was dry but with water and greenery. This place was Kufa, a name that Sa'd chose, meaning the mound of sand. Sa'd wrote to Umar that he had found Kufa. Kufa was a land of sand and pebbles.[69] At Kufa, the Muslims settled down and established their garrison. First of all, a mosque was built and next to the mosque a palace for Sa'd was built. Thousands of residential quarters were built for the Persian Muslim soldiers who had joined Sa'd and had become Muslims. Both the cities of Kufa and Basra were founded by the Muslims after the conquests of Ctesiphon, Tikreet, and Mosul. The Muslims had established their garrisons at Ctesiphon, Kufa, and Basra with small detachments at Hulwan, Seertan, Mosul, and Qirqeesia to guard against the Persians.

After the conquest of Iraq, according to Naumani, Umar introduced a system of revenue collection. The main sources of revenue were: (1) land revenue and (2) jizya. All the cultivated land was left in the local owner cultivators'

22 Ancient history of Afghanistan

possession, and they paid tax on the commodity produced. Tax was paid according to the type of the produce and the quality of the land production. The rent on land for production of wheat was 2 dirhams per jerib to 4 dirhams per jerib, depending on the productive quality of land. The rent on land for production of barley ranged between 1 dirham per jerib and 2 dirhams per jerib based again on the productive capability of land. The rent on land for the production of cotton, grapes, sesame, and vegetables was 5 dirhams per jerib, 10 dirhams per jerib, 8 dirhams per jerib, and 3 dirhams per jerib, respectively.[70] Umar maintained the relationships between the owner of the land and the cultivator of the land (share cropper) as were promulgated by the Persian Empire.

Jizya was imposed on the non-Muslims in return for the protection of their property and life and exemption from the military service. The people of Iraq in the east agreed happily to pay jizya at the rate of 1 dinar per person. This was paid by all the non-Muslims such as idolaters, Christians, Jews, and Zoroastrians. Umar's system of governance was a real democratic in which decisions were made through the consensus of the shura. At the end of every year, Umar used to call the ten nobles from the conquered areas and asked them to swear four times and declare that the taxes from the Muslims and the non-Muslims were not collected by using coercion.[71]

When Sa'd defeated the Persian forces at Babylon on his way to Ctesiphon, Hormuzan with his survivors fled to Ahwaz of which he was the governor and the prince. At Ahwaz, now known as the province of Khuzistan, he started gathering a big force for another confrontation with the Muslims. In the two districts of Ahwaz, Meisan and Daste Meisan, Hormuzan had established two bases.

Noman bin Muqarrin and Salma bin Al Qein established their two camps just opposite of the Persians' camps and simultaneously attacked the Persian forces. Hormuzan's forces were defeated and retreated toward Ahwaz and got deployed in the city along the left bank of Karun River. The Muslims followed them and secured the right bank of the Karun River. To buy time, Hormuzan sent a message to the two Muslim generals on the west bank for a peace treaty. Thus, the Muslims signed a treaty with Hormuzan according to which the area of Ahwaz and Mihirjanqazaf would be under the Muslims' rule and the Persians would pay jizya and other taxes and Hormuzan would still govern the area. The Muslims appointed Hurmila as the administrator of the area, whom they posted by the river Teri.

There was no clear-cut boundary between the Muslims' and Hormuzan's territories of Ahwaz. Hormuzan exploited the vagueness of the treaty and disputed the boundary line and refused to cooperate. Umar ordered for Ahwaz to be seized. Abu Musa marched toward Ahwaz and assembled his forces opposite Ahwaz and pushed the Persian forces across the Karun River. Ahwaz was the capital of the province of Khuzistan, which was stretched to the north and the east of Zagros Mountains, on its west was Iraq and to the south was the Persian Gulf. The Muslims crossed the Karun River by the northern edge of the city

Ancient history of Afghanistan **23**

and got engaged with the Persian army and defeated them. Hormuzan, with the surviving Persian army, left the battlefield and marched toward Ram Hormuz.

After the defeat of Ahwaz, the Persians decided to build up their forces for the next confrontation with the Muslims at Ram Hormuz and Tustar. Yazdjurd had arranged 300 cavalry men under the one-eyed Persian general Siyah and ordered him to support Hormuzan in his struggle against the Muslims. Instead of joining Hormuzan, Siyah moved to Kulhani in the north of Susa. Umar asked Abu Musa to send two armies led by Noman bin Muqarrin and Sahl bin Adhi against the Persians in Khuzistan to capture Tustar and arrest Hormuzan who had fled to Ram Hormuz. Noman's forces arrived in Ahwaz before Sahl, and Abu Musa ordered Noman to follow Hormuzan and kept Sahl's forces at Ahwaz as a reserve force.

Noman arrived in Arbuk on the east bank of the river and found the Persian forces ready for a battle. After a short engagement, the Persians were defeated and Hormuzan left Ram Hormuz and fled to Tustar. At Tustar, Hormuzan fortified the city for its defense. Hormuzan had planned for a long siege, and for this purpose he had gathered enough supplies. Noman easily captured Ram Hormuz.

Noman moved from Ram Hormuz toward Tustar. The two armies were engaged in battle on the plains in the southeast of Tustar. After a short engagement, the Persian army was defeated and was compelled to take refuge behind the ditch. Abu Musa then deployed the forces around the city to block the Persians' escape. The siege continued and the Persians sallied out but were unsuccessful and could not dent the Muslims. The Muslims crossed the ditch and stood between the wall and the ditch.

The siege prolonged and the inhabitants of Tustar were fed up with the siege and wanted a peace deal. One night, a Persian named Seema, taking advantage of the darkness of the night, left his house and went to the Muslims' camp where he met Abu Musa. Seema said that he would show the way the Muslims could enter the fortified city and capture it quickly on the condition that he and his family would be protected and that he would be paid pension for the rest of his life. Abu Musa wanted to be certain what he was saying. Abu Musa asked Ashras bin Auf to accompany Seema to see the way for the quick entry and capture of the city.

Seema took Ashras along and went to the west side of the city where there was a big stone-lined tunnel for the discharge of sewer water into the river. Both men entered the tunnel and at the end of the tunnel there was a way to the house of Seema. Seema took Ashras to his house and got Ashras attired in the Persian dress. He led Ashras around the city and showed him the entire perimeter of the wall from the inside and the position and the distance of the various gates. While walking inside the city's wall, they even passed by Hormuzan. Hormuzan looked at them but did not suspect. Ashras now understood the way and relayed back to Abu Musa.

Having now known the way to the fortified city, a plan of attack was designed for the next night. Two groups of soldiers were organized. First, a group of 40 men would attack which would be followed by a second group of

24 Ancient history of Afghanistan

200 men. The second group would wait for the signal of the first group for the attack. Then the commander posted at the gate near the tunnel would storm into the city as soon as the gate was opened by the first group. The Persians had no clue of what was going to happen inside the city. The 40 men who emerged from the sewer tunnel cried "Allah O Akbar" and pounced on the Persian guards at the gate and killed them and the chains and the locks of the doors were broken. The Persian soldiers rushed to the gate but were stopped by the second group of 200 men who had also emerged from the sewer tunnel by then. Now the main army posted at the gate near the sewer tunnel entered through the gate.

Hormuzan who led the siege fought bravely in the streets near the gate. Many Persians were killed and Hormuzan himself killed two prominent companions of the Holy Prophet. The Persians left the city and fled to Susa. Hormuzan with a select group sought refuge in the citadel. The Muslims took over the city, killing 1,000 Persians and capturing 600. Now the Muslims had to deal with the citadel's occupants. The Muslims surrounded the citadel and continued its siege. Hormuzan scaled the wall of the citadel and announced that he wanted to surrender but on one condition, that his fate should be decided by Umar, and whatever he wanted to do with it, it was up to him.[72] This was agreed to, and Hormuzan was captured and the Battle of Tustar came to an end.

Abu Musa marched toward Susa, also known to the Persians as Shush, taking along the captive Hormuzan. On arrival at Shush, Abu Musa was faced with a sizeable Persian army led by Hormuzan's brother Shahryar. The Muslims besieged the city and several engagements took place but nothing happened. Now a Persian general named Siyah, who had accepted Islam before the Battle of Tustar, gave a brilliant suggestion to Abu Musa, and a strategic plan based on Siyah's suggestion was prepared. The plan was to take Susa by guile as well as by force.

The night passed peacefully. Next morning the Persian guards near the gate found a Persian soldier lying on the ground in his bloodstained Persian uniform. Two soldiers left the gate to pick up their wounded soldier. As they got close to the ostentatiously wounded soldier, Abu Musa plunged at them and killed both and ran toward the half open gate. The supposedly wounded soldier was none other than General Siyah himself. General Siyah went to the gate and killed the sentry and got inside. Then another Persian soldier who was hiding nearby, named Khusro, joined Siyah. Both were at the half open gate at their back when the alarm was sounded and with more Persian soldiers rushing to the gate, General Siyah and Khusro attacked them. Siyah and Khusro fought bravely and became exhausted, then immediately another of Abu Musa's force that was positioned near the gate entered and started slaughtering the Persians inside the gate. The Muslims went into the city and scattered the Persians like birds and the Persian commander found no way to confront the Muslims any further and surrendered and requested for peace which was accepted and Susa was taken over by the Muslims in the middle of 20 Hijri.

Abu Musa admired Siyah's bravery, courage and fighting skills and said "One-eyed one, you and your commanders were not as we thought you were".[73] Siyah accepted the compliments but at the same time reminded Abu that they had come to his assistance when he needed the most and that they fought by his side against the Persians. Siyah then complained that he and his comrades were not being paid as the Arab fighters of their caliber were. Abu Musa wrote to Umar. Umar immediately approved a higher pay for the Persian commanders and their comrades, according to which, six leaders including Siyah got 2,500 dirhams per annum and 100 of them got 2,000 dirhams.

At Susa, Abu Musa also found the remains of the Prophet Daniel in a bier lying in a temple. Daniel[74] died in Susa and his remains had remained there. However, Daniel was not buried and his remains were kept in a bier lying in a temple. The body of Daniel was intact and Abu Musa found a parchment at his head. Abu Musa wrote to Umar about Daniel and sent the scroll to him. Umar sent instructions to Abu Musa that the remains of Daniel be properly enshrouded and buried. Under the orders of Umar, the Muslims dug thirteen graves and in one of them the remains of Daniel were buried and the remaining twelve graves were filled with dirt so that the location of the burial of Prophet Daniel remains unknown. As far as the scroll was concerned, Umar called for Ka'b al-Ahbar to translate it into Arabic. On an inquiry from the companions as to what was in it, Ka'b al-Ahbar said, "All your history and affairs, the melody of your speech and what is yet to happen".[75]

Now the only place in Khuzistan that was not under the Muslims' control was Junde Sabur. Abu Musa sent Aswad bin Rabee'a, with the nickname of Muqtarib, with a force to occupy Junde Sabur. Muqtarib accepted the surrender of Junde Sabur on the payment of jizya. On return from Susa, Abu Musa dispatched Hormuzan to Madina. He was escorted by the two companions of the Holy Prophet. Hormuzan was worried for his fate for breaking the promise twice. However, Hormuzan was a very intelligent Persian and was crafty enough to save his life. The escort arrived in Madina and went straight to Umar. After a long discussion, Umar said that Hormuzan would have safety if he becomes a Muslim. After this Hormuzan accepted Islam and took residence at Madina and was awarded a pension of 2,000 dirhams.[76] Later he was killed by Umar's son Ubaidullah on the suspicion of his involvement in the murder of his father.

Umar sent additional reinforcements to Noman which reached Mah for onward march toward Nihawand. Umar also announced the change of command in case of the fall of the commander. Noman immediately passed marching orders for his army with his brother Nueim as an advance group. The Muslims arrived at Isbeezahan, 11 miles short of Nihawand, and found the Persians ready for the battle. Isbeezahan was roughly at the site of the present-day village of Sa'd bin Abi Waqqas. The Muslim army encamped at Isbeezahan. The Persians' strength was 60,000 fighting men and the Muslims' strength was half of that, about 30,000 men.

26 Ancient history of Afghanistan

In December 641, the Muslim soldiers got ready for the battle in the land that stretched from Sheahan to Nihawand. The Muslim army was in the valley while the Persians positioned themselves on the top of a 500-foot high ridge, a more advantageous position for the Persians. As a part of their strategy, the Muslims used the guile of announcing the death of Umar and started packing for the withdrawal. This rumor was received by the Persian as good news. Mardanshah became more confident and the spirits of the Persians got boosted. The Persians saw the Muslims' outposts vacant. Mardanshah decided to finish the invaders once and for all and get back their land from them. Mardanshah ordered clearing of the belt of iron caltrops so that the Persian army could advance to attack the withdrawing Muslim army. For the Muslims this worked well, just as planned.

After the noon prayer, the Muslims attacked. Now a deadly war started between the two armies. Men fell like leaves from trees and the Muslims were determined to return to their families with victory. In the afternoon, the battle reached its climax when the Muslims hit hard at the Persians. The battlefield was covered with bodies lying here and there and the earth soaked in blood so much so that the horses and men slipped and fell. Noman was hit by an arrow and the horse and the master both fell. Noman was alive but unconscious. Nueim grabbed the army standard and took Noman's position in the center and continued the battle as if Noman was fighting in the center. The Persian commander-in-chief, Mardanshah, was killed. Many Persians were killed and many others managed to flee but the Muslims chased them. The fleeing Persian cried: "Wai khurd" meaning "I am finished". The Persians took refuge at a ravine which later took its name as Wai khurd.[77] The Muslims accomplished victory. Now the Muslim army arrived in Nihawand and the Persian commander Dinar just surrendered unconditionally and agreed to pay jizya and other taxes and peace returned to the city. Thus, the Battle of Nihawand ended in December 641 or January 642.

After Nihawand, the governor of Hamdan, named Khusro Shanam, surrendered and agreed to pay jizya. After the settlement of the payment details, Nueim appointed Khusro Shanam as the governor of Hamdan under the Muslim rule and he himself left for Nihawand. Now a large part of the hilly region of the Zagros Mountains was under the control of the Muslims. Nihawand was the last great battle fought between the Muslims and the Persians after Qadisiyya. This battle was known as the "Victory of the Victories".[78] A total number of 40,000 out of 60,000 Persians perished in the war. Umar granted the fighters of Nihawand the annual pay of 2,000 dirhams.

After the fall of Nihawand, according to Tabari as quoted by Akram, a veteran of Iraq named Ashraf bin Qeis said:

> O Commander of the Faithful.
> You have debarred us from settling in the land and made us withhold our hands from what we have conquered. But the Emperor of the Persia is alive behind them, and they will not cease to contend with us as long as

the Emperor is among them. Two kings cannot work together in harmony; one must oust the other. You have seen that we have not taken a city except in countering their moves. It is their Emperor who raises them against us, and this will continue until you permit us to settle in their land and push their Emperor out of Persia and out of the veneration of his people. Then the people of Persia will give up hope of his help and loose their firmness of purpose.[79]

The Muslims believed that the safety of Iraq would only be possible if the Muslims settle in the land so that the people of the conquered areas will cease to depend on the king of Persia, and we continue to destroy the king by destroying his empire.[80] The safety of Iraq depends on the destruction of the entire Persian Empire. This situation will not change until the king is driven out of the Persian Empire and his entire empire falls under the Muslims' domain.[81]

Umar was convinced and changed his policy by lifting the embargo on the Muslims for acquiring property and settling in Iraq. Until now the Muslims had been reacting to the Persians' move rather than acting directly. Now the Muslims would be able to act directly against the Persians to eliminate them. The Muslims already had Iraq and parts of Khuzistan under their control. The remaining of the Persian Empire stretched to Azerbaijan and Armenia in the north and Afghanistan in the center, and Makran and Sind (now in Pakistan) in the south.

Now Umar called Hormuzan. Hormuzan was the former Persian lord, the prince of Ahwaz, and the great Persian general who later became Muslim and lived in Madina. Umar asked Hormuzan, "How do you think, we should start? With Fars, or with Azerbaijan, or with Isfahan?" Hormuzan briefly replied, "There is a head and two wings". If one wing is cut, the head will stay with the other wing. And, if the head is cut then both wings will fall. So, start with the head.[82] Isfahan was the head and Fars and Azerbaijan were the wings. This was a very intelligent advice that Hormuzan offered to the Caliph Umar.

Umar decided to start with the head and to start it immediately. Umar ordered the start of the first of the four campaigns to destroy and bring the Persian Empire under the Muslim rule. In the last quarter of 21 Hijri, Umar ordered Abdullah bin Abdullah bin Utban to attack Isfahan, the head. Utban took the army from Iraq and marched via Nihawand to Isfahan. When the Muslims arrived in Isfahan, they found a big Persian army ready for the battle at Jayy, an outer edge to the east of Isfahan. Jayy still exists and later it was renamed to Sharistan. The Muslims immediately attacked the Persians who withdrew into the fortified city. The Muslims laid siege to Isfahan.

The siege of Isfahan continued for two weeks, and in the meantime the other two groups led by Ahnaf bin Qeis and Abu Musa from Basra joined Abdullah. Ahnaf bin Qeis was ordered to get positioned at Isfahan for the invasion of Khurasan. At the time of arrival of these two groups, the Persian general named Fazusfan challenged the Muslim commander for a single duel on the condition

28 Ancient history of Afghanistan

that the winner would have Isfahan. Abdullah bin Abdullah bin Utban accepted the challenge. Both the generals mounted on their horses and met for the duel. Fazusfan was the first to attack; Abdullah survived the blow, but it struck the front part of the saddle of his horse. The saddle fell down, and Abdullah also slipped off from the horse. But Abdullah immediately mounted on his horse again and the Persian general, instead of taking advantage of Abdullah's vulnerable position, told him that he was much too good a man to be killed and could have Isfahan in peace. The Persians surrendered and the Muslims took Isfahan.

Nueim with an army of 12,000 men advanced to Qazween and at Waj Ruz, a short distance from Qazween, found a large Persian army led by Isfandiar, the brother of the late Rustam. A battle ensued, in which the Persians were defeated. Some survivors fled to Rayy and some to Azerbaijan. Rayy was part of the present-day Tehran. Nueim ransacked Waj Ruz and advanced to Rayy which was fortified. The Muslims managed to get into the fort at night and made the Persians to yield. Rayy was ravaged and the Muslims collected a lot of booty. The inhabitants of Rayy agreed to pay jizya.

Nueim sent his brother Suweid to take control of the hilly region in the east that controlled communications with the northeastern part of the empire. Suweid took over one by one Demawand, Damghan, and Gurgan. The administrators of these districts surrendered and agreed to pay jizya. Now the whole of Tabaristan, the region now known as Mazandaran, was under the Muslims' rule. Now the head had been cut and the work on the wings started.

The work on the north wing of Azerbaijan started. After the Battle of Nihawand, Ammar bin Yasir was replaced by Mugheera bin Shu'ba as the governor of Kufa. Umar had appointed Hudayfah bin Al Yaman as the commander of this sector. Hudayfah captured Zanjan and Ardabeel thereafter. From here Hudayfah arrived in Bab, a few miles to the south of Darband. At Bab, Anushirwan had built a long wall from the shore of the Caspian into the hills of Azerbaijan with the sole purpose of keeping the Turks out of his empire. Bab surrendered and agreed to pay jizya. The Muslims advanced and captured Muqan by defeating the Turkish army. At this point in time, Hudayfah was replaced by Utba bin Farqad.

Utba continued the operation and took over all of Azerbaijan up to a little to the south of Darband and the eastern and the northern parts of Armenia as far as Tiflis on the south of the Caucasus Mountains. By the end of 22 Hijri, Azerbaijan and most parts of Armenia came under the Muslims' rule while some parts of Armenia remained with the Romans. Now the north wing of Azerbaijan was also cut and fell in the Muslins domain.

The third campaign in southern Persia was launched by Mujashe bin Masud. Mujashe advanced into Ardsheer Khurra district and confronted the Persians at Tawoos, also known as Tawwaj, and defeated them. He continued his advance and got to the town of Sabur, known to the Persians as Shapur, 10 miles to the northwest of Kazerun. In a few weeks, the people of Sabur surrendered and became part of the Muslims' kingdom. Now Uthman bin Abil Aas continued

Ancient history of Afghanistan **29**

where Mujashe had left and went deep into the region of Fars. Uthman defeated the Persian forces at Jor, also known as Ardsheer Khurra. Uthman advanced and captured Shiraz and Persepolis which were once destroyed by Alexander the Great. After Persepolis, Saria bin Zuneim led a campaign and captured the districts of Darabjurd (now Darab) and Fasa.

After this, Suheil bin Adi, supported by Abdullah bin Abdullah bin Utban, marched toward Kirman and defeated the Persian forces at Kirman. Suheil captured Jeeraft and then Beemand and Sheerjan in the north. Now was the turn of the great fighter and a brilliant hero of many campaigns in Iraq, Asim bin Amr, who scattered the Persian forces like flies at the border of Sistan, home of the late Rustam, and marched toward Zaranj, now called Zahidan, and laid a siege and the Persians surrendered to the Muslim rule.

Now only one province in the south named Makran and Sind in Pakistan was left for the Muslims to complete their operation in southern Persia. Umar arranged a strong force led by Hakam bin Amr, who marched toward Makran and confronted the forces of King Rasil of Sind in the Indian subcontinent. A battle took place, and the Muslims defeated King Rasil of Sind, who withdrew across the Indus River in Sind. This was the end of the Persian Empire and also marked the end of the Muslims' campaign against the Persians in the south. The Muslims did not go beyond this point and there was also no need for doing so as their mission to annihilate the Persian Empire had been accomplished.

After having eliminated the southern Persian Empire, the only task left for the Muslims was to occupy the province of Khurasan. The Muslims were determined not to leave an inch of land to be known as the Persian Empire. Umar ordered Ahnaf bin Qeis to march from Isfahan toward Khurasan. Ahnaf took a sizeable army with him and left Isfahan by avoiding Rayy to Nishapur, expecting a big confrontation by the Persians on that route. Ahnaf bypassed Nishapur toward Herat. On his way, he captured two towns, Tabas now known as Gulshan and Tus now known as Firdaus, and went straight to Herat leaving Nishapur behind him in the left. At Herat, the Persians gave a tough fight but were defeated and thus Herat opened the gates for Islam. Herat was the easternmost city of Khurasan Province.

After Herat, Anhaf marched toward Nishapur and captured it. After that he marched toward Merv in the north where Yazdjurd had taken refuge. When Yazdjurd heard about the arrival of the Muslims, he left for Balkh. Balkh was an ancient city located 14 miles to the west of the present-day Mazar-e-Sharif, the capital of Balkh Province in Afghanistan. Ahnaf took over Merv, now in Turkmenistan. Here Ahnaf stopped and waited for the arrival of reinforcements from Iraq. At Balkh, Yazdjurd had gathered a small army which was driven out by the Muslims across the Oxus River. Anhaf captured Balkh Province and a peace treaty was signed under which the inhabitants agreed to pay jizya. After conquering Balkh, Anhaf returned to Merv and made it his permanent station. Now the whole of Khurasan was under the Muslims' rule.

By the end of 23 Hijri, the Muslim empire stretched to Sind in the east, in central Afghanistan, Merv in the north, and to the Oxus River. Umar was

30 Ancient history of Afghanistan

happy with the spread of Islam in such farthest areas and the Persian Empire had now been converted into the Muslim empire. This was the end of the Sassanian dynasty of the Persian Empire, which was shattered by a wave of Islam that rose from Arabia and brought an area of 2,251,030[83] square miles under the domain of Islam. In the east it included Khuzistan, Armenia, Azerbaijan, Fars, Kirman, Khurasan (Iran), Afghanistan, Makran, and Sind in Pakistan. According to Tabari, the limit of the Muslims' rule was up till Makran in Pakistan. However, according to Balazuri, the Muslim forces reached Daybul near Karachi which was managed from Thatta.[84] The decline of the Persian Empire opened the gates for the spread of Islam to Central Asia, Armenia, beyond the Oxus River to Khurasan, Iran, Afghanistan, and South Asia, down to Sind in Pakistan. According to Lewis, during his reign, Mu'awyia continued with the conquests of Bukhara, Fergana, and Samarkand in Uzbekistan, across the Oxus River, and expanded trade through the Indian Ocean and the Silk Road.[85]

In the 9th century, the Saffarid dynasty was established under a Sistani leader, Yaqub bin Laith as-Saffar, who got control of Sistan and started conquering other parts of Iran, Afghanistan, parts of Pakistan (up to the Indus River), Tajikistan, and Uzbekistan. The capital of the Saffarid dynasty was Zaranj. During the rule of the Saffarid dynasty, Islam effectively reached Kabul and Ghazni. The Hindu dynasty, the Hindushahi, controlled Gandhara in the east. Afghanistan was influenced by the Persian language and culture. The independence of Khorasan resulted in the foundation of the Tahirid dynasty. Later, both the Saffarid and the Tahirid dynasties merged into the Samanid dynasty in Turkestan under its founder, Saman Khuda, with its capital at Bokhara. Ghazni became the center of power. The Samanids hired Turkish slaves in their army and Ghazni was the eastern limit of the Samanid kingdom, which was ruled by the Turkish on their behalf.

In 977, when the Samanid dynasty became weak, Sabuktedin, the Turkish warlord, established his own rule in Ghazni and remained the ruler until his death in 997. In 998, at the age of twenty-seven, the Turkish descendant, the greatest Sultan Mahmud Ghaznavi became the ruler of Ghazni. Mahmud Ghaznavi was born in Ghazni Province of Afghanistan in 971. He invaded India seventeen times successfully between 1000 and 1025. He expelled the Hindus from Gandhara and encouraged the people to convert to Islam both in India and Afghanistan. He destroyed the Somnath temple in Indian Gujarat and other temples in India and ravaged the idols. He also seized Multan from an Ismaili Muslim ruler. His empire spread from the Indian subcontinent to the Central Asian states of Bokhara and Samarkand. His summer capital was Ghazni and winter capital Lahore in Pakistan.

The Arab geographer Al-Biruni and the Persian poet Firdausi, author of *Shahanama*, adorned Sultan Mahmud's court. Sultan Mahmud Ghaznavi died in 1030. After Mahmud's death, the Ghaznavid empire was ruled by his son Masud I (1031–1041), who was a weak ruler and thus was challenged by the Seljuk Turks, who took control of Iran and the Central Asian territories under the Ghaznavid empire. Thus, the Ghaznavid empire was limited to eastern Afghanistan with its capitals in Ghazni and Lahore. Muizuddin Muhammad, also known in history by the name of Shahabuddin Ghauri, was born in 1150 in Ghor Province of modern-day Afghanistan. In 1173, the Ghaurids captured Ghazna, now Ghazni, and Shahabuddin Ghauri became its governor, while his elder brother Ghyasuddin Ghauri became the Sultan of the Ghaurid empire. Shahabuddin Ghauri captured Multan in 1175, Peshawar and Sialkot in 1181, and Lahore in 1187, which resulted in the complete elimination of the Ghaznavid dynasty.

After the death of his brother Ghyasuddin Ghauri, Shahabuddin Muhammad Ghauri became the Sultan of the Ghauri empire in 1202. In 1206, while he was coming back to Lahore, he stopped over at Damiak near Sohawa in the Jhelum District of Pakistan and was assassinated allegedly by a Hindu while he was praying. He is buried now at the place of his death according to his wish. He was succeeded by his general, Qutb-uddin Aibak, a Mamluk or slave of Muhammad of Ghor, as the first Sultan of India who ruled from 1206 until 1210. He died in Lahore while playing polo and is buried there. Aibak built the Qutub Minar and the Quwaatul Islam mosque in Delhi and Dhai Din Ka Jhompra mosque in Ajmer. The Ghaurids' Muiz-ud-din Mohammad Ghauri and his general Kutb-ud-din Aibak first established Islamic rule in North India. After Aibak's death, the Ghaurid empire was ruled by the regional rulers such as Nasiruddin Qabach as the ruler of Multan, Tajuddin Yeldoz as the ruler of Ghazni, and Ikhtiyaruddin Mohammad as the ruler of Bengal. In 1215, Ghor was captured by Mahmood Shah of Khwarizm Shah (Seljuk Turks) with their capital at Khiva. The Ghaurids' rule was finished by the Khawarzim Shahs. The empire of the Khwarizm Shahs had barely lived for five years when the people living between Lake Baikal and the Gobi Desert in the north of China, called Mongols, appeared on its soil.

Notes

1 Omrani, *Afghanistan: A Companion and Guide*, p. 32.
2 Ewans, *Afghanistan: A New History*, pp. 10–12.
3 Omrani, *Afghanistan: A Companion and Guide*, p. 32.
4 Romm, *The Campaigns of Alexander*, p. 26.
5 Ibid., p. 29.
6 Ibid., p. 31.
7 Ibid., p. 31.
8 Ibid., p. 67.
9 Ibid., p. 70.
10 Ibid., p. 71.
11 Ibid., p. 73.
12 Ibid., p. 78.
13 Ibid., p. 77, 2.12.7a.
14 Ibid., pp. 80–81.
15 Ibid., p. 101.
16 Ibid., p. 101.
17 Ibid., p. 111.

32 Ancient history of Afghanistan

18 Ibid., p. 113.
19 Ibid., p. 116.
20 Romm, *The Campaigns of Alexander*, p. 131.
21 Ibid., p. 141.
22 Omrani, *Afghanistan: A Companion and Guide*, p. 34.
23 Ibid., p. 137.
24 Omrani, *Afghanistan: A Companion and Guide*, p. 34.
25 Ewans, *Afghanistan: A New History*, p. 12.
26 Romm, *The Campaigns of Alexander*, p. 144.
27 Ibid., pp. 148–149.
28 Ibid., p. 178.
29 Dupree, *An Historical Guide to Afghanistan*, p. 27.
30 Ewans, *Afghanistan: A New History*, p. 12.
31 Dupree, *An Historical Guide to Afghanistan*, pp. 65, 237.
32 Romm, *The Campaigns of Alexander*, p. 186.
33 Ibid., p. 188.
34 Ibid., p. 184.
35 Ibid., p. 208.
36 Romm, *The Campaigns of Alexander*, p. 221.
37 Ibid., p. 219.
38 Ibid., p. 221.
39 Romm, *The Campaigns of Alexander*, p. 252.
40 Ibid., p. 260.
41 Ibid., p. 268.
42 Romm, *The Campaigns of Alexander*, pp. 279–280.
43 Ibid., p. 406.
44 Dupree, *An Historical Guide to Afghanistan*, p. 32.
45 Ewans, *Afghanistan: A New History*, p. 14.
46 Dupree, *An Historical Guide to Afghanistan*, p. 35.
47 Akram, *The Muslim Conquest of Persia*, p. 20.
48 Ibid., p. 20.
49 Ibid., p. 20.
50 Akram, *The Muslim Conquest of Persia*, p. 151.
51 Akram, *The Sword of Allah*, p. 218.
52 Ibid., p. 226.
53 Ibid., p. 232.
54 Al-Quran, Surah Anfal, Chapter 8.
55 Akram, *The Sword of Allah*, p. 242.
56 Ibid., p. 255.
57 Ibid., p. 261.
58 Ibid., p. 263.
59 Ibid., p. 274.
60 Ibid., p. 275.
61 Akram, *The Muslim Conquest of Persia*, p. 98.
62 Ibid., p. 100.
63 Ibid., p. 141.
64 Ibid., p. 142.
65 Ibid., p. 147.
66 Ibid., p. 171.
67 Ibid., p. 183.
68 Ibid., p. 194.
69 Ibid., p. 197.
70 Shibli Naumani, *Al-Farouk*, pp. 280–281.
71 Ibid., pp. 281–282.
72 Akram, *The Muslim Conquest of Persia*, p. 229.

73 Ibid., p. 232.
74 Ibid., p. 232.
75 Ibid., p. 232.
76 Ibid., p. 238.
77 Ibid., p. 265.
78 Ibid., p. 268.
79 Ibid., pp. 273–274.
80 Ibid., pp. 273–274.
81 Ibid., p. 274.
82 Ibid., p. 275.
83 Shibli Naumani, *Al-Farouk*, pp. 239–240.
84 Ibid., p. 220.
85 Lewis, *God's Crucible*, pp. 94–95.

Bibliography

Akram, A.I., *The Sword of Allah, Khalid Bin Al-Waleed, His Life and Campaigns*. Mr. Books, Islamabad, 1970.

Akram, A.I., *The Muslim Conquest of Persia*. Maktabah Publishers and Distributors, Birmingham, 1975.

Dupree, Nancy Hatch (ed.), *An Historical Guide to Afghanistan*. Afghan Tourist Organization, Publication Number 5, Jagra, Ltd., Tokyo, Japan, 1970.

Ewans, M., *Afghanistan: A New History*. Curzon Press, Richmond, 2001.

Lewis, D. Levering, *God's Crucible Islam and the Making of Europe*, 570–1215. W. W. Norton & Company, Inc, New York, 2008.

Naumani, S., Al-Farook (1898). Sheikh Ghulam Ali and Sons Ltd., Lahore.

Omrani, B., and M. Leeming, *Afghanistan: A Companion and Guide*. Odyssey Books and Guides, a division of Airphoto International Ltd., Odyssey Books and Guides, Sheung Wan, Hong Kong, 2007.

Romm, J., and R.B. Strassler, *The Campaigns of Alexander*. Anchor Books, a division of Random House, Inc., New York, 2010.

2

GENGHIS KHAN AND HIS DYNASTY

A sixteen-year-old beautiful girl of the Olkhunuud tribe named Hoelun got married to Chiledu of the Merkid tribe. She was going along with her newly-wed groom to her new home. On the road, the cart on which the newlywed couple was traveling was sighted by a raider named Yesugei of the Borijin clan. Yesugei wanted to find a wife for himself through kidnapping, which was normal practice on the steppe of the Mongolian region. Yesugei with the help of his two brothers attacked the cart which was carrying Hoelun and her new groom Chiledu. Hoelun immediately understood that she was being kidnapped and at the same time she wanted to save the life of her newlywed groom. She asked Chiledu to flee as quickly as possible. Hoelun then surrendered to her kidnapper Yesugei. Yesugei brought Hoelun home as his new wife.

Hoelun accepted her new life but at the same time she found out that her kidnapper already had a wife named Sochigel, who had one son. Both the wives of Yesugei lived in separate tents called gers in the Mongolian language. Soon after the kidnapping of Hoelun, Yesugei went on a hunting campaign against the Tartar, the most prestigious tribe of the steppe. Yesugei killed a Tartar named Temujin Uge. When he returned home, Hoelun bore her first son from Yesugei, whom he named Temujin. The name Temujin reflected a lingering hostility among the Tatars and the Mongols. There were many ethnic tribes, such as the Mongols, who were the descendants of the Huns, the Tartars on the steppe, the Khitan in the east and the Manchus in the far east, and the Turkic tribes of Central Asia, who were raiding against each other and stealing the wives and other possessions of each other.

When Temujin was born, the fingers of his right hand were tightly clutched and when his mother Hoelun opened his fingers there was a clot of blood in his hand which he brought from the womb of his mother. Whether this was a sign of a fortune or an evil, history would decide. When Temujin was nine years old,

DOI: 10.4324/9781003198376-2

his father took him in search of a wife. They decided to go to Hoelun's tribe, which was famous for its beauty. Hoelun's tribe was located at a great distance, and Yesugei wanted Temujin to be placed in the distant area in bride service. According to a tradition of the tribes on the steppe, a boy wishing for a wife was required to perform service to the parents of the girl for a few years after which the father of the girl would hand over the girl to him. While Yesugei and Temujin were on their way to Hoelun's tribe, they stopped by a family who had a beautiful daughter named Borte. Borte's father accepted Temujin in bride service, and Yesugei left for home.

Yesugei arrived home and fell ill. He then sent a man to bring Temujin back home. Temujin left Borte and returned home. When Temujin arrived home, he found his father dead. Yesugei left behind two wives Hoelun and Sochigel along with seven children. After the death of Yesugei, Hoelun and Temujin worked hard to feed their family. Temujin's family was abandoned by the Tayichiud tribe. Temujin developed a friendship with Jamuka whose family's camp was near them. Temujin and Jamuka took an oath of brotherhood and swallowed each other's blood to establish a firm friendship. According to tradition, after the death of a father, the eldest son took over command of the house. Temujin's half-brother Begter assumed that role which was not liked by Temujin. Temujin killed him. This was his first murder when he was so young. Murder on the territory of the Tayichiud tribe was a violation of their custom, and they arrested Temujin and imprisoned him. A cangue was put around his neck, and he was placed under the control of a slave family to guard him. One of the slave family members felt pity for him and gave him food and cut the cangue around his neck, burnt it, and helped him escape.

In 1178, Temujin took his half-brother Belgutei and left for his intended wife Borte, whom he had not seen for seven years after the death of his father. When Temujin arrived at Borte's place, he found out that Borte still had not married and was waiting for him. Borte's father gave her hand to Temujin. Both Temujin and Belgutei returned home with Borte as Temujin's wife. Borte brought a lot of gifts for her new family which included a very expensive fur coat. Temujin wanted protection for his family and for this reason he decided to give the fur coat as a gift to Ong Khan of the Kereyid tribe who overthrew his uncle Gur Khan and ruled central Mongolia. Ong Khan accepted the gift and accepted Temujin as his step-son, which ensured the protection of Temujin's family.

The Merkid tribe now decided to take revenge for the kidnapping of Hoelun married to Chiledu by not only recapturing Hoelun but also taking Borte to serve the tribe in return for Hoelun's kidnapping. The old lady who saved Temujin alerted him to the advance of the Merkid tribe. Temujin along with six companions and his mother and sister fled to take refuge in Mount Burkhan Khaldun. Temujin left behind his wife Borte, Sochigel, and the old woman. When the Merkid entered the ger of Temujin they found just the three women. They took Borte and returned.

36 Genghis Khan and his dynasty

In order to recover his wife Borte, Temujin sought help from Ong Khan and his boyhood friend Jamuka. The three forces of Ong Khan, Jamuka, and Temujin attacked the Merkid tribe. The Merkids fled, and Ong Khan, Jamuka, and Temujin's forces looted their gers. Temujin recovered Borte and found out that she was pregnant. She gave birth to a boy who Temujin named Jochi, meaning the visitor or the guest.

Later, Jamuka was prickled with jealousy of Temujin's capability. Jamuka considered himself superior to Temujin on the basis that he was from white bone and Temujin was from black bone. Temujin did not like this. Differences started popping up between the two sworn brothers. Temujin separated his group from Jamuka's. At this time, Temujin was nineteen years old. Temujin started building his own group and power structure.

In 1189, Temujin decided to become the khan of his own group. Temujin held a meeting of the council called a khuriltai which endorsed him with the title of khan. Temujin organized his group and appointed 150 elite guards. Jamuka refused to recognize Temujin as the khan of all the Mongol tribes.

In 1190, Jamuka was ready for battle with Temujin. As Jamuka's group was larger than Temujin's, Jamuka's forces pushed Temujin's forces across the steppe. Jamuka beheaded a prisoner from Temujin's group and tied it to the tail of a horse to humiliate the dead soul. The remaining seventy captured men were boiled in a big cooking pot, which was not liked even by his own people; they despised him and joined Temujin.

In 1196, when Temujin was thirty-four years old, he and Ong Khan of the Kereyid tribe attacked the Tartar tribe, which was a very famous and rich tribe on the steppe. The booty was so enormous that many people joined his group. After this, the Jurkin tribe stole Temujin's horse and killed ten of his followers, which formed the basis for a fight between the Jurkin and Temujin groups. The Jurkins were defeated and their leaders were later executed. After the Jurkins, Temujin captured a place called Avarga and made this place his base camp for further activities.

Jamuka was still not done with Temujin and did not recognize his leadership role. Jamuka called a meeting of a council that endorsed him with the title of Gur Khan, meaning the khan of the khans. Gur Khan was the title used by Ong Khan's uncle, who had ruled the Kereyid tribe but was killed by Ong Khan. By using this title, Jamuka challenged both Ong Khan and Temujin. Jamuka was also supported by the Tayichiud tribe. Both Ong Khan and Temujin set off against Jamuka, who later fled. Ong Khan's forces pursued Jamuka, and Temujin's forces pursued the Tayichiuds. After a big fight, the Tayichiuds fled and Temujin captured their leaders and executed them. Thus, Temujin had taken his revenge on the Tayichiud tribe, who had captured and imprisoned him thirty years ago when he was a boy.

In 1202, Ong Khan sent Temujin on his second campaign against the Tatars in the east. Temujin defeated the Tatars again and collected an enormous amount of the booty, which he managed himself and personally distributed to each of the warriors and to the widows and orphans of the warriors.

Genghis Khan and his dynasty **37**

In 1203, after the victory of the Tatars, Temujin thought that as Ong Khan was becoming old, it was time then to build a real relationship with Ong Khan so that after his death Temujin would have control of all the Mongol tribes. To implement his plan Temujin asked Ong Khan to give his daughter's hand in marriage to him. Temujin thought that if he accepted then that would mean the acknowledgment of his being the successor to Ong Khan. If not, then he would decide in battle. When Ong Khan received this message, he became furious and told the messenger to go back and tell him that he himself was just his vassal and how dare he ask for the hand of his daughter. Ong Khan said he would rather burn his daughter alive than giving her to Temujin.

Later, Ong Khan regretted sending the message to Temujin and worried that it could have disastrous consequences. Ong Khan sent a messenger to Temujin and said that he had changed his mind and asked him to come with a few members of his family to enjoy the wedding. Temujin left with a few companions and when he was a one-day ride away from Ong Khan, Temujin found out that Ong Khan had prepared a plan to kill him and had posted his men in hiding in different directions. Temujin ordered some of his men to go in those directions and he took a few companions and fled to the east before Ong Khan's army could reach him. Thus Temujin fled for the second time, this time from the warriors of Ong Khan of the the Kereyid tribe, while the first time he did it against the Merkid tribe when they kidnapped Borte. On hearing that Temujin had fled to the east, most of his followers, including his close relatives, broke the allegiance to Temujin and joined Ong Khan and Jamuka for the sake of their lives.

Temujin and his followers arrived on the distant shores of Lake Baljuna. They were exhausted after a long ride and were with empty bellies as they could not get anything to eat for many days. Suddenly they saw a wild horse and his men dashed to the horse, got hold of it, and skinned it. They gathered fuel to cook the meat. What they did was according to the steppe nomad custom. They put the meat in the hide and put water in it. They created a fire by burning fuel that they had collected from the desert. They put stones in the fire and when the stones became red hot, they put them in the hide which contained the meat and the water. The red-hot stones boiled the water that cooked the meat and the feast was ready to fill in the empty bellies. This feast was a blessing for Temujin in that it could be a sign of future victories. Temujin and his followers considered this feast as an intervention from nature and his followers pledged their loyalty to him, and this pledge came to be known as the covenant of Baljuna.

Now Temujin prepared a plan to counterattack Ong Khan, who was boasting that he had got rid of Temujin. Temujin sent word to his followers across the steppe and told the whole story as to what had happened while he was traveling to the wedding invitation and about the miracle of the horse and how it had saved and reenergized them.

Temujin and his followers, enkindled with new spirit, marched toward the land of Ong Khan. Temujin's followers had joined him from all the directions they had been hiding in. Ong Khan had arranged a big feast to celebrate the

38 Genghis Khan and his dynasty

victory over Temujin and to boast about his power. He was unaware of the plan of Temujin. Temujin's men marched toward the Kereyid land. Temujin and his followers instead of marching directly into Ong Khan's court took a difficult detour to reach Ong Khan. Temujin and his followers stormed Ong Khan's camp, and after three days of fighting the Kereyids fled. Ong Khan's son fled to the south and died in thirst. Ong Khan and Jamuka fled separately toward the Naiman tribe. Some followers of Ong Khan had deserted him and joined Temujin, who accepted them as long as they pledged loyalty. While Ong Khan was crossing the border alone toward the Naiman tribe, his border guard killed him not knowing who the man was. Temujin and his followers spread the news that Ong Khan was dead and that he was no longer a threat to them. Now the Naiman tribe ruled by Tayang Khan was Temujin's next target.

In 1204, the battle for the control of Mongolia was fought 300 miles to the west of Burkhan Khuldun. Jamuka had now joined the Naiman tribe. The number of Temujin's men was far less than Naiman's men. Temujin had used the strategy of hit and run. Temujin's men, albeit small in number, were committed to Temujin. Each of the soldiers said, "If he sends me into the fire or water, I go. I go for him".[1] Temujin was thus confident and asked his soldiers to enjoy a sound night's sleep before the decisive battle the next morning. Unlike the Mongols, the Naimans were very confused and fled in panic in the darkness of the night and their horses fell in the gorges one after another. The next morning the Mongols defeated the remaining forces of the Naiman tribe and completely destroyed Tayang Khan. Tayang Khan's son Guchlug and the forty-year-old Jamuka fled and took refuge in a forest. Later, in 1205, his followers captured Jamuka and presented him before Temujin. Temujin killed Jamuka and thus his last rival on the steppe was finished. Now Temujin had control over all the Mongol clans.

Temujin had killed his elder half-brother Begter to have control over the family. He had killed the Tatars who had killed his father. He had eliminated the Tayichiud tribe who had captured and enslaved him when he was a child. He had destroyed the Jurkin tribe. He had destroyed Ong Khan who had refused the marriage of his daughter to Temujin. He had destroyed the Jadaran clan by killing Jamuka for breaking the oath of the brotherhood. Temujin was now an undisputed ruler of the vast land of Mongolia. His territory had grassland with a population of 1 million people of different tribes and more than 15 million animals.

In 1206, Temujin summoned the khuriltai, along the Onon River in Burkhan Khaldun mountains, which had saved his life by offering him refuge when he fled against the Tayichiud tribe. Temujin had rejected all the Mongol titles like Gur Khan or Tayang Khan and chose the title that his followers chose for him, and that was Genghis Khan (Chinggis Khan). The installation of Genghis Khan was held in an open area on the steppe and was attended by hundreds of thousands of participants, who all bowed on their knees nine times in obeisance. From 1206 onward, Temujin became Genghis Khan. Genghis Khan, an orphan, demonstrated the courage and steadfastness of purpose that led him to become the leader of the Mongols in 1206. Genghis Khan was inspired by his ancestors of the Hun dynasty.

Temujin, now Genghis Khan, built strong institutions to govern his empire. He started from the military and provided an opportunity to all the cowherds, the shepherds, and the camel boys to rise to the position of a general in the army based on their courage, bravery, and performance. He announced that all the male members between the age of fifteen and seventy years would be active members of the Mongol army. Genghis Khan appointed trusted men for the protection of his family. He rewarded the people coming from the black-boned lineage to the highest position based on their performance.

Genghis Khan introduced new law based on Mongol customs and traditions and abolished customs which did not work. He prohibited the practice of kidnapping of women as a reaction to the kidnapping of his mother and his wife by the Mongol tribes. He prohibited abduction and enslavement of any Mongol as a reaction to his own capture and enslavement by the Tayichiud tribe. He prohibited the selling of women in marriage. He prohibited adultery. He declared that the matters of the ger should be decided within the ger and matters of the steppe should be decided on the steppe. The stealing of animals was prohibited. If anyone were to find an animal, he was to deliver it to the rightful owner. He also established the system of the lost and found. Anyone who found something and failed to report to the lost and found system was to be considered a thief and would be punished with execution. He further decreed that the whole family would collectively be culpable for the criminal deed(s) of any member of the family.

The Mongols were united as long as they had an enemy. Having enemies was the main cause for the collection of booty and the expansion of the empire. In 1207, Genghis Khan sent his eldest son, the twenty-eight-year-old Jochi, to Sibir in the north, which is now called Siberia. Jochi returned successful after submission of the Siberians and brought a lot of booty in the form of fur and feathers. Genghis Khan received a variety of goods from the Uighur people of the Taklimakan desert. Genghis Khan accepted submission of Uighur, now in the Xinjiang region in China. Genghis Khan built an alliance with Uighur by offering his daughter in marriage to Uighur Khan. In 1209, Uighur Khan came to Mongolia for the wedding with a caravan of camels laden with very precious gifts of gold, silver, pearls, and diamonds. Genghis Khan next targeted the south in an attempt to correct the imbalance of the goods available on the Mongol steppe.

In 1210, when Genghis Khan was forty-eight years old, he received an envoy from the new Golden Khan of the Jurched dynasty in China, whose capital was Zhongdu, now known as Beijing. The new Golden Khan ascended the throne after the death of the Golden Khan. The Jurched dynasty, founded in 1125, had ruled Manchuria, parts of Mongolia, and northern China. The envoy relayed the message of the Golden Khan, who demanded submission of Genghis Khan and the Mongols to the Golden Khan as a vassal nation. When Genghis Khan

40 Genghis Khan and his dynasty

heard the message, he became furious and spit on the ground with contempt. He made insulting remarks about the new Golden Khan. Genghis Khan was not the person to kowtow to anybody. He immediately mounted on his horse and moved toward the north.

In the 13th century, Jurched was the second largest kingdom to rule over 50 million people and to occupy a territory now called modern China with its capital at Zhongdu, now Beijing. The Jurched dynasty was second to the Sung dynasty based in Hangzhou in the Zhejiang province in eastern China, which ruled over 60 million people. To the west of the Jurcheds were the kingdoms of the Uighurs, the Tanguts, and the Black Khitans. Uighur had already committed to Genghis Khan and Tangut was subdued in a series of conquests between 1207 and 1209. The Tanguts were the Tibetan people who lived in modern-day Gansu Province in China. They were well fortified with the force of 150,000 soldiers, double the number of Genghis Khan's forces, but the numbers didn't matter for the Great Khan. Genghis Khan broke the siege and entered the city. With this, both Uighur and Tangut came under his control, which could provide him support against the Jurcheds.

In 1211, Genghis Khan's forces crossed the Gobi to invade the Jurched. Genghis Khan's entire army comprised 65,000 horsemen without any infantry, while the Jurcheds had a similar number of horsemen but with additional 85,000 foot soldiers. The Mongol soldiers moved without any food supply train and created their food supplies through the hunting and slaughtering of animals. They could travel for as long as ten days without stopping. According to Marco Polo, each Mongol soldier carried ten pounds of dried milk and dried strips of meat and yogurt. They ate a lot of protein which gave them strong bones and teeth. The Mongol soldiers were stronger than the Jurcheds, who ate just carbohydrates based on grains which stunted their bones and decayed their teeth.

In 1214, Genghis Khan laid a siege on the court of the Jurcheds. The new Golden Khan who had lost the support of his own people was in no position to stand against the Mongols. The new Golden Khan, who once wanted the allegiance of Genghis Khan, now had to think otherwise. He accepted himself as a vassal of Genghis Khan to have them withdraw. The new Golden Khan gave the Mongols massive gifts of silk, silver, gold, 3,000 horses, and 500 young boys and girls for service and as mates. In addition, he gave Genghis Khan one royal princess as a wife. After this Genghis Khan returned back to Mongolia.

When Genghis Khan had defeated Tayang Khan of Naiman, his son Guchlug fled to Black Khitan where he married the daughter of the ruler of Khitan. Later he overthrew the Khitan ruler and usurped his power. Guchlug was a Christian and harbored antagonistic feelings for Muslims living in the Black Khitan. Although Uighur had joined Genghis Khan, other Uighur Muslims living in the foothills of Tian Shan mountain of what is now Kyrgyzstan, Kazakhstan, Tajikistan, Kashgar, and the bordering region of Afghanistan and Pakistan were under Guchlug's rule. Guchlug prohibited the Muslims from the call for prayer, praying in the public, and having religious study centers. The Muslims of these areas sent their representatives to Genghis Khan and requested him to overthrow the Guchlug's rule for his anti-Muslim activities. Genghis Khan accepted their demand and sent General Jebe who overpowered Guchlug, defeated him, and finally beheaded him in the plains bordering Afghanistan, Pakistan, Tajikistan, Kyrgyzstan, and China and returned home.

The vast area from the mountains of Afghanistan to the Black Sea was ruled by a Turkic Sultan, Muhammad II, whose empire called Khwarizm covered most of Persia and Mawarannahr, now Uzbekistan, with its capital at Samarkand. Genghis Khan was interested in a trading partnership with the Sultan. Genghis Khan sent a trading caravan of 450 Muslim traders from Mongolia to Khwarizm. When the Mongols' trading caravan arrived in the province of Otrar in southern Kazakhstan, the governor of the province, who was the uncle of the Sultan and the brother of Sultan's mother, not only looted the caravan but also killed all of them. Genghis Khan brought the matter to the attention of the Sultan. Dupree reported Genghis Khan's message to the Sultan which said:

> I am the sovereign of the sun-rise, and thou the sovereign of the sun-set. Let there be between us a firm treaty of friendship, amity, and peace and let traders and caravans on both sides come and go, and let the precious products and ordinary commodities which may be in my territory be conveyed by them into thine, and those in thine into mine.

Sultan instead of punishing the governor rebuked Genghis Khan. This is what Genghis Khan wanted. He needed an enemy to fight with, and the Sultan had just provided him with that opportunity.

In 1219, Genghis Khan launched his campaign against the Khwarizm empire.

The strength of Genghis Khan's forces that entered the Khwarizm empire was between 100,000 and 125,000 horsemen with no infantry. This force was supplemented with the additional support from Uighur and the allied tribes plus a corps of Chinese doctors and engineers for a total of 150,000 to 200,000 men. Sultan's strength was 400,000 men gathered from all over his empire. In 1219, Genghis' sons Ogodei and Chaghatai captured the governor of Otrar and killed him by putting molten gold into his throat. Fletcher reported Genghis Khan's action as the "most brutal of all nomad invasions annihilated the armies of the Khwarizm Shahs". Genghis Khan's forces reached Bokhara. Sultan, deserted by the people, the army, and the family, fled and took refuge on an island in the Caspian Sea where he died. Genghis Khan captured Bokhara and Samarkand. The Khwarizm Shahs' empire with its capital at Urgench and all that it had was crushed[2] by the behemoth and the cutthroat Mongol Genghis Khan's juggernaut army.

In 1221, the Mongols marched through Azerbaijan and destroyed the Christian kingdom of Georgia with its capital at Tiflis (Tbilisi). The Mongols marched through the mountains of Caucasus and Crimea and routed out the Bulgars, the Turks, and the Russian princes on the northern shores of the Caspian Sea.

42 Genghis Khan and his dynasty

Later, Urgench, the homeland of the Shahs (Khwarizm) in Uzbekistan, was captured. Termez in the north of the Oxus River in Uzbekistan was captured and destroyed. Cities and crops were destroyed, the Khwarizm army was scattered, people were butchered, and all that was left behind was a barren land. The massacre of the Muslims by Genghis Khan in the Khwarizm empire was even greater than the massacre of the Jews.

The massacre committed by Genghis Khan was not different from the ones done by Christians against Jews. When the Christian Crusaders took Antioch in Turkey in 1098 and Jerusalem in 1099, they slaughtered the Jews and the Muslims without regard for age or gender. In 1160, when the Roman emperor Frederick Barbarossa of Germany attacked the Lombard city of Cremona in northern Italy, his men beheaded their prisoners and played football with their heads. In reaction, the defenders of Cremona got the German prisoners and pulled their limbs off in front of the captured soldiers. Similarly, the Germans got the captive's children and placed them on the catapult and hurled them at the wall.

After crossing the Amu (Oxus) River in 1221, Genghis Khan entered Bactria, now Balkh, in northern Afghanistan. Here, again, Genghis Khan repeated the same things that he did to the Khwarizm Shahs. Genghis Khan destroyed the irrigation system and left the land behind as pasture. He also seized Herat, though without much destruction, but when the people of Herat rebelled, the city was annihilated and about 160,000 (Heratis) residents were executed.

After Herat, Genghis Khan sieged Nishapur, the city of Omar Khayyam, a Persian poet. Genghis Khan gave a message to the citizens of Nishapur which Weatherford quoted as under:

> Commanders, elders and community, know that God has given me the empire of the earth from the east to the west, whoever submits shall be spared, but those who resist, they shall be destroyed with their wives, children and dependents.[3]

The citizens of Nishapur fought back and an arrow shot from the wall struck Genghis Khan's son-in-law Tokucher who was killed instantly. Genghis Khan called his daughter who was pregnant at the time of the death of her husband and asked her how she wanted to take revenge for her dead husband. She ordered death for all. On her orders, all the men, all the women, and all the children in Nishapur were killed. Then she ordered to pile up the heads of the men, the women, and the children in three separate pyramids. Having done this, she then ordered to get all the dogs and cats and kill them so that no living creature stays on this land. The number of citizens killed in Nishapur was 1,747,000,[4] more than the massacre of Herat.

After conquering city after city, Genghis Khan and his forces arrived in Bamian, a central province of Afghanistan, which was a Buddhist pilgrimage center. Here the Mongols destroyed the images of Buddha carved in the mountains. A battle broke out between the local residents and the Mongols. During the course of the battle, an arrow shot by a local resident struck the grandson of Genghis Khan, named Mutugen, who was the son of Chaghatai. Genghis Khan called Chaghatai and informed him about the death of his son and asked him how he would like to take revenge for his son's death. Genghis Khan told Chaghatai, "don't weep or cry, just kill". Under the orders of Chaghatai, no rich, no poor, no good, no bad, no man, no woman, and no child survived in Bamian. Later, the people of the Hazara tribe, who claimed to be the descendants of Genghis Khan, resettled in Bamian.

After Bamian, Genghis Khan crushed Ghazni and Peshawar. Genghis Khan crossed the Indus River, and, in the summer of 1222, reached Multan in the Punjab province of modern-day Pakistan. The weather here was too hot for the Mongols and the Mongol soldiers became sick and some of them died. Genghis Khan stopped here and decided to return back home. Genghis Khan left behind 20,000 soldiers (two tumuns – one tumun consists of 10,000 soldiers) and asked them to continue with the conquests of northern India. Marozzi reported that Genghis Khan's organization of his army was in "units of ten, one hundred, one thousand and ten thousand soldiers, a system which Temur retained".This remaining army of left-behind soldiers also started falling sick owing to the scorching heat and began dying, and the small army was depleted. The Mongols therefore decided to return back to Afghanistan.

During a period of four years, Genghis Khan conquered all the major cities in Central Asia and South Asia which included: Bukhara, Samarkand, Otrar, Urgench, Balkh, Banakat, Khojend, Merv, Nisa, Nishapur, Termez, Herat, Bamian, Ghazni, Peshawar, Qazvin, Hamadan, Ardabil, Maragheh, Tebrez, Tbilisi, Derbend, and Astrakhan. Genghis Khan eliminated any army that crossed his path from the Himalayan Mountains to the Caucasus Mountains, from the Indus River in Pakistan to the Volga River in western Russia.

Genghis Khan, though celebrated his victories, was more worried about his family which did not seem to be united for running the big empire that was spread from Hungary to the China Seas, from Serbia to the Persian Gulf and Indian subcontinent. Genghis Khan was now in his sixties and called a meeting of the family khuriltai to decide about his successor. Genghis had four sons, Jochi, Chaghatai, Ogodei, and Tolui. Jochi was the eldest son followed by Chaghatai. Now the difficult question for Genghis Khan was whom to ask first about the issue. Genghis Khan considering Jochi as the eldest son asked him first about the successor. The moment Genghis Khan asked Jochi, Chaghatai instantly jumped up and shouted how a bastard son of the Merkid tribe could be a successor of Genghis Khan. Both Jochi and Chaghatai quarreled with each other, and Genghis Khan calmed both of them and said Borte, their mother, did not run away to Merkid but was kidnapped by the Merkid tribe. When Genghis Khan recovered his wife from the Merkid tribe and brought her back home, she was pregnant. This was not the fault of Borte as she was at the mercy of her Merkid kidnapper. "Do not raise the suspicion of paternity of Jochi, he is the son of your mother". Chaghatai obeyed his father but would not accept Jochi as the

44 Genghis Khan and his dynasty

successor. Chaghatai then suggested to Genghis Khan that instead of Joshi and Chaghatai to pick up Ogodei as the successor. Jochi agreed to this. Ogodei was a heavy drinker. Nevertheless, Genghis Khan appreciated Ogodei's capabilities and picked him as his successor.

The Mongols had become used to foreign-produced goods and for this purpose they needed a foreign enemy to pick up a fight. Genghis Khan now launched a second campaign against the Tangut tribe which Genghis Khan had invaded for the first time in 1207. Genghis Khan had a plan in his mind, which was after conquering the Tangut, he would establish his base over there for his onward campaign against the Sung dynasty. During the winter of 1226–1227, while Genghis Khan was on his way to Tangut, he fell from a horse and got injured and later became sick. His Tatar wife Yesui because of his illness advised him not to go further, which he refused and continued his march against the Tangut. The name of the king of the Tangut tribe was Burkhan, which means God, was sacred to Genghis Khan. Once the Tanguts were defeated, he ordered that the name of the king be changed before his execution.

In 1227, a few days before the final victory over the Tanguts, Genghis Khan died. His Tatar wife Yesui washed his body, wrapped it in white cloth, placed his felt boots and the hat inside, added sandalwood to avoid the insects, and got ready for the burial. On the third day after his death, the body was placed in a cart that marched in a procession led by his spirit banner toward Mongolia for his final burial. The procession was followed by his horse with Genghis Khan's empty saddle.

According to the custom, Genghis Khan had distributed the territories that he had conquered among his four sons. Jochi, the eldest son, got the territories far away from Karakoram Mountain Range, in the west of the Irtish River known as the Golden Horde; Ogodei, the third son who was to be the future Great Khan, got western Mongolia; the second son Chaghatai got Central Asia, while the fourth and youngest son, Tolui, got the father's seat in Mongolia.

After the death of Genghis Khan, Ogodei became the Great Khan and the family took the name of the Golden Family. The finance of the Mongol Empire dwindled as the conquered territories stopped sending the tributes. Ogodei now started building his new capital at Karakoram. After the death of Jochi, his son Batu took over the command of his territory and he wanted the campaign of Eastern Europe which Ogodei resisted. At the same time, his brother Tolui died and Ogodei wanted to annex his territory by arranging a marriage of his son with the widow of Tolui, named Sorkhokhtani, who refused the marriage. To have an access to Sorkhokhtani's land would provide an opportunity to attack the Sung dynasty to extort more wealth.

Ogodei finally decided that the campaign of Eastern Europe and the Sung dynasty could start simultaneously. The European campaign was led by Batu who was supported by General Subodei, and the Sung dynasty campaign was led by the sons of Ogodei. The Sung dynasty campaign was not successful and Ogodei lost his favorite son. While the campaign of Europe led by Batu was successful, the booty was not as much as it was during the period of Genghis Khan. Batu and Mongke Khan, the two grandsons of Genghis Khan, participated in the European campaign. The strength of the Mongol force at that time was 50,000 Mongols and 100,000 allies.

In 1236, General Subordei led 400 Mongols and reached the Volga, the homeland of the Bulgars, and Mongke Khan, the eldest son of Tolui, marched toward the Kipchak Turks. From here the Mongols moved toward Russia and Ukraine. However, before attacking them, the Mongols sent envoys asking them to surrender. If they surrendered, they would enjoy the protection of the Mongols. They would also be allowed to rule themselves as a vassal state of the Mongols. In return, they would pay 10% tribute on their goods and wealth. By 1240, the Mongols had captured most of the Russian cities. Next the Mongols moved toward Kiev and captured it in December 1240.

After Kiev, the Mongols moved toward Hungary in the south with an army of 50,000 men. The 20,000 men were sent across Poland toward the German border in the north. On April 9, 1241, Duke Henry II of Selesia, a region formerly divided between Germany, Poland, and Czechoslovakia, gathered an army of 30,000 men from Germany, France, and Poland that met the Mongols at Liegnitz near the German-Polish border. The Mongols repulsed the first attack and retreated as part of a game plan. The Europeans thought that the Mongols had fled, and they relaxed and broke their rank. All of a sudden, the Mongols returned and attacked the Europeans, killing 25,000 of their army of 30,000 and captured some of them. After killing the entire army of Northern Europe, the Mongols returned to their campaign of Hungary.

The campaign of Germany was carried out to prevent the Germans and the Polish from sending their army to Hungary. King Bela of Hungary's forces was defeated by the Mongols and suffered more casualties than the northern Europeans. The Mongols slaughtered the Hungarians with their bodies lying helter-skelter. The Christian priest tried to keep the Mongols out of their capital city of Pest. The Mongols killed the priest and burnt the churches. Hungary lost King Bela, the bishop, and 100,000 soldiers. The Mongols' deeds of horror spread throughout Europe. From Hungary, the Mongols marched toward the Balkans on the way to Vienna. The Mongols crossed through the steppe of Central Asia, Russia, Ukraine, Poland, Germany, and Hungary and stopped where pastures ended.

On December 11, 1241, Ogodei died in a drunken stupor while Chaghatai also died about the same time. Now there was a competition among the grandsons of Genghis Khan for the office of the Great Khan. As all the grandsons were not capable to obtain power, this role was performed by their mothers. Sorkhokhtani, the widow of Tolui, the youngest son of Genghis Khan, ruled northern China as she had refused to marry the elder son of Ogodei. The widow of Chaghatai ruled Central Asia. During his life, as most of the time Ogodei remained drunk, he had passed on the administrative powers to his wife Toregene. Now with the exception of Eastern Europe, Genghis Khan's empire was ruled by the women of his household.

46 Genghis Khan and his dynasty

In 1250, Sorkhokhtani got her son Mongke Khan elected by the khuriltai. On July 1, 1251, Mongke Khan was installed as the Great Khan of the Mongol Empire. Sorkhokhtani had four sons, Mongke, Hulegu, Khubilai, and Arik Boke, and all of them were capable enough to become the Great Khan. Her son Hulegu became the Khan of Persia and created his own dynasty. Her sons stretched the Mongol Empire to Persia, Baghdad, Syria, and Turkey. They conquered parts of the Sung dynasty's Empire in the south and marched toward Vietnam, Laos, and Burma, and killed the Abbasid Muslim Caliph Al Musta'sim who ruled Baghdad. The power of the Mongol Empire had now been transferred from Ogodei to Tolui's family. Sorkhokhtani kept her four sons united until she died in February 1252.

Mongke Khan became the Great Khan of the Mongol Empire in 1251. On coming to power, Mongke Khan focused his attention on the unfinished agenda of Genghis Khan, which was about the conquest of the Sung dynasty and the Muslim states of Persia and the Middle East. Mongke Khan ordered his brother Hulegu to attack the Muslim cities of Baghdad, Damascus, and Cairo and subdue them. Mongke Khan ordered another brother Khubilai to conquer the Sung dynasty. In May 1253, both Hulegu and Khubilai Khan departed on their respective missions.

On February 5, 1258, the Mongols broke into the city and captured Baghdad. The Caliph was killed. Now Hulegu marched toward Damascus. Damascus surrendered without a fight. This was the lowest point in the history of the Muslims. The Mongols conquered most of the Muslim areas in Asia from the Indus River to the Mediterranean with the exception of the Arab Peninsula and North Africa, which did not come under the control of the Mongol Empire. Hulegu conquered Georgia, Armenia, and Azerbaijan in the west, Baghdad and Damascus in the south, and Khurasan and eastern Persia in the east. Hulegu was supported by his brother Mongke.

Up to this point the Mongols remained undefeated. In 1259, Mongke died. On September 3, 1260, the forces of the Sultan of Egypt named Baibars, also known as Al-Futuh, met the Mongols at Ain-al Jalut, also known as the Spring of Goliath, in modern-day Israel. The Sultan, who had already defeated the seventh crusade of the French king Louis IX, defeated the Mongols at Ain-al-Jalut. With this defeat, Hulegu's campaign of the Middle East ended as he could not conquer Cairo.

The second campaign against the Sung dynasty was led by Mongke's brother Khubilai Khan. Khubilai Khan's campaign was not successful. In 1257, Mongke Khan decided that he himself would lead the campaign of the Sung dynasty. But the weather did not support Mongke Khan; it was too hot and the soldiers started suffering from diarrhea, and Mongke Khan himself became sick of diarrhea and died on August 11, 1259. With his death, the Sung dynasty remained unconquered by the Mongols.

Khubilai in 1264 became the undisputed Great Khan and ruled China, Tibet, Manchuria, Korea, and eastern Mongolia. The Golden Horde of Jochi's descendant ruled Eastern Europe and refused to recognize Khubilai as the Great Khan. Hulegu ruled from Afghanistan to Turkey, his kingdom known as the Ilkhanate, meaning "vassal empire". The traditional Mongols ruled the central steppe known as Mogolistan. Thus, the great Mongol Empire of Genghis Khan was divided among the four rulers, viz. Khubilai, Hulegu, Golden Horde, and the traditional Mongols of the central steppe.

In 1272, Khubilai established a new capital of the Mongol Empire in Northern China at Khanbalik, where now modern Beijing stands. His administrative machinery included Chinese, Tibetans, Armenians, Khitans, Arabs, Tajiks, Uighurs, Tanguts, Turks, and Persians. To facilitate the promotion of trade, he introduced paper money instead of metal. With reference to business practices, the Mongols allowed the filing of bankruptcy for a maximum of two times, and on the third time the filer would be executed.

In 1261, Khubilai Khan set up an agricultural authority for the promotion of agriculture and the welfare of the peasants. The purpose of this authority was to find ways to increase the yield of the crops that could foster the welfare of the farmers. The Mongols brought the Chinese crops of tea and rice into Russia and the Middle East. The Mongols brought the seeds, the shoots, and the whole plants from China for adaptation to the soil and the climate of the Middle East. The Mongols also introduced new varieties of rice, millet, root crops, and citrus fruits from India, China, and Persia. In Southern China, the Mongols developed the lemon orchards, saplings for which were brought from the Middle East. The Mongols focused on the cotton crop, and in 1289, Khubilai Khan established a Cotton Promotion Bureau. The Mongols introduced new agricultural tools and implements like a triangular plow. The improved triangular plow was brought into China from Southeast Asia. The Mongols also set up agricultural research stations for development of new seeds' varieties and improvement in the yields of the crops as well as the publication and distribution of agricultural outreach material. He gave property rights to the landowners.

With Khubilai's reforms the Chinese became happy with the Mongols for their treatment of them. The Chinese generals, soldiers, and public officials deserted in favor of the Mongols. This led to the gradual weakening and erosion of the Sung dynasty, which eventually facilitated the complete conquest of the Sung dynasty by Khubilai Khan. Khubilai accomplished his goal through public politics and won over the population by manipulation of public opinion rather than military action. In 1276, the Mongols vanquished the Sung dynasty and occupied their capital at Hangzhou. China divided between the north and the south was now united, and Khubilai Khan proclaimed it as the Yuan dynasty which lasted until 1368.

Now Khubilai wanted to further add more lands to his empire which were across the waters and involved naval campaigns. In 1268, Khubilai sent an envoy to Japan and asked for submission to the Mongols. Khubilai had established a naval base in Korea which could be used against Japan. The Japanese refused to submit to the Mongolians. On Japan's refusal, Khubilai Khan sent an armada of

48 Genghis Khan and his dynasty

900 ships with 23,000 Korean and Chinese foot soldiers and Mongol cavalry. Khubilai's ships sailed in the water that separated Japan and Korea by 110 miles. The Mongols captured the Tsushima Island across the strait. Then the armada sailed into Hakata Bay and fought with the Japanese who fled. The Mongols were successful and then all of sudden a big storm came that destroyed the Mongols' ships and boats and 13,000 Mongol soldiers were drowned and killed. The Japanese chopped the heads of the envoys and this compelled Khubilai to launch another attack on Japan. The second campaign included two fleets, one from Korea with 900 ships carrying the 23,000 Koreans and the second one from China with 3,500 ships, 60,000 sailors, and 100,000 soldiers. Although the Mongols conquered the island in the channel, the entire armada was again wrecked by the storms. The Mongols ended their campaign against Japan which remained outside of the Mongol territory.

The Mongols had succeeded on the land and captured Burma, Annam in Northern Vietnam, and Laos. In 1289, Khubilai sent an envoy to the king of Java to surrender to the Mongols but the king refused to do so. In 1292, Khubilai then sent another armada of 1,000 ships and boats with 20,000 soldiers to Java. In 1293, the Mongols fought with Java forces and killed the king and conquered the island. While the Mongols were preparing for the celebration of the submission by the heir of the king of Java, the Mongols were suddenly ambushed by the people of Java and the key leaders of the Mongols were killed and the remaining troops retreated in humiliation. The Mongols were unsuccessful and Java remained outside of the territory of the Mongols. The four crucial battles of Poland, Egypt, Japan, and Java set the outer boundaries of the Mongol Empire instead of becoming part of their territory.

In 1294, Khubilai Khan died and after his death the Mongol Empire started dwindling. The great khans who succeeded Khubilai were lazy and entrapped in intrigues and coups. During the same time, the deadly contagious plague originated in South China. The Mongol warriors and the traders carried the disease to the north through the shipments of food along with the fleas which were the carriers of the disease. In 1331, 90% of the people of Hopei (Hebei) Province of North China died. China lost 60 million of its people and its population came down from 125 million to 65 million. The plague reached the capital of Golden Horde at Sarai in 1345. The inhabitants fled and carried the disease to Constantinople, from where it was further spread to Cairo in Egypt. By 1345 it had reached the cities of Italy and then entered England. By 1350 it had crossed the North Atlantic. It killed about 60% of the people of Iceland. In the sixty years from 1340 to 1400, the population of Africa declined from 80 million to 68 million and that of Asia from 238 million to 201 million. America was not affected by the plague. The population of the world declined significantly due to the plague.

The social impact of the plague was disastrous. Instead of identifying the real causes of the plague, the petrified people in the affected areas immediately jumped to the conclusion that the outbreak had a correlation with trade, and they started victimizing people associated with trade. In Europe, where the population declined from 75 million to 52 million as a result of death by the plague, Jews were targeted by the Christians, as mainly the Jews were considered to be the trading ones and they were considered responsible for bringing in the plague to Europe. In 1348, in Europe, more than 2,000 Jews were burnt. Some Jews converted to Christianity to save themselves and their children's lives. In Spain, the minority Muslims became victims and they were driven out to take refuge in Granada and Morocco.

The policies of Genghis Khan and Khubilai Khan in China were not followed by their descendants. The Chinese lost their hope in the Mongols and despised them and started action against the Tibetans who hated the Chinese. In the 1330s, the peasant leader Chu Yuan-chang started a movement against the tyrant Mongols. Chu Yuan-chang's movement marched toward modern-day Beijing and crushed any resistance that crossed its path. The people had no sympathy for their Mongol rulers. The movement was strengthened day by day, and by 1368 it had become an impregnable force that drove the Mongols out of North China. The last Mongol ruler, Sun Ti, went into exile. When the capital fell, the peasant leader Chu Yuan-chang had by then become so powerful that he changed his name and proclaimed himself as Emperor Tai Tsu, the founding ruler of the Ming dynasty, who routed out the Mongols-led Yuan dynasty. Tai Tsu ruled until his death in 1399.

After the overthrow of the Mongols, the Ming rulers ordered the Chinese to stop the Mongol practices of wearing Mongol dresses and naming their children in Mongolian names. The Ming rulers rejected the policies of the Mongols and revitalized the Chinese culture. The Ming rulers expelled the Muslims, the Jews, and the Christian traders who had been settled in China by the Mongols. They spent a lot of money on infrastructure and constructed the Great Wall for the defense of the Chinese against foreign invaders. The Ming dynasty shifted their capital to Nanjing and later moved it to the old Mongol capital of Khanbalik, now known as Beijing, which serves as the capital of modern China.

The weak Mongols were compelled by every country to leave and the natives took over the control of their governments. Korea, Russia, and China saw the resurgence of their native dynasties. The Muslim areas remained as Muslim states but without the domination of the Arabs such as the Ottoman empire in Turkey, the Safavids of Persia, and the Moghuls of India. The Golden Horde in Russia and the Mongols in Persia and the Middle East became the dominions of the Muslims. The Mongol Empire in Persia and the Middle East collapsed in 1335. The Mongols of the Persian Ilkhanate were either killed or absorbed as their subjects. In China, 400,000 Mongols were captured and killed. Those who were able to reach Mongolia embraced their traditional nomadic way of life. The Mongol rule in China collapsed in 1368. The Mongol Empire was captured and divided between China and Russia. China took the south of the Gobi Desert while Russia took the north of the Gobi Desert. The Ming dynasty ruled from 1368 to 1644, until it was overthrown by the Qing dynasty ruled by Manchu,

50 Genghis Khan and his dynasty

who intermarried with the real descendants of Genghis Khan to legitimatize as his heirs. The Qing dynasty ruled for 268 years from 1644 to 1912 until they were overthrown by revolutionaries.

Notes

1 Weatherford, *Genghis Khan and the making of the modern world*, p. 62.
2 Omrani, *Afghanistan: a companion and guide*, p. 58.
3 Weatherford, *Genghis Khan and the making of the modern world*, p. 111.
4 Ibid., pp. 117–118.

Bibliography

Dupree, N.H., *An Historical Guide to Afghanistan*. Afghan Tourist Organization, Jagra ltd, Tokyo, Japan, Publication Number 5, 1970.

Fletcher, A., *A Complete History of Afghanistan*. Cornell University Press, USA, 1966.

Weatherford, J., *Genghis Khan and the Making of the Modern World*. Crown Publishing Group of Random House, Inc., Broadway Books, US, 2004.

3

AMIR TEMUR AND HIS DYNASTY

After Genghis Khan, another warlord created a space for himself in the history of the world and that was Temur or Tamerlane. More than a hundred years after the death of Genghis Khan, on April 9, 1336, Temur was born, to Amir Taraghay of the Barlas clan in the village Khoja-Ilgar of the Shakhrisabz city, which is located 90 kilometers south of Samarkand and 32 kilometers from the ancient fort of Kesh. Kesh was a part of the Mawarannahr region that was under the control of the second son of Genghis Khan, Chaghatai, who ruled in Central Asia. However, Amir Temur was not the direct descendant of Genghis Khan but was from the Turkic Barlas tribe. Haji Beg was the chief of the Barlas tribe who ruled the Qashka Darya Valley, where Temur grew up and lived. At the age of ten, Temur learned martial arts, which would make him a great warrior. One day, Temur told his young friends that his grandmother dreamed that he had a great future and that he would rule the world from the east to the west. Amir Temur remembered a local proverb that one who could hold a sword could also hold a scepter.

In 1347, Amir Qazaghan overthrew the puppet khans of the Chaghatai ulus and ruled for a decade. Later, in 1358, Qazaghan was killed by a Moghul warrior on the orders of Tughluk Temur, the khan of Moghulistan. Tughluk Khan seized control of Moghulistan. Tughluk Temur planned to invade from the east to reunite the scattered Chaghatai ulus. Haji Beg of the Barlas tribe, who was unable to face the big force of Tughluk Temur, decided to flee to the south. Beg along with Temur fled toward the Oxus River. At the bank of the Oxus River, before crossing it, Amir Temur asked his tribal chief Haji Beg that he be allowed to go back to his homeland with a small party of his followers and fight the Moghul Tughluk. Amir Temur assured Haji Beg that he would successfully defend his homeland against Tughluk Temur. Haji Beg allowed him to go back to Shakhrisabz in Mawarannahr and defend it. When Amir Temur returned,

DOI: 10.4324/9781003198376-3

52 Amir Temur and his dynasty

what a daring volte-face he took; instead of fighting Tughluk Temur, he offered his services to him, who accepted. In 1361, at the age of twenty-five, Amir Temur became the vassal of Tughluk.

At the age of twenty-five, Amir Temur became the chief of his entire Barlas tribe. He made an alliance with Amir Hussain, the ruler of Balkh who was the grandson of Qazaghan, to strengthen their capabilities to confront the Moghul Khan. The common mission of Hussain and Temur was to get Mawarannahr back from the control of the Moghul Khan. To strengthen the relationship, Temur married the sister of Hussain named Aljai Turkhan-Agha. In the meantime, Tughluk Temur appointed his son Ilyas Khoja as the governor of Mawarannahr, which Temur did not like as he did not want to take a second-in-command position. Both Hussain and Temur revolted and went in hiding.

In 1363, Amir Temur was injured and became lame. There were different versions of this story. One version was that he was injured when he was serving the Sultan of Sistan in Khurasan as a mercenary. The territory now is known as the Dasht-i-Margo (desert of death) in the southwest of Afghanistan. Another version was that at night, Temur was taking the flock of his sheep when he was attacked by the Sistan men and got his limbs injured whence the name Temur the Lame or Tamerlane occurred to him. On June 22, 1941, the Russian archaeologist Professor Mikhail Gerasimov exhumed Temur's body and confirmed that both of his right limbs were injured.[1]

Temur and Hussain's forces that were raised from the local tribes of Sistan were about to confront the Moghul Khan's forces. Temur asked his men to light fire at night all around the battlefield that would show the enemy the existence of a big army around them. The Moghul Khan's army felt themselves surrounded by the allied forces of Temur and Hussain and fled the battlefield of Kunduz in northern Afghanistan. Temur asked his forces to tie the branches of the trees with their saddles so that they would create a great cloud of dust while chasing the Moghul forces. This ruse worked and the Moghul forces fled and Mawarannahr was conquered, and thus Temur got back his birthplace Shakhrisabz, the Green City, which was the capital of Mawarannahr. Temur and Hussain also overthrew the Sarbadars' leadership of Samarkand and captured it.

In 1365, Ilyas Khoja invaded again with a new Moghul army. The two armies confronted each other near Tashkent, to the northeast of both Samarkand and Shakhrisabz. Both the armies of Temur and Hussain were defeated in the Battle of Mire or Tashkent and lost 10,000 men during the retreat. Temur and Hussain fled across the Oxus River. This was the first defeat of Temur's forces against the Moghuls. Temur thought that Hussain had betrayed him, and this impression weakened their relationship.

In 1370, Temur marched toward the south and crossed the Oxus River at Termez (in modern-day Uzbekistan) and marched toward Balkh, the capital of Hussain and surrounded it. Hussain could not withstand Temur and was defeated. Hussain begged Temur's mercy for life which, albeit, was granted. However, another of Temur's warrior named Kay-Khusrau, who had a blood feud with Hussain, killed him.

Temur's great partner and rival was now dead and Hussain's wife Saray Mulk Khanum, the daughter of Qazaghan, the last khan of the Chaghatai dynasty, became Temur's new chief wife. Temur had already three wives and Saray Mulk Khanum became the queen. With Saray Mulk Khanum as his queen, Temur claimed the legitimacy as heir by claiming himself as Temur Gurgan, meaning the son-in-law of the Great Khan. In 1375, Temur married Dilshad Agha, the daughter of the Moghul Amir, Qamar-ud-din. In 1378, Temur married twelve-year-old Tuman-agha, the daughter of a Chaghatai noble. In 1397, when he was seventy years old, he married Tukal-khanum, the daughter of the Moghul Khan, Khizr Khoja, who became the lesser queen after Saray Mulk Khanum. In all, Temur had seven to eight wives and many concubines.

According to Genghis Khan's tradition, only a man of royal blood could become the Great Khan. Therefore, Temur installed a puppet khan of the Chaghatai clan named Suyurghatmish, with real powers vested in himself. Temur then summoned the khuriltai (council) at Balkh, which endorsed Temur as the Great Khan. On April 9, 1370, Temur crowned himself at Balkh as the imperial ruler of the Chaghatai ulus. Temur selected Balkh because it was important in that it once belonged to Alexander the Great and Genghis Khan. Balkh was the military base of Alexander from 329 to 327 BC. Balkh in the 8th and 9th centuries was known to the Arabs as the mother of cities. During the Islamic era of the Arab invaders, many Friday mosques and Islamic centers were established. Balkh also became the center of Persian poetry, and Maulana Jalaluddin Balkhi, a mystic Sufi poet known as Rumi, lived here. In 600 BC, Zoroaster practiced and preached his religion of fire worship at Balkh.

In 1866, after cholera broke out in Balkh, the residents moved to a new place in the east known as Mazar-i-Sharif, which is now the capital of Balkh Province of Afghanistan. The shrine of the 15th-century Khawaja Abu Parsa shows the architecture of the Temurid era. The tomb of the first Persian poetess, Rabia Balkhi, is still there in old Balkh. Rabia was killed by her brother for having a love affair with a slave. She wrote a poem with her blood while dying. Her tomb was built at the place where she was killed. Young Afghan lovers visit her tomb in remembrance of their love affairs.

Khwarizm was a very rich territory which had two capital cities – Kat and Urgench. Following the Muslim tradition, Temur, before the war, sent an envoy to the Khwarizm ruler Hussain Sufi to return the Khwarizm territory to the Chaghatai ulus. Hussain Sufi responded that it had been taken by the sword and that Temur could take it back by the sword only. This response was exactly what Temur had wanted. Temur wanted a casus belli for an attack on the Khwarizm which Hussain easily provided.

In 1372, Temur's army marched toward the north. After the confrontation, Temur captured Kat and every man was butchered while the women and the children were taken as slaves. Kat was plundered and destroyed. Hussain Sufi was

54 Amir Temur and his dynasty

defeated and fled to Urgench and died there. Yusuf Sufi, Hussain's brother, succeeded him and immediately submitted to Temur. Yusuf gave Hussain's daughter Khan-zada as wife to Temur's first son Jahangir. Khan-zada was a beautiful daughter of Uzbek, khan of the Golden Horde. Temur returned to Samarkand and waited for the arrival of the bride.

Khan-zada was sent with treasures. The marriage lasted for three years when in 1376 Jahangir became sick and died. Temur was absorbed in sadness as his first son, Jahangir, who was just twenty years old, had departed. In the three years of the marriage, Jahangir had fathered two sons of two different wives. Mohammad Sultan from Khan-zada took the position of Jahangir and became Temur's heir. The second son, Pir Mohammad, was born one month after the death of Jahangir from a different wife. Temur was so sad about the death of Jahangir that he forgot about his campaigns, which remained suspended for quite some time.

Now a refugee in a poor shape, named Tokhtamish, from the Golden Horde appeared in the court of Temur. Tokhtamish was a royal prince of the Genghis Khan house. Tokhtamish's father was killed by Urus, the ruler of the Golden Horde. Tokhtamish, fearing his death, fled to Temur for safety. Temur received Tokhtamish like a son. Temur gave him an army and resources to go back and fight Urus Khan. Tokhtamish made two attempts but failed.

Now Temur received an envoy from Urus Khan, who asked for the return of Tokhtamish to be arranged. Temur sent the envoy back with a message for Urus Khan that Marrozi reported as "he joined battle alongside Tokhtamish". Now Temur and Tokhtamish fought together against Urus Khan. Urus Khan was defeated and died. In 1378, Tokhtamish was installed as the khan with the support of Temur. Now the entire Golden Horde was under the control of Temur.

Herat, one of the four capitals of Khurasan, was ruled by the last ruler of the Kart dynasty, Malik Ghiyas-ad-din Pir Ali, as a vassal of the Mongols from 1370 until attacked by Temur in 1381. The Kart dynasty was founded by the first Kart leader, Malik Ruknuddin Abu Bakr, in 1245. Karts were the Sunni Muslims of Tajik origin. As always, Temur needed a justification for an attack. Temur sent a letter to Malik Ghiyas-ud-din Pir Ali asking him to attend a meeting of the khuriltai as a vassal of the Mongols. Malik Ghiyas-ud-din replied that he would come but he would need an escort to lead him to Samarkand. Temur sent his trusted leader Amir Sayf-ud-din to escort him to Mawarannahr. When the escort arrived in Herat, he found that Ghiyas-ud-din was just preparing for the defense of Herat by fortifying the walls and had no intention of giving up his land.

The campaign of Herat was the first campaign of Temur outside the Chaghatai ulus which was now his empire. Temur's forces marched toward the southwest and camped at Fushanj, the first military post established by Malik Ghiyas-ud-din for the defense of Herat. Temur smashed the garrison and the soldiers were cut into pieces. Ghiyas-ud-din retreated and took refuge in the fort. The city was surrounded by Temur. Temur sent a message that Marozzi reported as "all those who refused to fight him would be spared". Malik Ghiyas-ud-din, accompanied by the Kart nobles, came and surrendered in public in humiliation. Temur pardoned him, gave him a belt, and then dismissed him. The inhabitants of Herat paid a heavy ransom for their lives. The rich city was plundered and the treasure of Herat was taken home on camels' back. The Gate of Herat known as Darwaza Malik was pulled out and was taken to Shakhrisabz. The Ikhtiaruddin citadel was also destroyed by Temur. The defeated Malik was allowed to rule as a vassal of Temur. Herat was now part of Temur's empire. After two years, the Heratis rebelled against Temur and this time Temur sent his son Miranshah who cut them into pieces and beheaded the last ruler of the Kart dynasty, Malik Ghiys-ud-din, in the middle of a banquet in 1389. This ended the Kart dynasty.

Temur's son Shahrukh made Herat his capital. Queen Gohar Shad, the daughter of Amir Ghiyas-ud-din Tarkhan and the wife of Shahrukh, was an artistic woman and was interested in building religious and cultural buildings and gardens. She built the Musalla Complex, a mosque and mausoleum during 1417–1437. The four minarets which still exist, albeit, were damaged by the Russians. The tombs of Queen Gohar Shad, her husband Shahrukh, and their family members are located in Baghe Niswan in the Musalla Complex. The poet Jami and artist Behzad were the major contributors to the arts and the culture of the time. Artist Behzad is buried near the Mukhtar Mountain in the north of Herat.

The Great Mosque famous as Masjid-i-Jami was built by Sultan Ghiyas-ud-din Ghauri. The mosque was destroyed by the Mongols and was rebuilt by the Kart rulers, Malik Ghiyas-ud-din Kart and Malik Muiz-ud-din. It was restored by Temur. The Great Mosque covers an area of 16 acres with 460 domes and 400 pillars. The tomb of Abul Fath Sultan Ghiyas-ud-din Mohammad bin Sam is located in the northern part of the mosque. During the period of Malik Ghiyas-ud-din Pir Ali of Kart dynasty, a bronze cauldron was ordered. It was designed and made by Amal Al Abd Hasan bin Ali bin Hasan Ali Isfahani. It has six round handles installed on its sides. Fadaeian abd Nazarahari reported the dimension of the cauldron as "the upper mouth 0.85 centimeters, depth 100 centimeter, the inner radius 100 centimeters". The worshipers during the Kart dynasty were served sweet drinks from this cauldron. The cauldron is still sitting in the mosque.

The Qala-i-Ikhtiyaruddin, the citadel of Herat called Arg-e-Balahesar which was the residence of the kings, is located on a high hill in the northern part of the city between Ghetbichaq and Barduranis neighborhoods. The area of the citadel is 5,000 square meters, with its highest point of 20 meters, and has 13 towers. Genghis Khan and Amir Temur's forces fought their adversaries beneath this citadel. After its destruction by the Mongols, the citadel was rebuilt by the Kart prince Fakhruddin in the 14th century, which was restored by Shahrukh a hundred years later. The citadel had been home to Ghazanavid, the Seljuks, the Ghourids, the Mongols, Temur, the Safavids, and the Taliban, who used it as an army base and arsenal.

56 Amir Temur and his dynasty

In the east of the city, at Gazargah, Shahrukh built a shrine complex. Outside the complex, the young and old beggars asked the visitors for alms. Amir Dost Mohammad Khan, the former 19th-century king of Afghanistan, is buried here. The complex hosts the shrine of Khoja Abdullah Ansari, the 11th-century poet, philosopher, and saint of the city. Khoja Abdullah Ansari was born in Kohan Deh of Herat. He grew up during the periods of Sultan Mahmud Ghazanvi, the Seljuks, and the Ghouris. He followed Imam Shafei of Egypt. It is said that he spoke in the cradle and started preaching at the age of fourteen. He wrote thirty-two books. One was *Tafsir-e-Kashf al- Asrar wa Oddat-al Abrar*. Khoja Abdullah died in 1088 at the age of eighty-four and is buried at Gazargah.

After Herat, in 1382, Temur's forces moved toward Mazandaran and captured it by defeating its ruler. After Mazandaran, Temur's forces marched toward Isfizar, located 70 miles to the south of Herat. Isfizar fell in 1382. In the 1970s, Isfizar was known as Sabzavar, and during that time was renamed as Shindand. Sheikh Daud, who was a military man and had served in the Kart dynasty, rebelled against Temur after his governor of the town was killed. Temur's youngest son Miranshah, who was the governor of Khurasan, sent two of his Amirs to Isfizar to deal with the situation. Daud was sieged in the fortress. Temur himself led his army to Isfizar and took control of the siege. The fortress was destroyed, and when the walls of the fortress fell, Temur's forces entered and captured 2,000 men inside the fort and took them as slaves. According to Marozzi, this time Temur adopted a new method of execution. Marozzi quoting Yazdi reported: "There were near two thousand slaves taken who were piled alive one upon the other with mortar and bricks, so that these miserable wretches might serve as a monument to deter others from revolting".

After Isfizar, Temur's forces moved toward the southwest of Afghanistan's Nimroz Province with its capital at Zaranj. Temur himself led the battle, and in the battle his horse was hit and probably it may have hit Temur also in his right limb. Temur killed all the members of the army, and all the men, women, and children were slaughtered. The city of Zaranj was razed to the ground and the whole agricultural irrigation infrastructure was destroyed. The green province became Dasht-i-Margo (desert of hell). From Zaranj, Temur marched toward Kandahar in the south which fell in 1384. The governor of Kandahar was hanged.

After Kandahar, Temur moved toward the west across Persia and reached Sultaniya which was ruled by Sultan Ahmad. Sultaniya was founded in 1285 by Arghun, the sixth ruler of the Ilkhanate Persian empire. Sultan Ahmad surrendered. After annexing Sultania, Temur returned to Samarkand during the winter so that the soldiers could take rest and recharge for the next campaign.

Now Temur's protégé Tokhtamish had challenged him by taking over Tabriz with an army of 90,000 infidels and the victims were the Muslims. Tabriz was an international trading center. The trading caravans emerged on the Khurasan road on their way from Baghdad to China. The other caravans came from Cairo, Aleppo, Damascus, Antioch, and Constantinople. The traders from India came by crossing the port of Hormuz. Tabriz was a well-planned and financially developed city. Temur's army marched in the north toward Tabriz. Sultan Ahmad, the ruler of Tabriz, fled and was pursued but managed to escape and left the city at the discretion of Temur. The inhabitants of Tabriz avoided the war by begging for peace. Tabriz was surrendered to Temur and the inhabitants paid a heavy ransom. Tabriz was given to Mohammad Sultan, son of the late Jahangir.

After Tabriz Temur moved toward Georgia in the north which was a land of Christianity with its capital at Tiflis (Tbilisi). On his way to Georgia, Temur crushed Armenia. The Georgians decided to give a big fight to Temur. Temur led the army into Tiflis and the Christian king of Georgia named Bagrat was captured, chained, and was brought before Temur. Temur gave him a chance to convert to Islam which he accepted. Temur made Bagrat a vassal king. After six years, Bagrat died and his son Giorgi VII succeeded him and rebelled against Temur. Temur entered Tiflis and captured it and killed many more people than those who were captured.

After Georgia and Armenia, Temur took Isfahan and killed 3,000 soldiers and 70,000 men, women, and children lost their lives. In 1387, Temur captured Shiraz. Temur's name was read in Khutba (sermon) in the mosques. Temur returned to Samarkand. In Samarkand, Temur heard that his homeland Mawarannahr had been attacked again by Tokhtamish and Temur's eldest son, Prince Omar Sheikh, had narrowly escaped. Now Temur had to deliver the coup de grace to Tokhtamish. Temur assembled his army from Samarkand and Shakhrisabz and marched toward the north. Temur camped at Tashkent, or Shash as it was known then, for winter. Tashkent is the modern capital of Uzbekistan. Uzbekistan got independence in 1991. The statue of Amir Temur was inaugurated by the president of Uzbekistan on September 1, 1993, at the center square of the city. Across the square, the Uzbekistan government built a Temur museum in 1996 to celebrate Temur's 660th anniversary. I have visited this museum in Tashkent which has on display the historical glorious conquests of the conqueror of the world.

In the old city of Tashkent there is Khash Imam square, the heart of Muslim Tashkent. On the left side, there is a 16th-century Barak Khan Madrassa, a religious school which was founded by Shabanid, the ruler of Tashkent and a descendant of Temur. Opposite the Madrassa, there is the Tilly Sheikh Mosque, the grand Friday prayer mosque of Tashkent. Inside the mosque, there is a small library which holds 85,000 ancient books of the Islamic era. In this library, the oldest original Quran of Uthman sits in a climate-controlled glass case. This Quran was written in 646 under the orders of the third Caliph, Uthman, the son-in-law of the Holy Prophet Mohammad, peace be upon him.

Before this, the Quran was memorized by the Muslims and recorded on leaves, wood, camel bones, and leather. After the death of the Holy Prophet in 632, Abu Bakr, the first Caliph, got all the known suras (chapters) written by the famous scribes. During Uthman's sway, Uthman summoned the top four scribes and ordered them that suras of the Quran be collected and written down in one book called the Holy Quran. The Holy Quran was prepared in Medina. Uthman used this as his personal Quran.

58 Amir Temur and his dynasty

During the sway of Uthman, the Dar al-Islam stretched from Morocco in the west, Pakistan in the east, and in the north up to Armenia and Azerbaijan. Uthman swayed for twelve years until he was martyred on June 17, 656, by a mob who broke into his house while he was reciting the Holy Quran. At the time of death, Uthman was reciting the Sura Bakra verse 137: "And if they believe even as ye believe, then are they rightly guided. But if they turn away then they are in schism". His throat was cut and the blood fell on the Quran. Uthman was eighty-two when he died.

After Uthman, Ali became the fourth Caliph in 656 and took this Quran to Kufa where it remained for several hundred years. In 1393, when Temur conquered Baghdad, he found it there. Temur brought it and placed it in the Nur Madrassa in Samarkand where it stayed until the 19th century. Then war broke out between Britain and Tsarist Russia for supremacy over Central Asia. Russia expanded in the south, and Uthman's Quran was given to Tsar Alexander II by General von Kaufman, the governor of Turkistan, and was placed in a library in St. Petersburg. The Muslims of Turkistan appealed to Lenin for the return of their holy book Quran and finally they were able to get it. Uthman's Quran arrived in Tashkent where it was placed in the history museum. In 1989, Uthman's Quran was transferred from the history museum to Tillya Mosque where I have seen it during my visit in 2011.

Now Temur eyed the Sultanate of India, a task which Alexander the Great and Genghis Khan could not do. Temur assembled an army of 90,000 for the campaign of India. The mission was for honor and wealth. Delhi was a thousand miles far away to the southeast and to reach there required passing through the difficult terrain of the snowy Hindu Kush mountain range and the huge rivers that acted as a bulwark for Delhi. Once there, another obstacle was the beasts of India, especially the elephants. The campaign was not easy, but for Temur nothing was impossible with the help of Allah. Temur accepted this challenge in March 1398.

After the death of Firoz Shah Tughlaq of the Tughlaq dynasty in 1388, Delhi was engulfed in internal conflicts that led to the spread of fratricide among the sons and grandsons of Firoz Shah. Firoz Shah was a Turkic Muslim ruler who ruled over the Sultanate of Delhi from 1351 to 1388. Firoz's father Rajab was the younger brother of Ghazi Malik, who had founded the Tughlaq dynasty in 1320 and had taken the title of Ghiyas-ud-din Tughluq. Consequently, the small independent kingdoms of Bengal, Kashmir, and Deccan emerged. This was an opportunity that Temur wanted to exploit. In 1397, Temur sent Pir Mohammad, son of Jahangir, to Multan in Punjab of modern-day Pakistan, as an advance party.

In March 1398, an army of 90,000 left the Gate of Samarkand on M-39 southward through crumbling and potholed roads. The number of horses was twice the number of men. Temur's forces reached the 5,500-foot Takhtakaracha Pass in Uzbekistan. A ride from Samarkand to Shakhrisabz, the birthplace of Temur, takes two hours. I have passed through Shakhrisabz on my way to

Samarkand, once a very famous city but now reduced to a small village. In the south of Shakhrisabz are the Hissar Mountains. After two days of the ride from Shakhrisabz, Temur's forces passed through the famous Temur Darwaza or Iron Gate of Derband in the Baysun Tau mountains. The two iron gates of Samarkand and Derband were rich sources of the customs revenues of Temur's empire.

Temur's forces now headed toward Termez. Temur arrived at Termez in the spring of 1398. He crossed the Oxus River, also called the Bridge of Friendship between Afghanistan and Uzbekistan, a long bridge that I have walked through to enter Uzbekistan. After crossing the Oxus River, Temur's forces marched from Balkh and reached Andarab, from where they crossed the heavy snowy 12,600-foot Khawak Pass, once crossed by Alexander the Great, where his army suffered a lot of casualties and lost many horses that could not walk on snow and fell. By August 1398, Temur's forces arrived in Kabul. In Kabul, Temur stayed and received the gifts and the tributes from the vassals of his conquered areas.

In September, Temur crossed the Indus River at Attock. But still there were other rivers like Jhelum, Chenab, and Ravi waiting for Temur for his crossing. In October 1398, Temur met his grandson Pir Mohammad who was occupied in siege of the city of the saints, Multan. Siege of Multan continued for six months and the inhabitants ran out of supplies and had to eat whatever they could get. The inhabitants of Multan defended their city with great courage and bravery but later surrendered to Temur. The villages and the people who opposed his grandson were no more to be seen on the face of the earth.

Temur's forces marched toward Delhi and camped at Loni in the north of the city. The Sultanate of Delhi was weak due to internal strife. The Sultan of Delhi had an army of 10,000 horses, between 20,000 and 40,000 infantry, and 120 well-trained battle elephants. Temur wanted to take Delhi as quickly as possible without laying siege to the city. Temur had taken 100,000 Indians as slaves and killed them all to avoid any rebellion at the time of the attack on Delhi.

Before the battle, Temur recited Sura Yunis (Jonah) from the Holy Quran. On December 17, 1398, the forces of Mallu Khan and Sultan Mahmud left the gates of Delhi for the battle. The elephants carrying the armed soldiers on their backs were deployed in the center of the Indian forces. The Tatars took their battle formation positions in the center and the left and the right wings, while Temur himself occupied a position on a high ground from where he could monitor the battle. Before the start of the battle, Temur dismounted from his horse and prostrated and begged Allah for victory. When the Indians were overpowered by the Tatars, they moved their elephants forward. Temur's archers struck the mahouts but the elephants kept moving forward. Temur then ordered the unloading of the camels and untied their ropes and sent them forward. The camels ran toward the elephants who got panicked and in their attempt at fast retreat trampled their own soldiers. The elephants were also affected by the caltrops.

At this moment, Pir Mohammad attacked the Indians who had no choice but to retreat as many of their soldiers had already been trampled by their own elephants. The battle was over and Temur accomplished what Alexander the Great

60 Amir Temur and his dynasty

and Genghis Khan could not. The Tatars chased the fleeing Indians and killed them and heaps of dead Indian soldiers were scattered all over the battlefield.

Temur entered Delhi victoriously in 1398. His standard was installed on the walls of the city. A court was held wherein the nobles of India were present in the ceremony of the surrender of the Sultanate of Delhi. The nobles of India pleaded for their lives as their rulers Mallu Khan and Sultan Mahmood had abandoned them. The victory was celebrated and all those elephants which were used in the battle were brought in before Temur. Temur distributed those elephants throughout his empire. Among the recipients were the princes of Tabriz, Shiraz, and Herat. The Tartars collected huge amounts of gold and silver as booty.

Temur remained in Delhi for two weeks and then announced his return to Samarkand. Khizr Khoja, who founded the Syed dynasty, was installed as the governor of modern-day Sind and Punjab in Pakistan. Temur returned with a heavy load of booty. Later, Temur captured Meerut and killed 48,000 Hindus. The Muslim Shah of Kashmir submitted and presented gifts and tributes to Temur. The Hindu Raja of Jammu was captured and did not take a second to convert to Islam. Now Temur attacked Lahore to punish a prince who had already submitted and later did not appear when called by Temur. Lahore was recaptured and the prince was executed. Temur crossed the Oxus River and reached Termez. He was received by the royal family members and a delegation of the nobles and officials from Samarkand. All clapped and congratulated Temur on his victory over India. Temur next marched toward Samarkand.

The next campaign of Temur was Egypt. Since the time of Salahuddin Ayubi, Egypt was the leader of Dar-as-Salaam. Salahudin, in the 12th century, had recaptured Jerusalem and united Egypt and Syria. Under the Mamluk dynasty, Egypt spread from the Nile to Iraq, Palestine, Jerusalem, and Syria and from southeastern Anatolia to the Hijaz in the west of Saudi Arabia, Tabuk, Medina, Jeddah, and Mecca. The Ottoman sultan Salim I conquered Egypt in 1517 and Napoleon conquered it in 1798. Egypt was occupied by the British in 1882 and became an independent country in 1922. After the death of Burquq, his ten-year-old son Faraj was at the mercy of the nobles who were struggling to capture power by overthrowing the young prince. Temur thought that this was the most appropriate time for his attack on Egypt.

On hearing about the arrival of Temur, Faraj requested assistance from Bayazid. Bayazid sent him a large force. Temur wrote a letter to the young prince Faraj and demanded him for the return of the envoy Atilmish, who had been captured and imprisoned by his father Burquq, and save himself and his empire, or be prepared for an attack by the Tatars. Faraj's advisor ignored the warning of Temur and instead the viceroy of Damascus, Sudun, captured the envoy who brought the message and cut him into pieces. Temur ordered his army to march toward Aleppo, 165 miles southwest of Malatiyah. Aleppo was a very famous cultural and commercial center and had a very well-built citadel, which still

Amir Temur and his dynasty **61**

existed at the time of my visit in 2010. According to Ibn Batuta, the Messenger Ibrahim (Abraham) had worshiped Allah here at this citadel.[2] The Syrians gathered their forces from Antioch, Acre, Hama, Homs, Ramallah, Canaan Gaza, Tripoli, Baalbek, and Jerusalem.

In October 1400, Temur's forces camped near Aleppo. Both the Muslim armies started the battle with a loud shout, "Allah O Akbar" (God is great). After the severe fight, Damurdash, the governor of Aleppo, surrendered the city to Temur. Temur had treated Damurdash well but did not spare Sudun who had killed Temur's envoy and executed him. Now Aleppo was Temur's territory. After Aleppo, the road to Damascus was now clear for Temur's forces. In January 1401, Temur camped near the city and the Sultan of Egypt made a despicable attempt to assassinate Temur. The Sultan sent one assassin disguised as a dervish (a poor, austere religious person of Islamic order) accompanied by two other persons to execute the evil design. When they reached the court of Temur, who suspected the main assassin, he was patted down and a dagger was recovered from him. He was immediately killed and Temur got the nose and ears of the accomplices cut off and sent them back to the sultan.

Temur then sent another envoy to Prince Faraj demanding him that he must return the envoy Atilmish and coin money in Temur's name and surrender to the Tatars. Marozzi quoted extract of the message of Temur to Prince Faraj as:

> This you ought to do, if you have any compassion for yourself or your subjects. Our soldiers are like roaring lions, which hunger for their prey. They seek to kill there enemy, pillage everything he owns, raze his buildings to the ground. There are only two ways to choose. Either peace, the conquences of which are quiet and joy; or war, which will lead to disorder and desolation. I have set both for you. It is upto you which path to follow. Consult your prudence and make your choice.

Faraj promised to comply but at the same time procrastinated the decision. Temur ordered that the city be taken immediately and took it after twenty-nine days of the siege of the city. Damascus faced massive destruction now. The governor submitted but there was no mercy now and was beheaded. The citadel offered an enormous amount of treasury to Temur. An agreement between the nobles and Temur was reached, according to which a ransom of 10 million dinars was agreed. After the completion of booty collection by the officers, it was found to be about one-third of the total. Temur ordered the collection of everything available with the residents. Each person was brutally tortured until he declared his true possession. A great treasury of gold and silver was collected. With the collection of booty over, the houses and the mosques were burnt down and destroyed. The Great Mosque of Umayyad was disgraced.

Temur took the city of Baghdad. The tomb of Shia Imam Musa al Kazim and other shrines were burnt and destroyed. The governor and his daughter tried to escape but their boat was fired upon and was overturned. Temur visited

62 Amir Temur and his dynasty

the tomb of Imam Abu Hanifa in eastern Baghdad and prayed. Antioch, Acre (Jerusalem, Israel), Baalbek (modern-day Lebanon in the north of Beirut), Beirut, Hama (western Syria), Homs (also known as Emessa), and Antioch (city of southern Turkey) were destroyed and 90,000 people were killed in Baghdad alone.

Temur now demanded of Bayazid I, the Ottoman Sultan, to return the rebel Turkoman tribal chief Qara Yusuf, who had taken refuge under Bayazid I. He was wanted by Temur. Temur asked the Ottoman Sultan to either execute him or expel him or hand him over in chains to Temur. The noncompliance with Temur's demand would provide Temur with a casus belli to attack the Ottoman Empire. Temur also mentioned that as Bayazid I is engaged against the infidels of Europe, he would not attack him just then as it would damage the cause of Islam.

The Ottoman Sultan, who had taken the Christian territories such as Serbia in the Battle of Kosovo in 1389, and Bulgaria in 1393, was a great threat to the Christians of Europe. The Ottoman Sultan Bayazid was now fighting the combined army of the European Christians including France, Germany, England, Hungary, Croatia, Bulgaria, Wallacia, Poland, Bohemia (Czech Republic), Italy, and Spain. The total strength of the European combined army was 16,000. Both the armies of the crescent and the cross met at Nicopolis in the Bulgarian empire. On September 25, 1396, the Christian crusade failed and the crescent defeated the cross. After this victory, Bayazid, whose nickname was Yilderim, was ready to carry expeditions over the whole of Europe. Europe had become very weak and was looking for a messiah which they found in Temur who had challenged the Ottoman Empire.

Bayazid heard that Temur had reached Qir Shahr (now Kirsehir) in the southeast of Ankara, which surprised Bayazid so much that he became mad with anger. The Ottomans were away to the east. Ankara was now under siege. When the Ottoman forces arrived at Ankara, they were exhausted and had already lost 5,000 men before the start of the battle. Another diplomatic maneuver that Temur made was that he remained in touch with the Tatar soldiers of Bayazid's army. Temur offered them the lucrative booty if they switched sides to join their Tatar brothers in Temur's army at the start of the battle. Temur had worked on this plan many years before the confrontation with Bayazid. This proved to be a decisive tactic which decided the fate of the battle even before it started.

On July 28, 1402, the battle began in the plains of Ankara and the setback to Bayazid was the desertion of the Tatar's contingent of his army which had badly impacted the Ottoman forces and this resulted in the collapse of the left flank led by Prince Sulayman Chelebi. Consequently, Bayazid's janissaries (royal guards) were captured. Though Bayazid bravely resisted, the circumstances did not favor him and he was captured and delivered to Temur as a prisoner.

Prince Sulayman Chelebi, the son of Bayazid, acknowledged that his father was well treated by Temur and that Temur had made both the sons of Bayazid as vassal kings. Prince Chelebi received his father's European lands and his brother Isa Chelebi got the land in the northwest of Anatolia, also known as Asia Minor.

In March 1403, when Temur heard about the death of Bayazid in captivity, Temur broke into tears as he was planning to restore his empire to him.

After the Ottoman Empire, the Ming dynasty of China was next on his agenda. After a difficult journey, Temur arrived in Otrar in Kazakhstan in mid-January. Here Temur got the cold in his litter. His doctor, Maulana Fadl of Tabriz, gave him some prescriptions which did not work well and the cold brought on fever. Temur became weak and lost his voice and knew that his time on earth was over and that he was being summoned back by his God who had created him.

Temur summoned his family who were with him and the nobles for a final audience with him. Temur told the audience, "at my death do not weep, do not tear your clothes but just offer fateh (prayer) to make my soul in peace". Then he announced Pir Mohammad as his successor. He ordered all the generals and the noblemen to obey him and help him in the discharge of his duties as an emperor. At this last moment when most people lose their senses, Temur was mindful of the saying of the Holy Prophet Mohammad, peace be upon him, that at the last moment of his life if he could say "La ilaha illallah" (there is no god but God), he would go to the paradise. And Temur did say "La ilaha illallah" when angel Izrael approached him and said "we belong to God and to God must we return". With these words Emperor Temur died on February 18, 1405, and was buried in Gur Amir Mausoleum in Samarkand. During his rule, Temur patronized the scholars, poets, painters, and architects and being a Sunni Muslim encouraged Sufism, dervishes, saints, and protected Shiism.

Soon after the death of Temur, the royal in-house competitors became indulged in a blood feud over the throne. Khalil Sultan ignored the nomination of Temur and captured the throne by defeating and killing the designated prince Pir Mohammad. Without the spoils, the army was not interested in serving Khalil Sultan and started deserting him. By 1409, Sultan Khalil became bankrupt and went to his uncle Shahrukh who welcomed him only to poison him.

Shahrukh was ruling Khurasan and transferred his capital to Herat, leaving Samarkand in the hands of his son Ulugh Beg. The next forty years were a period of glorious history. Under Shahrukh's rule (1405–1447), Herat became the center of trade, art, literature, calligraphy, and painting, and his wife Gawhar Shad took a special interest in architecture and built mosques, school, gardens, and mausoleum with high minarets which exist even today in Herat. Gawhar Shad is buried in Herat and her tomb reflects the finesse of Islamic architecture, and people still visit her maqbara (tomb). The tomb is also a place of interest for tourists. Ulugh Beg ruled Samarkand until 1447 as the governor and beautified Samarkand where his grandfather Temur is buried. Shahrukh died in 1447 and his successors ruled Herat for twenty-one years.

Thereafter, the last Temurid, Sultan Husayn Baiqara (1468–1506) took control of the empire and ruled for another thirty-eight years. Husayn continued the Temurid renaissance and his court was adorned by the famous painter Bihzad and the poet Abdul Rehman Jami. Husayn died in 1506 and his sons were incapable to rule Herat, and this resulted in the end of the Temurid renaissance. Herat was

64 Amir Temur and his dynasty

conquered by the Uzbeks in 1507, and three years later Herat was taken over by the Persian Safavids, who they were able to rule until the end of the18th century.

With the dwindling of the Temurid renaissance, a new chapter emerges with the birth of Mohammad Zahir-ud-din known as Babur, a Tiger, in 1483 in Ferghana, about 200 miles east of Samarkand. He was the descendant of both Genghis Khan and Temur. He was twelve years old when his father, the ruler of Ferghana, died and he became the ruler of Ferghana. At the age of fifteen, Babur planned to capture Samarkand. In 1497 after a siege of seven months, he captured Samarkand, but in the meantime his followers had deserted him and Ferghana was taken away from him. Samarkand was taken away from him by the Uzbek leader Shaibani Khan.

In 1504, Babur moved toward the Hindu Kush and captured Kabul, and the ruler of Kabul, Zunnum Arghun, after surrendering to Babur went to Kandahar. Babur made Kabul the first seat of his empire. Babur liked Afghanistan and established a Babur's garden on the western slope of Mount Sheri-Darwaza. Babur later captured Ghazni and Kandahar from Arghun. Babur was summoned by Husayn, the last ruler of the Temurid dynasty, to help restore and stabilize the dwindling Temurid renaissance, but before Babur could arrive in Herat, Husayn died in 1506. After Husayn's death, his two sons began fighting against each other to have control of Herat. Babur offered them to fight a war against the Uzbeks on their behalf but his offer was not accepted by them and Babur dropped the idea of winning back the empire of Temur and returned back to Kabul. Having been disappointed by the north side, he focused his attention to the south, toward India.

After establishing his control in Kabul, Ghazni, and Kandahar, Babur attacked and defeated the last Sultan of Delhi, Ibrahim Lodi (Lodi was an Afghan Pushtun tribe) at the First Battle of Panipat (Haryana) in 1526 and became the ruler of Delhi and thus laid the foundation of the Moghul dynasty. Thus, the Lodi dynasty that was established by Bahlul Lodi (1451–1489), followed by Sikandar Lodi (1489–1517) and Ibrahim Lodi (1517–1526), came to an end to make space for the Moghul dynasty. In 1527, Babar defeated the Rajputs at Khanua, in the west of Agra. Babur was announced in the Great Mosque of Delhi as the Badshah (king). When the Moghul dynasty was established by Babur, it was at the same time that Shah Ismail founded the Safavid dynasty in Persia. Both the Moghul dynasty and the Safavid dynasty lived as neighbors irrespective of their different creeds of Sunni and Shia. Kabul was with the Moghul dynasty and Herat was with the Safavid dynasty, and this kept the land of Afghanistan as a buffer state between the two dynasties. Kandahar changed hands many times between the two dynasties. The Moghul Akbar conquered it in 1595 and Shah Abbas of Safavid took it back in 1622. Shah Jahan retook it in 1637, which was again taken by the Persians in 1649. The territory of Afghanistan was divided into three parts. The north was ruled by the Uzbeks, the west (Herat) was ruled by the Safavids, and the southeast was ruled by the Moghuls. All the time, Kabul remained with the Moghuls. Babur wrote his biography, an extraordinary piece

Amir Temur and his dynasty **65**

of work, known as *Baburnama*, also known as Tuzk-e-babri, that covers historical events of his time and his life story.

Babur ruled as the Moghul emperor for a period of four years until his death on December 26, 1530, in Agra. Babur had expressed his wish to his wife Bibi Mubarka that no matter wherever he dies, his body be brought back to Kabul for burial. Babur loved Kabul so much for its beauty and climate. Bibi Mubarka complied with Babar's wish and brought his body back to Kabul and buried him in the garden that he had established himself known as Bagh-i-Babur (Babur's Garden). Afghans and tourists visit his grave on weekends or holidays. Later King Nadir Shah (1929–1933) laid marble stones on Babur's grave.

After the death of Babur, his son, Humayun ascended the throne in 1530. Humayun was born in Kabul on March 6, 1508. he ruled from 1530 to 1540, when he was banished by an Afghan soldier Sher Shah Suri, who had established his control in Bihar and Bengal. Sher Shah Suri defeated Humayun at Chaunsa in 1539. In 1540 after his expulsion from India, Humayun became homeless. First, he went to Sind to get support and then to Iran. His illustrious son Akbar was born in Sind in 1542. Humayun reached Iran in 1544 and got support from Iranian Shah Tahmasp. He conquered Kandahar in 1545 and Kabul from his brother Kamran in 1550. In 1555, he captured Lahore from the descendant of Sher Shah Suri, Sikander Suri, the rebel governor of Punjab at Sirhand, and then recaptured Delhi. His second rule was from 1555 until his death in 1556. He is buried in New Delhi.

Humayun was succeeded by his fourteen-year-old son Jalal-ud-din Mohammad Akbar in 1556, as the third Moghul ruler. Akbar was born on October 15, 1542, at Umarkot, Sind, when Humayun was under refuge in Sind. Juvenile Akbar was assisted by his guardian Behram Khan in governing the Moghul empire. Behram Khan had defeated the Hindu king Hemu at the Second Battle of Panipat in 1556. When Akbar became a grown up, he fired Behram Khan and started ruling in 1556. Akbar was the greatest Moghul emperor who vastly extended the Moghul Empire spread over areas which are now in Afghanistan, Pakistan, and northern India and Bengal. He was a very religious person, practiced religious tolerance, and avoided proselytizing. He ruled until his death in 1605.

Jalal-ud-din Mohammad Akbar was succeeded by his son Nur-ud-din Mohammad Salim, also known as Jehangir. Jehangir was born on August 31, 1569, at Fatehpur Sikri in India. He became the fourth Moghul emperor in 1605. In 1611, he married Mehrunnisa known as Nur Jahan, a widow of an Afghan officer. She was very beautiful and intelligent. She was born in Kandahar. She became Jehangir's favorite queen. She got her family inducted into the government with her father, Itimad-ud-daula, as the chief minister and her brother, Asif Khan, as the advisor. Jehangir was challenged by his son Khusrau. Jehangir defeated him and made him blind. Jehangir became a wine and opium addict and this affected his governance. Thus, Nur Jahan effectively took control of the government. Jehangir relied heavily on her advice. Under the strong influence of his Persian wife Nur Jahan, he promoted Persian culture. He became sick and died in 1627 in Lahore. Nur Jahan died in 1645 and is buried in Lahore.

66 Amir Temur and his dynasty

After the death of Jehangir, his third son Shahabuddin Mohammad Shah Jahan, also known as Prince Khurram, became the fifth Moghul emperor in 1628 with the support of his father-in-law Asif Khan. Shah Jahan married Mumtaz Mahal, also known as Arjumand Bano Begum, the daughter of Asif Khan and the niece of Nur Jahan. Shah Jahan was born in 1592 in Lahore.

The Moghul empire had grown in size with each successive ruler. In the 1640s, Shah Jahan diverted his attention to northern Afghanistan. He fought the Uzbeks in Balkh, but even after seven years of war efforts he could not defeat the Uzbeks. He made three attempts to capture Kandahar from the Persian Safavids but he failed again. He built Taj Mahal of white marble in Agra in memory of his beloved queen Mumtaz Mahal. It took seventeen years to be completed, and reflects intricate patterns of Islamic and Moghul architecture. In 1648, he moved his capital to Delhi. He built Qila Mubarak (great palace fortress) just opposite Jamia Mosque, Delhi. This mosque stands to the present date. He provided quick justice to the poor people.

Shah Jahan had four sons. Dara Shikoh, the eldest son, who lived with Shah Jahan in the palace, was declared as his heir. The second son, Shuja, was the governor of Bengal, Bihar, and Orissa. The third son, Aurangzeb, was the governor of Deccan. The fourth son, Murad, was the governor of Gujrat. In 1658, Shah Jahan became ill and a struggle for ascension to the throne ensued among the four brothers. Aurangzeb defeated Dara Shikoh and got control over all his brothers and put his father behind the bar. Shah Jahan ruled from 1628 through 1658 and died in 1666. Both the queen Mumtaz Mahal and Shah Jahan are buried in the Taj Mahal, Agra.

After overpowering his three brothers, Aurangzeb Alamgir succeeded Shah Jahan as the sixth Moghul emperor in 1658. Aurangzeb was born in 1618 in India. Aurangzeb not only defeated the first contestant, his elder brother Dara Shikoh, but also tried him on the charges of apostasy from Islam and executed him after one year of his usurping the throne. He sent Dara Shikoh's head to their imprisoned father Shah Jahan. The main resistance to Aurangzeb came from the Marathas. But this resistance faded soon due to the sudden death of the Maratha chief. The other resistance came from the Rajputs of Jodhpur and Mewar who had declared their independence. Aurangzeb prepared his army under the command of his son Akbar to fix Rajput's resistance. Akbar showed tepid interest as he himself was planning to become the emperor. Akbar fled to Deccan to seek Maratha's assistance against his father. Finally, Aurangzeb took command of his army by himself and drove his son out to Persia wherefrom he never came back. The son of Maratha chief Sambaji, who had supported Akbar, was defeated and killed by Aurangzeb in 1689. Aurangzeb ruled for forty-nine years until he died in 1707 in India. After his death, the Moghul empire started dwindling due to weak and incapable successors.

After the death of Aurangzeb, his son Bahadur Shah I became the seventh Moghul emperor in 1707. Bahadur Shah was born in 1643 in India. He ruled from 1707 until he died in 1712 in Lahore. After his death, his son, Jahandar

Shah became the eighth Moghul emperor but ruled for a short period and died in 1713 in Delhi. After Jahandar Shah's death, Farrukhsiyar, the grandson of Bahadur Shah I, became the ninth Moghul emperor and ruled from 1713 until he was killed in 1719 by the powerful Sayed brothers, Abdullah and Hussain Ali. Farrukhsiyar had granted a license to the British East India Company to import duty-free goods into Bengal, and this free trading right to the British helped them to strengthen their position in Bengal. After his death, Mohammad Shah, the grandson of Bahadur Shah, became the tenth Moghul ruler in 1719. Mohammad Shah was born in Ghazni in Afghanistan in 1702. In 1720, the assassination of Hussain Ali and the defeat of Abdullah led Mohammad Shah free of the Sayed brothers' interference. In 1721, Mohammad Shah married the daughter of Farrukhsiyar. Gradually, his empire started disintegrating as most of the provinces started declaring their independence from the Moghul empire: the Nawab of Oudh became independent; the Afghan Rohilla tribesmen took control of Rohilkhand in the southeast of Delhi; Bengal started paying a very little amount of the annual tribute; Marathas gained control of Gujrat; and so on. Muhammad Shah died in 1748, and after his death the Marathas acquired control of northern India and the Moghul rule became more or less limited to Delhi.

After Mohammad Shah's death, his son Ahmad Shah Bahadur became the eleventh Moghul ruler at the age of twenty-two in 1748. He was a very ineffective ruler and was defeated by the Marathas at the Battle of Sikandarabad. He fled in 1754 and lived in confinement until his death in 1775 at Delhi. After Ahmad Shah Bahadur, Aziz-ud-din Alamgir II, son of Jahandar Shah, became the Moghul ruler in 1754 and ruled until his death in 1759. After his death, his son Ali Gauhar, known as Shah Alam II, became the Moghul ruler in 1760. He was a very weak ruler and granted the East India Company rights to collect the taxes. Shah Alam remained a puppet ruler until his death in 1806. After his death, his son Akbar II became the Moghul ruler, who ruled from 1806 to 1837. He was the second son of Shah Alam II. He was a king by name and his movements were limited to the Red Fort in Delhi as he was under the complete control of the British through the East India Company. During his regime, the East India Company stopped calling itself the subject of the Moghul emperor and stopped minting coins in his name. After the death of Akbar II, his second son Bahadur Shah Zafar became the last Moghul ruler in 1837. He too was a king by name, and due to his involvement in the Indian Rebellion of 1857, the British exiled him to Rangoon, Burma, which was under British control. He died in Rangoon in 1862, and with his death the Moghul dynasty came to an end.

Notes

1 Marozzi, *Tamerlane: Sword of Islam, Conqueror of the World*, pp. 31, 421.
2 Marozzi, *Tamerlane: Sword of Islam, Conqueror of the World*, p. 292.

68 Amir Temur and his dynasty

Bibliography

Dupree, N.H., *An Historical Guide to Afghanistan*. Afghan Tourist Organization, Jagre Ltd., Tokyo Japan, Publication Number 5, 1970.

Ewans, M., *Afghanistan: A New History*. Curzon Press, Richmond, 2001.

Fletcher, A., *A Complete History of Afghanistan*. Cornell University Press, USA, 1966.

Marozzi, J., *Tamerlane: Sword of Islam, Conqueror of the World*. Harper Perennial, London, UK, 2005.

Omrani, B., and M. Leeming, *Afghanistan: A Companion and Guide*. Odyssey Books and Guides, Sheung Wan, Hong Kong, a division of Airphoto International Ltd., 2007.

4
RISE AND FALL OF DURRANI DYNASTY

During the 16th century, Afghanistan remained a buffer state between the Moghuls in Kabul and the Persians in Herat and for almost two centuries both of these Safavid (Shia) and the Moghul (Sunni) dynasties simultaneously existed as neighbors. When both the Moghul and the Safavid dynasties started becoming weak, the Pushtuns started emerging on the scene. First, the tribe of Yousafzais declared independence in 1667 which was followed by Afridis who were joined by the Khattaks, Sherannis, and Ghilzai tribes who declared independence in 1672. These tribes destroyed the Moghul army and made Akmal Khan their king. But this revolt did not survive for a long period and was crushed by Moghul emperor Aurangzeb.

At this time, Kandahar was ruled by the Safavids. The Safavid Governor Gurgin Khan, a Georgian descendant, received reports that Ghilzai Pushtuns in connivance with the Moghuls were plotting against the Safavid rule. Gurgin Khan crushed the plot in 1704 and arrested their leader Mir Wais, chief of Hotaki tribe, and sent him to Isfahan as a prisoner[1]. Normalcy prevailed in Kandahar and after some time Mir Wais was released, who, against the expectations of Safavids, was received back with a big reception by the Pushtuns.

Mir Wais organized his forces and killed Governor Gurgin Khan and his retinue in 1709. He captured Kandahar city and at the same time Abdali Pushtuns captured Herat city from the Safavids[2]. Mir Wais died in 1715 and his eighteen-year-old son, Mir Mahmud, became the ruler. Mir Mahmud, half insane and cruel, ran amok attacking Persia and first compelled Abdali Pushtuns of Herat to surrender to him as there was no love between the two Pushtun tribes of Ghilzai and Abdalis. Then he attacked Kirman and thereafter Isfahan, the capital of the Safavid empire. After the siege of Isfahan for six months, the Safavid king Sultan Hussain, in 1722, surrendered to Mir Mahmud[3]. Mir Mahmud carried

DOI: 10.4324/9781003198376-4

70 Rise and Fall of Durrani Dynasty

out atrocities by looting, plundering, and butchering the people. He killed all the members of the Safavid family.

Local Persian Shia people hated him for his atrocities and started organizing against him. In the meantime, his cousin Ashraf killed Mir Mahmud. But it was too late, as widespread damage had been done by the madness of Mahmud. At this point in time, Nadir Quli Beg of Turk Afshar tribe living in northern Iran, who was serving in the army of the last Safavid king Tahmasp, rose to the position of a General. Quli Beg organized his army in connivance with Abdali Pushtuns who had been hit badly by Mir Mahmud. Nadir Quli Beg is also known as Nadir Shah. The people considered him as the Persian Napoleon. Nadir Shah defeated the Ghilzais at Mehmandost (Zargan) in 1730[4] and annihilated the Ghilzais army. The surviving Ghilzais fled to Balochistan's deserts and died there. The Safavid king, Tahmasp, became a puppet in the hands of Nadir Quli Beg who later deposed him and became the king under the name Nadir Shah. Nadir Shah, a great warrior, started his series of expeditions and captured Kandahar from the Ghilzais and asked the Ghilzais to settle in Herat and the Abdali Pushtuns to settle in Kandahar. In 1738[5], Nadir Shah captured both Kandahar and Kabul and turned towards the Moguls in India.

Nadir Shah forayed into India and defeated the Moguls in 1739 and captured Delhi[6]. Shah got hold of the famous diamond, Koh-i-Noor, and brought back a lot of plundered wealth from India. Although he succeeded in destroying the Moghul dynasty, he failed to stabilize and establish the Persian empire. He was despised by the Persians because of involvement of the cruel Afghan and Turkomen soldiers in his army. Later he raided Bokhara, Samarkand, and Kiev. He was very suspicious by nature and became paranoid. "In June, 1747[7] a group of his own Persian officers assassinated Nadir Shah Afshar", writes Dupree. The Abdali Pushtuns who served as a detachment of Nadir's army, became worried, fearing that if they went back to Herat they would be confronted by the Persians. So, they decided to go to Kandahar instead of Herat. In this way, after the death of Nadir Shah, the birth of Afghanistan became obvious.

In Kandahar, the Abdali Pushtuns convened a meeting of the chiefs of the nine Abdali subtribes, at the mazar (shrine) of Sheikh Surkh[8] near Kandahar. The purpose of the meeting was to elect a leader of their own to create a country for themselves which would be free of any foreign hegemony. Their opponent, the Ghilzais, were so weak after their defeat by Nadir Shah that the Abdalis now did not face any threat from them. The Ghilzais submitted and accepted the Abdalis as their leader. On the other hand, the Moghul dynasty had been immensely weakened by their defeat at the hands of Nadir Shah. In the fall of the Moghul dynasty and the weakness of the Ghilzai Pushtun tribes, the Abdali Pushtuns saw a potential of enormous opportunity for themselves. The two of the Abdali tribes who contested for leadership were the Popalzai and the Barakzai. Finally, Ahmad Khan Sadozai[9] of Popalzai, who was the erstwhile commander of Abdali detachment in Nadir Shah's army, and possessed a lot of Nadir Shah's resources, was elected unanimously as the leader of the Afghans. Saddozai was declared the first king of the Afghans and therefrom his name became Ahmad Shah Abdali. But as soon as he became the king, he changed the name of his tribe from Abdali to Durrani [Durr-i-Durran (pearl of the pearls)], and his new name emerged as Ahmad Shah Durrani, who laid the foundation of an independent Afghanistan in 1747.

When Ahmad Shah became the king, he was 23 years old. When he was born, his father, Mohammad Zaman Khan, who was the chief of the Popalzai tribe, was living in exile in Multan. At the age of 14, Ahmad Shah was captured by Nadir Shah, who found the young boy a very talented and audacious soldier and trusted him and made him the captain of an Abdali detachment in his army.

Soon after Ahmad Shah became the king of the Afghans, "he was also fortunate enough to capture a caravan, which, in total ignorance of Nadir Shah's fate was returning through Kandaghar en route for Persia, loaded with treasure from India", writes Ewans. The leader of the caravan was Taqi Khan Akhtabeghi, a Turk descendant, who was unaware of the death of Nadir Shah. All the treasure that Taqi Khan brought from India for Nadir Shah was pillaged by Ahmad Shah, who paid this to his army that served under his command in Nadir Shah's army.

The young Ahmad Shah gained a lot of experience from Nadir Shah's governance and based on that experience he tried to develop, organize, and establish his country with built-in allowances for the Afghan's culture and temperament. First of all, Ahmad Shah marched toward Kabul which was governed by Nasir Khan on behalf of Nadir Shah. Nasir Khan decided not to yield to Ahmad Shah but confront him. Nasir Shah tried to organize his force of the tribes of Ghilzai, Hazara, and Qizilbash. Ghilzai and Hazara had no love for each other and Qizilbash did not think Abdalis as bad. Thus, Ghilzai, Hazaras, and Qizzilbash showed tepid interest in defending Nasir Shah. Ahmad Shah captured Kabul and Nasir Shah fled to India. When Nasir Shah heard that the Durranis treated his harem, the women and the children of his family with respect, he came back and pledged allegiance to Ahmad Shah. After this, the Afghan army captured Peshawar without any resistance.

After the death of Aurangzeb, the Moghul empire started to decrease in strength due to the incapability of the successive leaderships and this resulted in rampant treachery and disloyalty within the Moghul empire. One example was Shahnawaz Khan, the Moghul Governor of Punjab. He connived with Ahmad Shah for an attack on India. "In December 1748, an Afghan army made up primarily of Durrani horsemen galloped out of Peshawar and raced toward Lahore", writes Fletcher. On reaching the river Chenab, they were surprised to see the Moghul army on the other side. For two days both the armies stayed face to face and on the third night the Afghan forces managed to cross the river and to head toward Lahore by ignoring the Moghul army. Ahmad Shah captured Lahore and Shahnawaz fled to Delhi.

On hearing the news of the Afghan attack on Lahore, the Moghul emperor Mohammad Shah sent his son, Moghul Ahmad Shah, to reinforce Shahnawaz's remaining army. Moghul Ahmad Shah's forces met the Afghan forces at Sirhind

72 Rise and Fall of Durrani Dynasty

(a city in Fatehgarh Sahib district of modern-day Indian Punjab). Here Ahmad Shah had an upper hand but unfortunately an incident happened that changed the game. The incident was that an Afghan soldier mistakenly ignited the powder train and the resultant explosion killed hundreds of Ahmad Shah soldiers. Consequently, Ahmad Shah had to retreat and Lahore stayed with the Moghuls. Later, Moghul emperor Mohammad Shah died and his son Moghul Ahmad Shah, who had recently celebrated his victory against Ahmad Shah, became the new Moghul king.

In 1749, the Afghan army again crossed Indus and this time Ahmad Shah was very careful about his gunpowder. Now, the new Moghul Governor of Punjab, Muin-ul-mulk, was ordered by Moghul Ahmad Shah to seek peace in exchange for offering all the territories held by Nadir Shah including Sind. Ahmad Shah was satisfied and returned back to Afghanistan much richer. Thus far, Ahmad Shah had captured Kabul, Peshawar, Lahore, and Delhi.

In 1750, Ahmad Shah moved with the Baloch army toward Herat which was ruled by Governor Mohammad Amir Khan on behalf of another Shah Rukh, the grandson of Nadir Shah from Meshed, which was the capital of the Persian empire. The governor surrendered to the Durranis. Ahmad Shah moved to Meshed and Shah Rukh yielded to him. After Meshed, Ahmad Shah marched toward Nishapur. It was winter and Ahmad Shah had no experience of winter siege and consequently his army disintegrated due to bad weather. He came back to Herat and recruited a new army of the Chahar Aimak and the Durranis. Ahmad Shah again raided Nishapur in 1751 and captured it. From Nishapur, Ahmad Shah came back again to Meshed and Shah Rukh yielded the provinces of Torbad, Bakhaz, and Khaff to Ahmad Shah Durrani and promised to coin money in the name of the Afghan king. Ahmad Shah was very happy with the end result of his expedition and dispatched another unit of his army under the leadership of Beghi Khan toward the north over the Hindu Kush and defeated the Uzbeks and captured Maimana, Andkhui, Balkh, Bamian, and Badakhshan, and allowed the old satraps (khans) to rule their areas as vassals of Ahmad Shah. At that time, Badakhshan was ruled by Sultan Shah, the Uzbek khan of Badakhshan who possessed the shirt of the Holy Prophet Mohammad, peace be upon him. This shirt is still kept in a shrine in Kandahar.

In 1751, Ahmad Shah Durrani returned to Punjab as the promised revenue was not delivered by Muin-ul-Mulk, the Governor of Punjab. Muin-ul-Mulk resisted for four months and then Ahmad Shah sent a message to Delhi to either hand over Punjab or get ready for a battle. Moghul Shah yielded to Ahmad Shah's demand. In the meantime, Ahmad Shah Durrani's army led by Sardar Abdullah Khan took over Kashmir. After the fall of Punjab, Ahmad Shah made Muin-ul-Mulk the Governor of Punjab. With the death of Muin-ul-Mulk in 1753, his wife Mughlani Begum became the Governor of Punjab. She was weak, and Moghuls retook Punjab from Mughlani Begum in 1755. Mughlani Begum asked Ahmad Shah for help. Ahmad Shah came back and, instead of raiding Punjab, went straight to Delhi. Moghul Shah did not resist and yielded to Ahmad

Shah. Ahmad Shah's soldiers roamed in the streets and looked upon everything, be it gold or any precious thing or women, as their property and grabbed it.

Like Babur, Ahmad Shah Durrani also wanted to make Delhi the capital of his empire but unbearable heat compelled him otherwise. He decided to go back to Afghanistan. He left Delhi in the hands of Najib-ud-daula, the Moghul Nawab of Oudh. He arranged the marriage of the Moghul emperor's niece to his son Timur Mirza. He named the eleven-year-old Timur Mirza as the Viceroy of Punjab with mentor Sardar Jehan Khan vested with the real power.

While Ahmad Shah Durrani was busy in Afghanistan consolidating his empire, the Sikhs in Punjab started getting stronger and the Marathas got control of the Deccan with their capital at Poona. The Marathas raided Lahore and drove out Timur Mirza and Sardar Jehan Khan and appointed the Moghul Adina Beg Khan as the Governor of Punjab. After that the Marathas reached Delhi and drove out Najib-ud-daula, the Afghan viceroy.

Sardar Jehan Khan and Najib-ud-daula sent messages to Ahmad Shah Durrani about the problems in India. Ahmad Shah replied that presently he was occupied in dealing with the rebellions of Darwesh Ali Khan in Herat and Nasir Khan of Kalat. As soon as he was done with them, he would come to India and fix their problems. Darwesh's problem was minor which was fixed immediately but the problem of Nasir Khan was too big to handle. Nasir Khan, not a Pushtun but a Baloch Sardar of Kalat, had announced an independent sovereign state of his own. Ahmad Shah sent his army under the command of Shah Wali Khan. Both the Afghan army and Nasir Khan's army met at Mustung and Nasir Khan defeated the Afghan army. Ahmad Shah was very annoyed and he then sent his huge army to bring Nasir Khan for a pledge of allegiance. This time Nasir Khan yielded and renewed his allegiance to Ahmad Shah with the promise that he would not pay any annual tribute to Ahmad Shah, which was accepted by Ahmad Shah as he was not interested in fighting with the Balochs.

Now Ahmad Shah turned toward India. Knowing that a fight with the Marathas will be a crucial one, he gave a call for Jehad against the Maratha Hindus, which was responded to by all the tribes of the Durranis, Ghilzais, Balochis, Chahar Aimaks, and Qizilbashs. In August 1759, Ahmad Shah left Peshawar for Lahore. On January 9, 1760, his army waded through the Jumna river and attacked the Marathas, wherein their leader Dattaji Sindhia was killed and his army fled to the Deccan. The Maratha ruler, also called Peshwa, gave a call to all the chiefs of the Marathas for a joint crusade against the Afghans. The Maratha army was led by General Sadashiv Rao, also called Bhao, under the leadership of Peshwa's sixteen-year-old son, Vishvas Rao. The Maratha army was also supported by a Muslim unit under Ibrahim Khan Gardi, who was a French army-trained soldier and who despised Ahmad Shah Durrani.

Knowing the strength of the Marathas, Ahmad Shah also sought local support from the Moghuls and Rohillas (Afghans living in India) and these local forces joined him including Shuja-ud-daula of Oadh. On January 13, General Bhao ordered for war shouting "hur, hur, hurree" and the first attack was made

74 Rise and Fall of Durrani Dynasty

by Ibrahim Khan Gardi. The war did not take long, it ended soon in favor of Ahmad Shah and Peshwa's son Vishva Roa was killed and General Bhao ran away. When Ahmad Shah's army entered the Maratha camp, they found 25,000 women of the noble Maratha families now at the mercy of the Afghans, five hundred elephants, and lots of treasuries. This battle was the third battle that was fought at the field of Panipat, 50 miles, or 80 kilometers, north of Delhi. This victory was important for the Afghans by way of glory and power. This war ended the Marathas' power and they never again got back their position. Similarly, this war also marked the beginning of the decline of Afghanistan as well. Ahmad Shah made Ali Guahar, also known as Shah Alam II, a puppet ruler of the Moghul throne and returned to Afghanistan.

In the meantime, the Sikhs obtained their strength by developing their army in the name of Khalsa and started looting village after village and the Moghul governors proved ineffective in checking and controlling them. Ahmad Shah came back to India and defeated the Sikhs at Ludhiana. He then moved to Amritsar and destroyed their temple, the religious place of the Sikhs. Ahmad Shah appointed a Hindu, Kabuli Mal, as the governor to rule Punjab on his behalf and he himself returned to Afghanistan. On Ahmad Shah's return to Afghanistan, the Sikhs revenged themselves and searched for and slaughtered the Muslims wherever they found them and destroyed their mosques and prayer places. In 1764, Ahmad Shah along with Nasir Khan of Kalat returned to India and defeated the Sikhs again and made Alha Sing the governor of Sirhind. The Sikhs emerged again. Ahmad Shah returned in 1766 and emerged victorious yet again.

In 1769, Ahmad Shah planned another attack on India which he postponed later. Had he carried out this attack, this would have been his tenth attack of India. Ahmad Shah was fifty and thought that it was time to hand over the power to someone else. In February 1772, he called a meeting of the tribal Jirga and nominated his second son Timur Mirza as the head of the Afghan government. He handed over power to Timur Mirza and went for a summer retreat at the Suleiman mountains, where he died on April 14, 1772. His body was brought back to Kandahar, where he was buried in a tomb at the center of the city. Ahmad Shah was a very religious person and was accessible even to the poorest of the poor. In addition to his military strategic capability, he was a poet who took a keen interest in art, literature, and philosophy. As the father of the nation, he is known as Baba, meaning "Father", and the Afghans called him Ahmad Shah Baba.

Timur was in Herat when Ahmad Shah died. He heard that Shah Wali Khan, father-in-law of his elder brother Suleiman, had nominated Suleiman for the throne. Timur left Herat for Kandahar. When he reached Kandahar, all the tribes who had originally supported Suleiman had submitted to him and this included Shah Wali Khan also. But Timur did not forgive Shah Wali Khan and executed him and his elder brother fled away to save his life.

Now Timur Mirza became Timur Shah. Timur Shah was born in 1746 near Meshed, one year before the birth of Afghanistan. Ahmad Shah had provided his promising son with a good education. The first thing Timur Shah did was that he shifted the capital from Kandahar to Kabul. Timur was not interested in warring, but he did provide help to the Afghan vassals whenever they needed it. He invaded India five times from 1774 through 1785 to crush the Sikhs' rising. He sent his army three times to Khurasan to support Shah Rukh. Similarly, he responded to the Amir of the Kalhora tribe in Sind who was deposed by Fateh Ali Talpura. However, on the advice of his army, Timur appointed Fateh Ali as the Amir of Sind.

Timur ruled for twenty years and during this period there occurred only two internal conspiracies against him. The first one was the rebellion of the Durrani Sardar Abdul Khaliq, supported by the Baloch leader, Khan of Kalat, Nasir Khan. This was crushed by Timur. The second one was when Sahibzada of Chamkanni, who was a guard in the royal palace in Peshawar Fort, connived with Faizullah Khan of the Khalil tribe of Peshawar to kill Timur Shah. Their plot was to replace Timur Shah with Sikandar Mirza, the son of his elder brother Suleiman. This attempt too was foiled by Timur Shah.

Timur Shah died of cholera in 1793 and left behind thirty-six children which included twenty-one sons who became involved in competing for the throne. However, the main contestants were Humayun Mirza who was the Governor of Kandahar from the Sadozai tribe; the second one was Mahmud Mirza who was the Governor of Herat from the Sadozai tribe; and the third one, a half-brother, was Mohammad Zaman Mirza, who was the Governor of Kabul from the Yusufzai tribe. With the strong support of the Barakzai subtribe of Durrani, Mohammad Zaman Mirza was nominated. Mohammad Zaman Mirza also enjoyed the support of Paindah Khan of the Mohammadzai tribe. He was twenty-three years old and audacious and arrogant. He was not willing to share the power with the tribal chiefs and wanted to be a despotic leader by ruling from the central capital. Because of the practice of polygamy, there were numerous brothers and half-brothers who were a source of persistent rivalry among themselves and this led to weakness in the governance.

Like his predecessors, Zaman Shah had a problem with the Sikhs of Punjab. He visited India and after assessing the situation he thought it worthwhile to reconcile with the Sikhs, and as a result of the reconciliation, he made Ranjit Singh the Governor of Punjab. While he was in India, he heard about the internal rebellion by his brothers. On his return he handled them and brought stability.

Now Zaman Shah started the implementation of his plan of centralization of power by abolishing the role of the feudal lords. As a first step in this direction, he removed the chiefs of Mohammadzai tribes from the key positions they had held long since Ahmad Shah Durrani. Durrani tribes did not like this. They convened a meeting of the chiefs including Paindah Khan of the Mohammadzai tribe, Mohammad Sharif Khan of the Qizilbash tribe, Sultan Khan of the Nurzai Durrani tribe, and Rahim Khan of the Alizai Durrani tribe. An informer informed Zaman Shah of the said meeting, who took immediate action and

76 Rise and Fall of Durrani Dynasty

arrested all of them and finally executed them. Through the execution of the plotters, he sent across a strong message to the conspirators.

Now trouble started for Zaman Shah. Fateh Khan, the elder son of Paindah Khan, went to Persia and convinced Zaman's brother Mahmud Mirza to make another bid for the throne. Fateh Khan and Mahmud held a meeting with the chiefs of the Barakzai, Alizai, and Nurzai tribes and organized an army, which attacked and captured Kandahar. After Kandahar, the rival group moved toward Kabul. Here they met with the royal forces commanded by a Nurzai chief who betrayed Zaman Shah and switched sides by handing over his army to Fateh Khan and Mahmud. Zaman Shah fled to Peshawar and took refuge with a tribal chief, but the host later violated the tribal tradition of sanctuary and handed Zaman over to Mahmud's administration.

Zaman was tortured, blinded, and put in prison. Later, he escaped from prison in connivance with Mahmud and went to Bokhara where he was tortured by Uzbeck ruler Hyder Turi, who was interested in information about the hideout of the Koh-i-Noor diamond. Zaman managed to escape from Bokhara to Herat which was governed by his half-brother Haji Feroz-ud-din, who finally sent him to India where he stayed till his death.

After ascending to the throne, Mahmud Shah reversed the centralization policy of Zaman and delegated power to the tribal chiefs. The power was distributed between Fateh Khan of the Barakzai tribe and Sher Mohammad Khan, son of Shah Wali Khan, also of the Barakzai tribe. With this distribution of power, Mahmud Shah enjoyed royal privileges.

At that time, Peshawar was governed by Shuja-ul-Mulk, who was the brother of Zaman Shah. Shuja-ul-Mulk had an access to the royal treasury and he used the resources to make an alliance with the local tribes. Shuja raised an army of the Afridi, Mohmand, and Yusufzai tribes and crossed the Khyber Pass. His forces met the royal forces led by Fateh Khan at Surkh Rud in Jalalabad. Shuja's forces were victorious but then, all of a sudden, his army started plundering the treasury of their own commander. This created chaos and confusion among Shuja's forces. Fateh Khan understood the situation and quickly assembled and arranged his army and attacked and drove the rebel army out, thereby capturing Peshawar. Shuja-ul-Mulk took refuge with an Afridi tribe in the Tirah Bagh area of North Waziristan.

The Pushtuns and the Qizilbashs were hostile toward each other because of their creed. The Pushtuns were Sunnis and the Qizilbash were Shias. Sher Mohammad Khan of the Mohammadzai tribe had protested to Shah Mahmud against the appointment of Fateh Khan as a wazir. Sher Mohammad Khan had invited Shuja to come and take over Kabul. At this time Mahmud Shah was confined in Bala Hissar. Shuja-ul-Mulk left his exile with the Afridis and moved toward Kabul where he was greeted by the deserted army of Fateh Khan. When Fateh Khan heard the news, he went back to Kandahar. Shuja captured the throne and ruled from 1803 to 1809. Shah Mahmud's period of rule was from 1799 through 1803.

Shuja did not take any action against his predecessors with the exception of the tribal chief who had handed over his brother Shah Zaman to Fateh Khan's army. Shuja even forgave Fateh Khan. Another event that shocked Shuja was the escape of Mahmud from Bala Hissar arranged by Fateh Khan's brother Dost Mohammad. Another trouble to Shuja came from his wazir, Sher Mohammad Khan. When Shuja was in Sind, Sher Mohammad overthrew Shuja by installing Shuja's nephew Kaissar Mirza. Shuja came back and defeated Sher Mohammad Khan and executed him. His head was carried on a pole through the streets of Kabul, and Shuja survived another internal rebellion. In 1809, Fateh Khan and Mahmud captured Kandahar and moved toward Kabul. Shuja who was in Peshawar led his army and crossed Khyber Pass and met Fateh Khan and Mahmud's forces at Gandamak, where he was defeated. Shuja fled to India and spent the rest of his life with his brother Zaman.

Shah Mahmud came back into power again in1809 and delegated his powers to Fateh Khan to rule as a despotic ruler. He practiced nepotism and gave different areas of Afghanistan to his twenty brothers to rule. In 1811, Fateh Khan invaded Kashmir with the help of Ranjit Sing, who was very powerful in Punjab and who expected to be given the governorship of Kashmir. Fateh Khan, however, gave this position to Mohammad Azim Khan of the Barakzai tribe and Ranjit Sing was very much disappointed and decided that from now onward he would never work on behalf of Afghanistan.

Fateh Khan and his twenty brothers ruled unopposed all over Afghanistan. Herat was governed by Feroz-ud-din who maintained diplomatic relations with Mahmud. In 1805, the Persian army led by Mohammad Khan Kajar invaded Herat but retreated due to mismanagement. However, Feroz-ud-din still agreed to pay a small amount of annual tribute to the Persian King. In order to credit a victory, the Persian king Fateh Ali Shah sent his army again in 1816 to capture Herat. But before the Persian army arrived in Herat, Fateh Khan marched from Kabul toward Herat. Fateh Khan was greeted by Feroz-ud-din but was asked not to enter the city. Fateh Khan did not like this and entered the city and arrested Haji Feroz-ud-din and captured Herat. Fateh Khan then sent Feroz-ud-din to Kabul. Fateh Khan got hold of all the treasury of Feroz-ud-din and then asked his amok brother Dost Mohammad Khan to enter Feroz-ud-din's harem and collect whatever could be found there. This was clearly a violation of the Afghan tradition. Dost Mohammad Khan, considered a Gurkek or "little wolf", entered the harem and misbehaved with the daughter of Shah Mahmud and sister of Prince Kamran by pulling jeweled girdle off her hip. Dost Mohammad Khan had exceeded the limits of Afghan norms.

When this news reached Kabul, Mahmud ordered the arrest of his wazir and sent Kamran on this mission to Herat. In the meantime, Fateh Khan defeated the Persian forces. Kamran was received respectfully by Fateh Khan. Kamran invited Fateh Khan to his court, and when he arrived, Kamran ordered the guards to arrest him and then he was blinded right there.

78 Rise and Fall of Durrani Dynasty

The reaction from Fateh Khan's brothers was knee-jerk. All of Fateh Khan's brothers left Herat and reached Saadut and called a meeting of the Barakzai tribe, and Dost Mohammad Khan went to Kabul to seek the Qizilbashs' support to oust Mahmud. Mahmud arrived in Herat and both Mahmud and Kamran killed the blinded Fateh Khan. Mahmud and Kamran thereafter started ruling Herat. Later Mahmud was poisoned by his son Kamran and died in 1829. Kamran became the ruler of Herat in 1829 and ruled with the help of his wazir, Yar Mohammad Khan, who was the chief of the Alizai Durrani tribe. He ruled until he was murdered by Yar Mohammad Khan in 1842. The Barakzai brothers declared Dost Mohammad as the Amir-ul-Mominin, or "commander of the faithful", in 1837[10]. That was the end of the Saddozai or Durrani dynasty that had been founded by Ahmad Shah Durrani. "When the dynasty tore itself apart, many of his male descendants had been killed", write Omrani and Leeming.

Notes

1 Omrani, *Afghanistan: a companion and guide*, p. 67.
2 Fletcher, *A complete history of Afghanistan*, p. 39; Ewans, *Afghanistan: a new history*, pp. 20–22.
3 Ibid.
4 Omrani, *Afghanistan: a companion and guide*, p. 69.
5 Ewans, *Afghanistan: a new history*, p. 22.
6 Omrani, *Afghanistan: a companion and guide*, p. 69.
7 Ewans, *Afghanistan: a new history*, p. 22.
8 Fletcher, *A complete history of Afghanistan*, p. 42.
9 Omrani, *Afghanistan: a companion and guide*, p. 70.
10 Fletcher, *A complete history of Afghanistan*, p. 71.

Bibliography

Dupree, N.H., *An Historical Guide to Afghanistan*. Afghan Tourist Organization, Jagra Ltd., Tokyo, Japan, Publication Number 5, 1970.

Ewans, M., *Afghanistan: A New History*. Curzon Press, Richmond, 2001.

Fletcher, A., *A Complete History of Afghanistan*. Cornell University Press, New York, 1965.

Omrani, B., and M. Leeming, *Afghanistan: A Companion and Guide*. Odyssey Books and Guides, Sheung Wan, Hong Kong, a division of Airphoto International Ltd., 2007.

5

THE BRITISH INTERFERENCE IN AFGHANISTAN

The British had settled in the Indian sub-continent through the East India Company which initially started as a trading concern during the regime of the Mughal emperor Jehangir. The British Commander Robert Clive defeated the Nawab of Bengal, Siraj-ul-daula, at the Battle of Plassey on June 23, 1757, and got control of Bengal. Dunbar writes, "Mir Jafar entered Murshidabad in triumph and executed Siraj-ud-daula when he fell into his hands". The company first got exemption of customs duties and later started collecting taxes on behalf of the Mughal emperor. The Company pillaged the once very rich Bengal and made it the poorest place through indiscriminate extortion. During the Bengal famine of 1943–44, 4 million of Bengalis starved to death, writes Shashi Tharoor. The Company made a big fortune and started diverting money into military expeditions. The Company then became an official agent of the British Government and brought the pillaged Indian subcontinent under British imperialism. Now the British were concerned about the protection of their possessions in the Indian subcontinent.

The British feared threats from the Franco-Russian alliance and Persia. The Franco-Russian accord was reached between Napoleon Bonaparte and Czar Alexander II according to which Russia was to send its forces to Persia where the French forces would join them via Constantinople. Once they took over Persia, their forces then would move to India via Afghanistan. Moreover, Russia was not to engage in trading activities with Britain. This agreement was reached after the defeat of Russia by the French Commander, Napoleon. These threats could only be implemented through Afghanistan, a corridor for the Central Asian invasions. The British entered into an agreement with Persia which said that no armies would be permitted to pass through Persia into India; the British would be indifferent with regard to the Persian–Afghanistan dispute; and that the British will provide arms to Persia in the case of any European attack on Persia.

DOI: 10.4324/9781003198376-5

80 The British Interference in Afghanistan

Russia had taken over the Persian province Gokcha in 1825, and the next year Persia attacked Russia to get its territory back. The Persian army was led by Abbas Mirza, the oldest son of the Shah. Dupree writes, "Russia defeated Persia in 1828 and their growing political influence at the Persian court was viewed with such mistrust and concern by the British in India". Persia asked Britain to provide arms to Persia in accordance with the treaty of 1809. The British denied them their request. The agreement was that Britain would provide arms to Persia in case of any European attack on Persia. They reasoned that, here, as Persia had been attacked not by Europeans but by Russians, their appeal for arms was a moot point. The Persians were disappointed with the British and considered them an unreliable ally.

The Persians then turned to Russia, signed a treaty of Turkmanchai in 1828, and surrendered its territory of Erivan and Nakshivan districts to Russia and also agreed to pay them indemnity. That is what the British were very concerned with the threats of attacking India by Napoleon, Russia, and Persia. Now Afghanistan became a cornerstone of their policy and thus the British started getting involved in Afghanistan to bring it under its control through briberies and conspiracies. The British interference in Afghanistan started during the period of Dost Mohammad Khan.

During Dost Mohammad Khan's rule, Peshawar was administered by his brother Sultan Mohammad Khan. An American, Josia Harlem, who was on the payroll of the British as their sleuth bribed Sultan Mohammad Khan and convinced him to leave the post at night so that it could be taken over by Ranjit Sing in connivance with the British. When Peshawar was seized by Ranjit Sing, Dost Mohammad Khan was shocked by the disloyalty and the treachery of his brother. In 1837, he sent his army under the command of his son Mohammad Akbar Khan, who defeated the Sikh army at Jamrud and Sikh general Hari Sing was killed. Afghan army could have taken back Peshawar, but fearing the presence of the British decided to go back without taking Peshawar and thus Peshawar remained with Ranjit Sing.

Dost Mohammad Khan was ready to terminate all kinds of links with Russia and Persia and wanted to sign a treaty with the British if the British could help him in getting Peshawar back from Ranjit Sing. Peshawar was very important for him in that it was a rich province and, most importantly, it was inhabited by the Pushtuns who were a source of strength for him. The British did not accept this proposal saying that they could not possibly interfere in others' affairs, rather it could only offer its good offices. Dost Mohammad Khan answered that he did not need that. Now the British and Dost Mohammad were on different paths.

The British thought it prudent to get rid of Dost Mohammad Khan. The idea was developed by the British secret sleuth William Hay Macnaghten. The plan was to replace Dost Mohammad Khan with an exiled Afghan Shah Shuja who once ruled Peshawar. The British had thought that Shah Shuja would act as the British puppet ruler to facilitate their policies to have control over Afghanistan. This was the biggest blunder of the British that reflected their ignorance of the

The British Interference in Afghanistan   **81**

Afghan Pushtuns. The British did not have the slightest idea where the Afghan Pushtuns were coming from. Bribing, aid, tricks would not work for the Afghans.

To implement this plan, Auckland, the Governor General of India, visited Lahore in May 1838 and met with Ranjit Sing to develop a strategy to oust Dost Mohammad Khan. A tripartite treaty was signed on July 16, 1838, between Shah Shuja, Ranjit Sing, and Britain.[1] According to this agreement, Shah Shuja was to relinquish all those areas that were under Sikh control and Ranjeet Sing was to support Shah Shuja to capture the throne from Dost Mohammad Khan. When the details were being worked out, the British asked Ranjit Sing to send Sikh army under the command of Shuja's son Timur Mirza to cross the Khyber Pass for Kabul while Shuja himself was to move toward Kandahar. Ranjit Sing neither wanted to participate in a big way, nor wanted to let his army cross the Khyber Pass to fight the Afghans. He was scared and did not want to confront the Afghans beyond Khyber Pass. He understood the Afghans better than the British did. Knowing the tepid response from Ranjit Sing, Auckland decided now there should only be the British effort in this matter. Auckland on October 1, 1838, issued the Simla manifesto stating the reasons for British action in Afghanistan. Auckland's plan was based on complete ignorance of the Afghans' character and Afghanistan and this fact was proved by history later.

At Ferozepur, Auckland recruited and assembled an army of about 30,000 soldiers consisting of Shah Shuja's retinue and followers both men and women, Nepalese Gurkhas, Bengalis, and Marathas under the command of Sir Harry Fane. On hearing the news that Persian army had moved toward Herat, the British became concerned and handed over the command of the army from Fane to Sir Willoughby Cotton. On December 10, 1838, Shah Shuja accompanied by his blind brother Shah Zaman and followed by the British army marched toward Kandahar. The British hypocritical declaration was that they were neither attacking Afghanistan nor was it at war with Afghanistan. It was just following Shah Shuja as an allied escort. After crossing the Indus, the Shuja-led British army passed through Bakhar and Shikarpur and then entered the Bolan Pass that connects Jacobabad and Sibi with Quetta where it was confronted by the Balochi tribes. Bolan Pass was one of the main routes used by traders and invaders and was not safe as the caravans were robbed by the local residents whose livelihood was dependent upon such robbery. The British army reached Quetta on March 26; here again the command of the army changed hands from Cotton to Sir John Keane.

When the British army left Quetta, and passed through Kojak Pass that connects Qila Abdullah with Chaman, the army was confronted by the Ghilzais. When the army reached Kandahar, it was vacated by the Barakzai princes who had fled to the west. Shah Shuja accompanied by Macnaghten entered Kandahar in triumph on April 24, 1839, and the people in the streets offered their tepid greeting as Shah Zindabad.[2] The Kandaharis and their chiefs stayed away from Shah Shuja. According to Ewans, Macnaghten reported to Auckland that "Shah Shuja had been received with feelings nearly amounting to adulation".

82 The British Interference in Afghanistan

Dost Mohammad Khan was anxiously waiting for Shah Shuja and the British army. The British army left Kandahar on June 27, 1839, for Ghazni by leaving a small unit as a reserve force in Kandahar. Dost's son Ghulam Haider Khan was ruling Ghazni then. The British forces defeated Ghulam Haider Khan and killed 500 Afghans and 17 British soldiers died. After capturing Ghazni, the British forces moved toward Kabul. At Argandeh, the British and Dost's forces faced each other. Dost's followers started slipping away from their positions and he was able to manage a safe run to an unknown destination. The British wanted to pursue and apprehend him but were unable to do so. Then Haji Khan Kakar, who had previously worked with Dost, volunteered to guide the British to find and get hold of Dost. Haji Khan Kaker in fact misguided the British by deviating them from the actual path and he made the British wander on different irrelevant paths for one month without any result. The British became suspicious of Haji Khan Kakar and punished him by exiling him to India.

On August 7, Shah Shuja in the company of British envoy Macnaghten entered Kabul.[3] The people in the streets were bewildered and watched him pass through the streets with their long faces seemingly telling the new Shah that it was okay, but it was not okay. After reaching Kabul, General Keane ordered the reserve unit that was left at Kandahar to march toward Herat to negotiate a treaty with Yar Mohammad Khan, the ruler of Herat. Yar Mohammad Khan accepted the presence of the British. General Keane then ordered the Bombay soldiers to go back to India via Kandahar. When the Bombay soldiers left Kandahar, they wanted to teach a lesson to Khan of Kalat, Mehrab Khan, for not providing supplies to the British army on their way to Kandahar. Mehrab Khan was removed and a puppet Nawaz Khan was installed as the Khan of Kalat. Mehrab Khan's son rebelled and killed Nawaz Khan. The British could not do anything. After a month, General Keane left Kabul for India via the Khyber Pass.

In Kabul, Shuja acted as the puppet ruler of the British and power was divided between Shuja and the British. Defense, foreign and tribal affairs were with the British while civil administration and criminal law stayed with Shuja. Shuja had very much resented his role as a puppet and started thinking about how to get rid of the British. Shuja gave the key positions to Durrani and Barakzai sardars including Osman Khan Barakzai, the nephew of Dost Mohammad Khan; Abdullah Khan, chief of the Achakzai Durrani tribe; and Aminullah Khan, a very powerful and strong Malik of the Ghilzai tribe. Practically, Macnaghten was at the helm of the affairs in organizing and ruling the government.

But for Macnaghten to rule Afghanistan was not an easy business. Soon the Ghilzai tribes started rebelling against the British, and Macnaghten institutionalized the policy of bribery and subsidies to the tribal chiefs to make them quiet. But at the same time, Macnaghten was worried about Dost Mohammad Khan who could stage a comeback at any time.

Later, the British heard that Dost Mohammad Khan was hiding in Khulm in Balkh Province and pursued him. Dost Mohammad Khan fled to Bokhara where he raised a small army of the Uzbek horsemen and came back to Khulm in July

1840. Dost Mohammad Khan found the British in Bamian where they were punishing the Hazara people of Bamian for not providing the supplies for their army. After the confrontation, Dost fled to Kohistan where he raised an army of the Tajiks and confronted the British at Parwan, 40 miles to the north of Kabul. Here the Bengal soldiers deserted the British side to fight. With a minor victory, Dost Mohammad Khan left the scene.

After two days, Dost Mohammad Khan met Macnaghten and surrendered his sword. Now Macnaghten was satisfied that a dangerous hawk was in their hands. Later Dost was exiled to India escorted by Commander Cotton. The British realized that they should have not played any role here and instead should have withdrawn after installing Shah Shuja. Auckland received a message ordering him to either withdraw from Afghanistan or increase the force to have complete control. Auckland did nothing.

The British proved to be very cruel in their handling of the Afghans. One young British officer destroyed a whole village because the people of that village supposedly looked at him with contempt. The British meddled with their women, which was highly unacceptable in the Afghan custom. One Afghan murdered his wife on the charge of an affair with the British. The British asked Shuja to execute the wife murderer which the puppet Shuja did in spite of the fact that this was against the Afghan tradition. Before the arrival of the British, the Afghans were tolerant toward non-Muslim religions. But when the British missionaries started proselytizing the Afghans, it became unbearable for the Afghans to compromise on their faith. Thus, the British had sown the seeds of hate, anger, and mistrust among the Afghans, the fruit of which they had to harvest later.

After the settlement of the British with the puppet Shah Shuja in Kabul, British General Richard Sale was asked to get back to India with his army unit. General Sale's return journey proved to be horrible for the British. On October 9, when the British left Kabul and reached Khurd Kabul, about 17 miles from Kabul, the British army was attacked by Afghan tribes. After three days of fighting the passage was cleared. All the way from Kabul to Jalalabad, the British army was attacked by the Afghan tribes at different points such as Tezin, 29 miles from Kabul, and Jagdalak valley by the Mohmands, Safis, and other tribes from the top of the hills alongside the road. When Sale sojourned at the Gandamak valley, he received a message from Kabul that there was serious trouble from rebel sardars and was asked to come back for aid. Sale, himself wounded, discussed this with his wounded soldiers who were terribly scared to repeat the same deadly passage again and asked Sale to not comply and move forward toward Jalalabad as they were unable to fight anymore. Sale replied to Kabul that his soldiers were seriously wounded and that they were left with no ammunition to fight with and thus had decided to move forward to Jalalabad.

The rebel sardars who were in the court of Shah Shuja believed that the puppet Shuja is helpless. The main opponents were Abdullah Khan, a chief of the Achakzai Durrani tribe; Aminullah Khan, a Ghilzai; and Zaman Shah, a cousin of Dost Mohammad Khan. All three men were good in intrigues. At

84 The British Interference in Afghanistan

that time, the cantonment was at Sherpur, now part of Wazir Akbar Khan area in Kabul. That cantonment is now housed by the US military. Bibi Mehro's hill was just a thousand yards away, which was used by the Afghan tribes to attack the British forces. When Alexander Burnes, who was the governor of Kabul city, heard about these people, he decided to exile them to India as they had links with Dost Mohammad Khan. Not only that, another blunder that Burnes made was that he had protected those Afghan women who had left their husbands to stay with the British. This meddling with their women compelled all the Afghan tribes to become part of Abdullah's conspiracy against the British. When a British agent, Mohan Lal, told Burnes that the opponents' alliance was growing rapidly, Burnes jumped out of his chair and said it was time to leave the country.

While Burnes was just planning to get out of Kabul, the next day Abdullah Khan with one hundred armed Afghans stormed Burnes' residence and killed Burnes and his retinue. The Afghan women living there with the British were also killed as no aid from Macnaghten came. Only one Afghan, Mohammad Hussain, survived with twenty-six wounds. After the annihilation of Burnes' army, Abdullah Khan and his group proceeded to the adjacent treasury and bagged £17000, but the group let go of the two British officers Johnson and Trevor along with their wives and children safely. The Afghans had bitter hatred against Burnes because of the invasion of Afghanistan and their meddling with the Afghan women. This situation was further aggravated by the call of Mullah of Kabul, Mohammad Shah Khan, to the Afghans to drive out the infidels from the soil of Afghanistan.

The rebel group led by Abdullah Khan chose Zaman Shah as the puppet leader while the real power vested in Abdullah Khan and Aminullah Khan. When the story of Burnes' killing and his army spread, the regional tribal leaders rose to the occasion. In Ghazni, Musa Khan, the malik of the Suleiman Khel Ghilzai tribe, led his force to the citadel and killed 130 British soldiers. In Charikar, the capital city of Parwan Province, the Gurkha and the Punjabi forces of the British army were attacked by the Kohistani Tajiks led by the chief, Khoja Mir Khan. The British officers fled and let the Gurkha and the Punjabi Muslim officers face them. The Muslim Punjabi soldiers defected to the Afghans but the Gurkhas had no option but to be brutally killed by the Afghans.

Now the events were joined by Dost Mohammad Khan's son Mohammad Akbar Khan who, like his father, was a very brave, bold, and good strategist. With Akbar Khan's coming, the intensity of sniper attacks from the top of Bibi Mehro hill on the cantonment, the house of the British army, increased rapidly. The British soldiers became panicky and asked the viceroy Macnaghten to start immediate negotiation for their safe exit. Macnaghten met with the eighteen tribal chiefs and tried to reach an agreement according to which the British were to leave Afghanistan and the Afghan chiefs to provide the supplies. The agreement was disregarded as neither of them honored the agreement. Neither did the British leave nor did the Afghan provide supplies. Even Macnaghten, a sleuth,

The British Interference in Afghanistan **85**

who was from the secret department and was famous for his make-and-break techniques, through bribery and intrigues could not do anything successfully.

Shah Shuja was confined to Bala Hissar. He asked Commander Cotton to remove all the British forces from Bala Hissar as he thought that the British forces should not stay near his zannana (harem). Cotton complied and moved the forces to the cantonment in the Sherpur area. While other tribal chiefs rebelled against the British, 10,000 Shiite Qizilbash led by their chief Sherin Khan did not become a part of the attacks on the British. Actually, Qizilbash supported Macnaghten. Macnaghten, an expert in intrigues, had put 10,000 to 15,000 rupees as head money for Abdullah Khan, Aminullah Khan, and the other key sardars. As a result of this intrigue, Abdullah Khan and Mir Musjidi were killed.

On December 22, 1841, Mohammad Akbar Khan prepared a plan for Macnaghten. Akbar Khan sent his representative Sultan Khan to Macnaghten to make a deal. The so-called deal was that Akbar Khan will deliver the head of Aminullah Khan to Macnaghten and in return British will pay him 30 lakh rupees. Also, Akbar Khan will be made a wazir and the British would leave within eight months. The venue of the meeting was set by the side of the Kabul river in Kabul city. Macnaghten was allured by this deal and easily fell into Akbar Khan's trap. When Macnaghten accompanied by Lawrence, Trevor, and Mackenzie reached the rendezvous, on December 23, 1841, Akbar Khan with his key people was already waiting. During the course of the discussion, the people started gathering around.

Macnaghten asked Akbar Khan about the people standing around. Akbar Khan said, do not worry, these people are part of the secret. While talking, Akbar Khan asked his men in Dari language "begeer", or "catch" him, writes Fletcher. When he uttered these words, Akbar Khan got hold of the left hand of Macnaghten, whose face had turned red in horror. According to Captain Lawrence, Macnaghten uttered his last words in Persian language as "Az barae Khoda" meaning for God's sake, writes Fletcher. Akbar Khan shot him right there and the other three British officials fled with the help of the accompanying Afghan horsemen.[4] By killing Macnaghten, Akbar Khan took revenge for deposing his father Dost Mohammad Khan and the invasion of Afghanistan by Macnaghten. Macnaghten's head was cut and his headless body was displayed on a pole by walking through the streets of Kabul.[5] Macnaghten was replaced by Pottinger who was asked to immediately negotiate with Akbar to withdraw from Afghanistan. Akbar Khan agreed and asked to forget about what had happened.

Now the horrible withdrawal of the terrified British forces from Afghanistan started. The British contingent included 4,500 army personnel of different units and 12,000 other civilian families and support staff. Their journey was from Kabul to Jalalabad via the Kabul-Jalalabad road passing through dangerously narrow passages and hills. On January 6, 1842, the British forces started their withdrawal. When they reached Butkhak, Akbar Khan met them and took Pottinger, Lawrence, and Mackenzie hostage. At Khurd Kabul, they were attacked by the Afghans from the heights and 3,000 bodies fell. Akbar Khan

86 The British Interference in Afghanistan

asked his countrymen to stop attacks but they did not follow his instructions. Akbar Khan then advised the British that the women along with their husbands and the children should accompany him for safety which was accepted. In Kabul Khurd, the British reached Targh-i-Taraki, a 50-feet-long and 10–feet-wide gorge, where they were attacked by the Afghans almost annihilating everybody with the exception of a few who were able to make their way to meet the advance party at Kubbar-i-Jubbar.

The British army under Brigadier Shelton continued their retreat until they reached Jagdalak and sojourned in a ruined fort. Here they received a message from Akbar Khan that Shelton and Johnson should come back and take the dying General Elphinstone along. On their retreat, the army had to pass through many gorges where they were attacked from the heights by the Afghan tribes. Akbar Khan asked the attacking tribesmen to stop their strikes against the British and even offered them 60,000 rupees, but his request and monetary offer remained ineffective. The British left 70 wounded soldiers behind and continued their retreat toward Jalalabad. After a short journey they reached another gorge and they were confronted again by the Afghan tribes. Here the soldiers ran amok in disappointment and cut to pieces their own mates and camp followers and then deserted. Twenty soldiers along with 300 camp followers, who remained steadfast, continued their journey toward Jalalabad.

The army reached Gandamak where it stopped and held a meeting with the Ghilzais' chief to secure a safe passage. Here Major Charles Griffith successfully negotiated and got the promise that they will not be further attacked on their way to Jalalabad. Then all of a sudden one person of a tribe tried to snatch a musket from a soldier and in this effort the tribesman was killed. This infuriated his tribe and they took some soldiers captive. Six soldiers were able to make it to Fatehabad, still 16 miles away from Jalalabad. Five of them decided to stay there forever, and one man, Dr. Byrdon, who was an Assistant Surgeon embedded with the army reached Jalalabad. He was almost half dead and for some time he did not talk. He was considered the sole survivor of this retreat. But it is reported that some other soldiers that were held captive by Mohammad Akbar Khan were released later and made to Jalalabad after Dr. Byrdon's arrival.[6]

After this humiliation, Auckland was replaced by Lord Ellenborough who arrived in Calcutta on February 28, 1842. Ellenborough announced the reversal of Auckland's policy. Ellenborough wanted to restore the image and the reputation of the army. For this purpose, he prepared two army units – one to support general Nott in Kandahar and the other to leave for Jalalabad via Khyber Pass. But then, on May 17, 1842, he had to recant himself and ordered General Nott at Kandahar to withdraw via Kabul and the Jalalabad force was sent for his assistance. The purpose of traveling back to Kabul was to get their prisoners held by Mohammad Akbar Khan released and taken back to India.

In Kabul, Shuja reconciled with Zaman Khan and made him wazir just to be united against the rising Mohammad Akbar Khan. Shuja then offered Mohammad Akbar Khan to take the position of Commander-in-Chief. Akbar

The British Interference in Afghanistan **87**

Khan refused to accept unless, "the Shah came to Jalalabad", writes Fletcher. When Shuja left Kabul, he was confronted by an Afghan tribe, led by Shuja-ud-daulah, son of Zaman Khan, who killed him and tossed his body in a ditch. That was the end of the expedition of Afghanistan that had started from Ferozepur and it marked the end of the Saddozai rule as well. After that, the Barakzais ruled Afghanistan. Now, an internal war for power among the different Afghan tribes started.

The British army next became involved in seeking revenge by engaging in barbaric and uncalled for unethical acts. On August 9, 1842, General Nott left Kandahar for Kabul. The army camped outside the city and they were joined by the Jalalabad forces, led by General Pollock, who had confronted Mohammad Akbar Khan at Tezin and had routed him out to continue toward Kabul. The city wore a desolate look. They waited until the people had come back to the city. When the people started appearing in the city's bazaar, the army was ordered to destroy Kabul. The beautiful bazaar of Kabul and the entire city, including the mosque of Ali Mardan, were destroyed and burned down; the men, women, and children were killed with the exception of the Qizilbash tribe, whose people and houses remained safe. The British started looking for the prisoners held by the Afghans in Bamian. The Qizilbash chief, Sherin Khan, offered to get them released. The British agreed and Sherin Khan took 600 horsemen and left for Bamian. However, before Sherin Khan's arrival at Bamian, the Afghan who was in charge of those prisoners had released them on payment of 20,000 rupees.

The British did not stop here, as their thirst for vengeance was not satiated as yet. The British army moved to the village Istalif where they killed every male person and raped the women and the soldiers kept shouting that they were nothing but assassins. The army then moved to Charikar, where they repeated what they did at Istalif. They destroyed the city, killed the people, raped the women, and came back to Kabul.

Unlike the British's callous, barbaric, atrocious acts of destroying, burning wounded soldiers and cities, killing men and raping women, the Afghans acted quite differently in a civilized but brave manner. Afghans did not rape any British woman, the two British minor girls who were left behind stayed there and became a part of Afghanistan and they did not complain about any sort of excesses from the Afghans. Similarly, the Afghans did not harm the prisoners of the war. Although the British thought that they had restored the morale, prestige and reputation of the British army, these acts will never be justified by history.

On October 12, 1842, the British started their retreat to India, taking along blind Shah Zaman and Shah Shuja's family. The British army had destroyed Jalalabad and when they entered the Khyber Pass, they were attacked by the Afghans. The British army crossed the Sutlej river on December 18, 1842, and was greeted by Lord Ellenborough. The army took along the doors from Ghazni and boasted that these were the doors that were taken by Sultan Mahmud Ghaznavi from the Somnath Temple in 1026. These were not the doors from Somnath Temple but were the doors made of deodar wood and carved according to the

88 The British Interference in Afghanistan

Islamic tradition. On their way to India, the British army was crossed by the Afghan horsemen led by Dost Mohammad Khan, who had been released from British captivity in Ludhiana. Dost Mohammad Khan was now heading toward the north to build a new Afghanistan. In the first Anglo-Afghan War, the British had lost 20,000 soldiers and 50,000 camels with humiliation on their credit. This was the end of the first Anglo-Afghan War.

Dost Mohammad Khan returned and started uniting his people and building a new Afghanistan on the rubbles left by the British. When Dost ascended to the throne in 1842, at the same time Kohendil Khan captured Kandahar from Shuja's son Safdar Jang. While Dost was concentrating on rebuilding his country, his implacable son Mohammad Akbar Khan was insisting his father to take revenge by attacking the British who were engaged in the Anglo-Sikh War. Dost had come to know the power of the British while he was their captive at Ludhiana; he therefore decided to refrain from this adventure. The disappointed Mohammad Akbar Khan left for Persia to raise an army with the help of the Persian Shah but died there. The Afghans became suspicious that Dost Mohammad Khan had become pro-British during the course of his captivity in India. The Sikhs were defeated by the British in the Anglo-Sikh War of 1845.

The Sikhs wanted to be revenged for their defeat by the British. Therefore, the Sikhs' leader, Diwan Mulraj Sing, approached Dost Mohammad Khan that if the Afghans could help them against the British, the Sikhs would cede Peshawar and all the territories to the west of the Indus River to Afghanistan. This alluring offer was accepted by Dost Mohammad Khan and sent his army under the command of Ghulam Haider Khan, the younger brother of Mohmmad Akbar Khan. The Afghan army occupied Peshawar and Attock and stopped there as they did not want to go beyond that in support of the Sikhs. When the British destroyed Khalsa, Dost Mohammad had to withdraw his army from Attock and Peshawar. The British retook Peshawar and the other areas. With the death of Kohendil in 1855, Dost Mohammad Khan got Kandahar back. Now Dost turned his attention to the north ruled by the Uzbeks. By 1858, his forces reclaimed the land between the Hindu Kush and the Oxus (Amu) River. Now his target was Herat, which was being ruled by Yar Mohammad Khan's son Syed Mohammad. Instead of facing Dost Mohammad Khan, Syed Mohammad asked for the Persian Shah's protection and offered to rule as Shah's vassal to which Shah agreed.

Herbert Edward, the Commissioner of Peshawar, convinced Lord Dalhousie that it was in the British interest to have an alliance with Afghanistan so that the latter did not fall under Russian influence. Lord Dalhousie agreed and an invitation to visit Peshawar was sent to Dost Mohammad. Dost accepted the invitation and sent his son Ghulam Haider to Peshawar. Ghulam Haider reached an agreement with the British which was to be based on mutual respect.

In the meantime, Syed Mohammad of Herat was deposed by Mohammad Yusuf, a grand nephew of Shah Shuja. Like his predecessor, Yusuf Khan also asked Persia for protection. Instead of providing protection to Mohammad Yusuf Khan, the Shah of Persia just entered Herat and captured it. In disappointment,

Yusuf Khan raised the British flag on his palace showing that he has British protection. The British immediately reacted and rejected Yusuf Khan's claim of having British protection. Yusuf Khan was deposed by another Saddozai Isa Khan who was killed by the Persians, and thereby the Persians seized the control of Herat.

In another movement, the British captured the island of Kharak in the Persian Gulf and then landed their armies at Bushire to confront the Persian army. The Persian army was defeated and a peace treaty was signed between the British and the Persians according to which Persia surrendered its claim on Herat. Persia vacated Herat on March 4, 1857, which was then handed over to Sultan Ahmad Khan, also known as Sultan Jan, the son of Kohendil, the former ruler of Kandahar. Sultan Ahmad Khan had no love for his father-in-law Dost Mohammad Khan.

During the Anglo-Persian tension, the British sent another invitation to Dost Mohammad Khan to visit Peshawar. This time, Dost Mohammad visited Peshawar himself in January 1857and reconfirmed the treaty of 1855 that was signed between the British and Ghulam Haider Khan. According to this agreement, the British confirmed their promise to help Afghanistan in case of any foreign invasion. Dost Mohammad captured Herat in 1863, but soon after the capture of Herat he died. Dost Mohammad's relations with the British remained cordial until his death in 1863. Dost Mohammad was succeeded by his third son, Sher Ali Khan, as Amir. Dost Mohammad Khan left behind 16 sons from his five wives. He is buried at Herat in the same graveyard where there is a tomb of Khawaja Abdullah Ansari, a Persian sufi who lived in the 11th century in Khurasan, now Herat, in Afghanistan and his shrine was built during the reign of the Temurid dynasty. There is a saying on his gravestone, "Is Dost dead that there is no justice".[7]

Although Sher Ali Khan ascended the throne, he was not accepted by his two half-brothers, Afzal Khan and Azim Khan. Afzal and Azim's mother was from the Mohmand tribe, who lived in the areas which are now in Pakistan. Both of them revolted against Sher Ali Khan. Azim Khan was interested in the governorship of Afghan Turkestan and, in this effort, he was supported by Abdur Rahman, son of Azam Khan. Anyway, Sher Ali Khan was victorious in this tussle. In 1864, Mohammad Amin, brother of Sher Ali, rebelled and that was also suppressed, but Sher Ali's son Mohammad Ali was killed. Sher Ali was very depressed at the loss of his son. In the meantime, Abdur Rahman raised an army of Afghan Turkestan and came to Kabul when Sher Ali Khan fled to Kandahar. Afzal Khan's forces led by Abdur Rahman defeated Sher Ali Khan at Sheikhabad and again in 1867 at Kalat-i-Ghilzai. Sher Ali fled to Herat and Afzal Khan became Amir. Afzal Khan died in 1868 and Azim Khan became Amir. Azim Khan did not have the ability and courage to rule and his people started deserting him. Azim Khan fled to Persia and died in 1869.

Abdur Rahman fled to Russia and lived in Tashkent. Sher Ali Khan returned back as Amir again in 1869. He sought protection from the British but the British

90 The British Interference in Afghanistan

were indifferent. Sher Ali then turned to Russia for assistance, which was when the British became alert. The British recognized Sher Ali Khan and sent him a gift of 20,000 rupees and 3,000 shoulder guns. This act of the British strengthened Sher Ali Khan a little bit and he devoted his attention to developing his country. He introduced for the first time postal service in Afghanistan and started a weekly magazine called *Shamsun-Nahar*. He tried to organize his army on the pattern of the Europeans but failed due to lack of discipline in the Pushtuns.

The British annexed Punjab in 1849 and thus concentrated their focus on ensuring the stability of their Indian empire and hence were no longer interested in the affairs of Afghanistan. But when the Russian policy changed toward the Central Asian states by bringing Bokhara and Tashkent under their influence, this compelled the British to rethink their policy about Afghanistan. The British invited Sher Ali to Ambala but the talks were fruitless as the British did not promise to protect Sher Ali Khan. However, with the passage of time, the new viceroy Lord Lytton said that the British were neither interested in the land of Afghanistan nor did they want to harm the independence of Afghanistan. At the same time, the British would never like to let Afghanistan fall under the influence of Russia. Ignoring the British, the Russians continued their advance to Afghanistan's borders. In 1875, the Russians annexed Khokand and renamed it Ferghana and later also annexed Khiva.

Now the British were anxious to get involved in Afghanistan's affairs, but Sher Ali Khan was reluctant. When the viceroy wrote to Sher Ali Khan that the British were planning to send a mission to Afghanistan to discuss the matters of common interest, Sher Ali replied that the viceroy could discuss these matters with his agent, Atta Mohammad, in Kabul. According to Omrani and Leeming, "the refusal of Sher Ali in 1878 to receive the British mission whilst at the same time agreeing to meet an unexpected Russian delegation was seized upon as a pretext". On September 10, a messenger reached Kabul announcing that a British mission was arriving in Kabul. Kabul was mourning the death of Abdullah Jan, the son of Sher Ali Khan. The British mission reached Peshawar and stopped at Jamrud Fort and sent their political officer Cavagnari along with his escorts to cross the gorge to Afghanistan. The group was stopped by the Afghan border commander, Faiz Mohammad, who said he would not allow them to proceed further until he had approval from Kabul. Cavagnari informed back that they were being held up at the border by the Afghan commander.

Lytton was asked to issue an ultimatum to Sher Ali Khan with an expiry date of November 20, 1878. Sher Ali had given his approval of entry to the British delegation on November 19, 1878. But before the receipt of Sher Ali's response, the British delegation had already entered and started their march toward Kabul. The British entered Afghanistan through three different routes: the north, the central, and the southern gorges. The north route was through Khyber Pass, the central route was through Kurram agency, and the southern route was Kandahar through Kojak Pass. This was the beginning of the second Anglo-Afghan War. Sher Ali Khan tried to stand up against the British but failing in his efforts he got his son Yaqub Khan to ascend the throne in 1879. Sher Ali himself fled to the Russian Turkestan to get their support. The Russians refused him permission to proceed further. He had a heart problem and died on February 21, 1879.

With the demise of his father, Yaqub Khan decided to negotiate with the British. He met the British political officer Cavagnari at Ghadamak on May 20, 1879, and signed a treaty. According to the treaty, the British were allowed free travel within Afghanistan and the British envoy was placed in Kabul. After this treaty, the British asked the army to withdraw through the northern pass. The armies that were supposed to withdraw through the central and the southern passes were told to wait until further orders. Cavagnari was announced as an envoy to Afghanistan and was housed at Bala Hissar with an escort of seventy-five soldiers. This place was near the Amir's house. The British soldiers were seen in the streets of Kabul by the Afghans with hate and scowl showing that they had a different plan in their mind for the British soldiers.

On September 2, 1879, a group of the Amir's soldiers, who had not been paid for the last eight months protested in front of the Amir's house for payment of their salaries. The Amir's Qizilbash guards repulsed them. The soldiers were told that for the time being they will be paid only one month's salary. This did not pacify them. They marched toward the British mission to register their protest where they were fired at by the British guards. These soldiers were unarmed. They came back to their units and picked up their guns, and then the other citizens of Kabul joined them. Yaqub Khan sent his Commander-in-Chief, Daud Khan, to the soldiers and the protesting citizens to convince them but it did not help. Yaqub Khan was helpless. The mob stormed the British mission and killed the envoy Cavagnari and his escorts. Poor Yaqub had nothing to do with this revolt. However, the British blamed that Yaqub was involved in the intrigue that killed Cavagnari and his escorts.

When this news reached India, General Roberts was ordered to advance toward Kabul. On September 27, 1879, Yaqub visited Roberts when he was received coldly. Roberts continued his march toward Kabul. General Roberts' army entered Kabul, and Amir Yaqub was deposed. General Roberts was not concerned with the killers of Cavagnari. He just ordered that the city be destroyed and anybody who opposed the British be killed. The massacre of Kabul continued until it was stopped by orders from London.

The massacre of Kabul by the British compelled the Afghans, who were driven out of the city in cold winter, to look for leaders to ensure and provide them protection. The Afghans came across two such leaders, Din Mohammad (Mushi-i-Alam), a Mullah from Ghazni, and Mohammad Jan of Wardak. General Macpherson repulsed an attack from Mullah Din Mohammad but his army was repulsed by Wardak Mohammad Jan at Chardeh near Kabul. On Jan's victory, the Afghans from all the nearby villages started marching toward Kabul. General Macpherson crushed the villagers' raid and caused them heavy casualties. The villagers went back carrying the dead bodies of their own. Unlike the tumultuous Kabul, Kandahar was peaceful. But for the British the main problem

92   The British Interference in Afghanistan

was Herat, which was governed by Ayub Khan, the younger brother of the deposed Yaqub Khan.

The British had realized that it was not only difficult to control Afghanistan but also very much expensive, and the Indian taxpayers were reluctant to bear the burden of these expensive military activities in Afghanistan. Now, the British mulled on how to get out of this dirty mud. The British came across a person in the name of Abdur Rahman who was in exile in Tashkent, Russia. And the Russians had no objection if Abdur Rahman got power in Afghanistan. The Russians had provided him the supplies for 200 men and made him cross the Oxus River, into Afghanistan.

In Afghanistan, Abdur Rahman was received by Sultan Murad Khan, the governor of the Afghan Turkestan, and Ghulam Haider Khan, the commander of the Afghan northern army. The British political officer, Sir Lepel Griffin, was instructed by the British viceroy to meet Abdur Rahman and know as to what his plans were and try to negotiate an agreement with him. Abdur Rahman said that both the Russians and the British should ensure the independence of Afghanistan. The British reacted that they did not see and expect any interest of Russia in Afghanistan. However, Griffin assured Abdur Rahman that the British were ready to accept him as the Amir of Afghanistan. But the British included one clause in the agreement under which Kandahar had to be separated from Kabul. Abdur Rahman did not like this but convinced the Ghilzais that for the time being let the condition be accepted and get the British out of Afghanistan, and after their departure this issue of separating Kandahar from Kabul could be resettled.

On July 17, 1880, Abdur Rahman met Griffin at Charikar, now the capital city of Parwan Province, where he was accepted as the Amir of Kabul. On July 22, 1880, Ayub Khan, the governor of Herat, proceeded to Helmand for the onward march to Kandahar via Maiwand. The British army met his forces at Mahmudabad near Maiwand and the battle known as the Battle of Maiwand started. At the same time, other tribes emerged and attacked the units of Jacob rifles which were destroyed. Burnes tried to reorganize his forces but most of his troops had fled. Burnes kept his 66th regiment intact, which fought till their ultimate defeat. The British defeat at the Battle of Maiwand was the biggest defeat of the British army. Ayub's soldiers pillaged the British camps.

The British left the wounded soldiers at the mercy of the Afghan women's knives and stones. The soldiers that survived took refuge behind the walls of the fort and waited for help from India to rescue them. On August 6, Roberts left Kabul for Kandahar and Ayub's forces took their position on the hills. Roberts' forces attacked Ayub's forces and they fled toward Herat. The British forces evacuated Kabul on August 11, 1880. On April 21, 1881, Kandahar city was handed over to Hashim Khan, an officer of Abdur Rahman. Sher Ali Khan, the governor of Kandahar, accepted the Britishs' pension and refuge in India. Now, Russia had set up its mission in Kabul. The war had cost the British 20 million pounds and 3,000 soldiers.

The British Interference in Afghanistan **93**

Abdur Rahman's cousin Ayub Khan, who was famous for his Maiwand victory, ruled Herat. The Ghilzai tribes were the main opponents of the Durrani tribe at the center. The infidels who lived in Kafristan and the Mongol-Hazaras were always at war with the Pushtuns and Tajiks. Given the overall situation, it was a gigantic task for Abdur Rahman to restore, unite, develop, and rule Afghanistan as a strong nation.

Abdur Rahman was born in 1844 and his father Afzal Khan was the son of Dost Mohammad. Abdur Rahman's mother was from the Bangash tribe of Kurrum valley. Afzal Khan served as the governor of the Afghan Turkestan. When Abdur Rahman was thirteen years old he was made the governor of Tashkurgan. When Afzal Khan heard that his son Abdur Rahman has become alcoholic and drug addicted, he put him behind the bar for one year. After his release he was asked to command an army against the Uzbek leader of Badakhshan.

After the evacuation of Kandahar, Ayub Khan, the ruler of Herat, marched toward Kandahar and at a place near Girishk defeated Rahman's forces and occupied Kandahar. Knowing that Ayub Khan had brought the entire army from Herat and left behind just a small garrison, Abdur Rahman thought it was an opportunity to attack Herat. Abdur Rahman's forces easily occupied Herat. Next Rahman raised another army of the Ghilzai tribes and expelled Ayub Khan from Kandahar as Ayub's army deserted him and switched to Abdur Rahman's side. Ayub Khan fled to India and never came back.

During his sway from 1880 until his death in 1901, Abdur Rahman was confronted with four conflicts and rebellions. The first one was from the Ghilzai tribes who thought that Abdur Rahman had become the ruler as a result of a deal with the British. They wanted their own indigenous leaders, which they found in the persons of Mullah Din Mohammad known as Mushki-i-Alam (fragrance of the universe) and Mohammad Jan Wardaki. Abdur Rahman arrested Mohammad Jan Wardaki and got him killed, while Mullah Din Mohammad died a natural death. Mullah Din Mohammad was succeeded by his son Mullah Abdul Karim whom Abdur Rahman used to call as Mushi-i-Alam (mouse of the universe).

The Ghilzais' revolt started in the summer of 1886 and was led by Mullah Abdul Karim near Ghazni. Abdur Rahman's forces defeated them and exhumed the grave of Mullah Din Mohammad and his body was tossed in a ditch. This was the style of Abdur Rahman to terrorize his opponents.

The second revolt was bred by Abdur Rahman himself as a test of his opponents. Abdur Rahman wanted to test one of his cousins, Ishaq Khan, who was the son of Azim Khan, whole brother of Afzal Khan. Ishaq Khan was a Hafiz-i-Quran (learned Quran by heart) and was more religious than others. Abdur Rahman thought that Ishaq Khan was a religious person and would not be interested in becoming a ruler of Afghanistan. To test this hypothesis, Abdur Rahman went to Laghman on a vacation, from where he spread a fake rumor about his death. On hearing the fake news of the death of Abdur Rahman, Ishaq

94 The British Interference in Afghanistan

Khan expressed his intention as a claimant to the throne. Thus Abdur Rahman's hypothesis was successfully tested.

Abdur Rahman sent two armies; one under the command of Ghulam Haider Charkhi, the commander-in-chief, and the other under Ghulam Haider Tokhi, the governor of Badakhshan, to deal with Ishaq Khan. These armies confronted Ishaq Khan's forces at Tashkurgan. Initially, Ishaq Khan's forces had an edge over Abdur Rahman's forces as Ishaq's forces fought more courageously. In the meantime, the Uzbeks captured some of Abdur Rahman's soldiers and thought to take them to Ishaq. When Ishaq mistakenly saw and thought the Uzbeks to be Rahman's soldiers, he got scared and to avoid his arrest he jumped on his horseback and galloped toward the north. Ishaq's soldiers were confused and did not understand why their leader fled while they were fighting bravely. For some time they continued to fight without their leader, but later surrendered to Abdur Rahman's forces. Ishaq Khan crossed the Amu River and spent the rest of his life in religious activities in Russia.

The third rebellion was put up by the Mongol Hazaras, who were against both the Pushtuns and Tajiks, and had declared their independence in 1891. Their movement was crushed by Ghulam Haider Charkhi at Uruzghan.

The fourth internal conflict was with the Kafirs of Kafiristan who were never subdued even by Temur. Abdur Rahman secretly arranged four armies at Panjsher, Badakhshan, Laghman, and Chitral and attacked the Kafirs of Kafiristan from different directions in 1896. The Kafirs were taken aback and defeated. After the defeat of the Kafirs, Abdur Rahman renamed Kafiristan as Nuristan, which first was a district of Nangarhar and has now become a province in Afghanistan. Many of the Kafirs converted to Islam and settled in Laghman and Paghman. The British protested that these Kafirs were Christians and Abdur Rahman responded that he did not see any Christian among them.

After settling the internal conflicts, Abdur Rahman now considered organizing the structure of his government. He tried to develop the national army based on the concept of "Hasht Nafri" (eight men). Under this scheme, each village was supposed to nominate one person out of the eight persons to the national army. The state had promised to provide military training for two years, uniform, and maintenance allowance (salary). He also planned to equip his army with weapons. But he did not have enough resources for ammunition. His soldiers had rifles without ammunition and thus they could not practice improving their shooting skills.

As far as the civil administration was concerned, he had divided the treasury department into two units, the state and the royals, and both were located within his palace. He had set up the houses of representation in the form of the supreme council and the general assembly represented by the tribal chiefs and maliks. However, these bodies were just superficial and never discussed any issue of public interest and Abdur Rahman never bothered to seek advice from these bodies. His legal system was supposedly based on Imam Abu Hanifa's interpretation of Islam. Although justices known as Qazi were supposed to dispense justice, in practice, Amir himself was making the judicial decisions by fiat.

The British Interference in Afghanistan 95

On the north side, Abdur Rahman was under pressure from Russia's threat and on the south side he did not have good relations with the British. Finally, he got an invitation from the Viceroy of India to visit India. He met Viceroy Lord Dufferin at Rawalpindi. Abdur Rahman asked the viceroy that London and Kabul should have direct communications for improvement in relations between the two countries. He had an impression that the Viceroy of India did not forward his concerns to the British government in London, and that's why he made this request.

In 1894, Abdur Rahman received an invitation from the British government to visit London. He sent his son Nasrullah Khan who was Hafiz-i-Quran (learned Quran by heart). When Nasrullah landed in London, there public gathering on the street to see the person coming from a country which had slaughtered the British ambassadors, army generals, political officers, army officers, soldiers, civilians, men, women, and children through the Khyber Pass and had defeated the British army. Nasrullah presented a letter from his father Abdur Rahman to Queen Victoria. The letter requested for establishment of diplomatic relationships between the two countries. The British responded that this was not possible in the light of the fate of the previous ambassadors who were posted in Kabul. Nasrullah thus returned unsuccessful.

Abdur Rahman restored and united the territories of Afghanistan as a nation and ruled his country with an iron hand. But for one thing he was disliked the most by the Afghans and that was the Durand Agreement that he had signed with Mortimer Durand, the Foreign Secretary of the Government of British India, on November 12, 1893, at Rawalpindi. This agreement was about the Durand Line representing a long border between modern-day Pakistan and Afghanistan. Under this agreement, most of the Pushtun tribes including Yousafzais, Afridis, Orakzais, Wazirs, and Mohmands were bifurcated on both sides of Afghanistan and Pakistan, which was then part of British India.

In May 1901, Abdur Rahman suffered a stroke which affected his right arm and the flaccid Amir decided that it was time now to hand over the reins to his eldest son Habibullah, who was thirty-two years old. Abdur Rahman died on October 1, 1901, at the age of fifty-six. He was buried in Kabul and his tomb was put on fire many times by the Afghans who despised him because of his cruel rule and signing of the Durand treaty with the British.

After the death of Abdur Rahman, Habibullah ascended the throne in October, 1901. Habibullah realized the threats of Russia and British India's paranoid fear of Russia and managed it diplomatically for nineteen years of his rule in Afghanistan. During the rule of Abdur Rahman, Afghanistan's relations or dealings with foreign countries were through British mediation. Habibullah ignored this and announced that he was sending his own representatives to twenty-four countries. Lord Curzon did not like this and recommended an immediate attack on Afghanistan. The British government sent a message that they were sending a mission to Kabul. Instead of receiving the mission Habibullah sent a message back that he was sending his sixteen-year-old son Inayatullah Khan to India which the British did not like.

96 The British Interference in Afghanistan

On December 12, the British sent a mission led by Sir Louis Dane to Kabul. The purpose of this mission was to sign a new treaty with Habibullah Khan. The new treaty would restore: the boycott of Quetta-Chaman railroad that was announced by his father Abdur Rahman; the stoppage of the tribal intrigues across the Durand Line; the demarcation of the frontiers of the Mohmands; and a new treaty similar to that which was signed with his father Abdur Rahman. Habibullah threw this draft treaty aside and produced his own draft written in Persian on the lines of Abdur Rahman's agreement with the British with his name as the new king of Afghanistan. Habibullah further declared that his draft is the final draft, take it or leave it, with no other option. The British were surprised but accepted it as it at least ratified the Durand Line Agreement that his father Abdur Rahman had signed with the British India foreign secretary. The British ratified this treaty on March 21, 1905. Habibullah was happy over his victory that in this treaty British did not get anything except the confirmation of the Durand Line Agreement that was signed by his father.

Habibullah was again invited by the British to visit India in June 1906. Habibullah accepted this invitation. He left his brother Nasrullah Khan and his son Amanullah at Kabul. He himself left for India in January 1907 with an entourage of 1,100. His junket was for two months. The British toured him through the military, civilian, and other interesting places. Habibullah offered to marry various English women he met with as he was fond of harem comforts. He left behind more than one hundred children from many wives. The British thought that as a result of this visit Habibullah would not despise the British. But the British were mistaken. He was the same Habibullah when he entered and left India. Whenever Habibullah wanted to show his displeasure with the British, he used the tribal chiefs to raid the North-West Frontier Province to create discomforts for British India.

In 1913, the Mangal tribes of Khost rebelled against Habibullah due to the high taxes. Habibullah crushed this revolt with the assistance of the chiefs of Suleiman Khel, Shinwaris, and Khugiani tribes. The Mangals were unable to handle the onslaught by these tribes and Habibullah's army led by Commander Nadir Khan. The Mangals then requested a truce, which was granted by Nadir Khan. Later Nadir Khan was made the Commander-in-Chief of the Afghan army.

During the rule of Abdur Rahman, twenty-one Barakzai brothers were exiled in India and the Tarzi family in Syria. Habibullah not only gave them political amnesty but also welcomed them back and gave them key positions in the government as they were well educated in India and Syria. Now Habibullah's inner circle included his brother Nasrullah Khan and his two sons, Inayatullah Khan and Amanullah Khan, the latter was the most favored by the Amir. External circles included the Barakzai brothers and the Tarzi family led by Mohammad Beg Tarzi, the descendants of the Dil brothers who had ruled Kandahar during the rule of Dost Mohammad. Mohammad Beg Tarzi published a newspaper called *Siraj-ul-Akhbar*. The third family was Charkhis, the descendants of

Ghulam Haider Charkhi, the Commander-in-Chief of the Afghan army during Abdur Rahman's rule. Ghulam Haider Charkhi's two sons, Ghulam Nabi and Ghulam Siddiq, were the generals in the army. Habibullah successfully controlled all these groups while also running his government.

In August 1915, a delegation of Turkish-German group of eight men reached Kabul and tried to convince the placid Amir Habibullah to attack British India. The group assured him that he will be supported by the German and the Turkish armies. The group included defense strategists and secret agents. They stayed at Bagh-i-Bala. While the leaders of the Turkish-German group were busy in discussion with Habibullah, the other members of the group were busy with other Indian agents such as Mahendra Pratap and Barkatullah who were Indian revolutionary leaders. Habibullah Khan was assured that if his attack on India was successful, he would be made the king of India.

Although the meeting with Habibullah was not much successful, the meetings of other members of the group with Indian agents were successful in that they sow the seeds of freedom of the Indian subcontinent from the British. The group left Kabul on May 22, 1916, with a draft agreement under which Habibullah would get 50,000 canons and 20 million pounds in gold. The group leader Oskar von Niedermayer knew that Habibullah was not going to act, so this agreement will not hold in effect. When the British heard that the Turkish-German group had announced jihad from Instanbul, Karbla, and Najif, they took immediate action and bribed the Mullahs and the tribal chiefs. The Afghans considered Habibullah's inaction to support the Muslim cause in WWI as his treachery to Islam.

On February 2, 1919, Habibullah wrote a letter to the Viceroy of India that he had supported the British by not taking the side of the Turkish-German alliance during WWI and therefore Afghanistan merits the grant of full sovereignty by allowing it to deal with the international community. The British replied that they would continue looking after the foreign affairs of Afghanistan.

After Peshawar went to British India, Habibullah made Jalalabad Afghanistan's winter capital. Habibullah along with his brother Nasrullah and his son Inayatullah left Kabul for Jalalabad. He left his son Amanullah in Kabul as in charge of the treasury and the garrison. Habibullah was fond of hunting, so he left Jalalabad for Laghman district on February 19, 1919, and camped at the foot of Khula Ghos Pass. There he was shot in the ear while sleeping by an unknown killer. Based on the different conspiracy theories, the Russians identified Mustafa Saghir, the British agent, as the assassin, while the British alleged Amanullah Khan, Nasrullah, Mohammad Beg Tarzai, and Nadir Khan as being part of the plot.

Habibullah died at the age of fifty and had ruled for nineteen years. The cause of his death could have been his failure to respond to the vox populi of the Afghans to support the Muslim Turkey by taking action against the British. However, he gave political amnesty to all those who were exiled in India and Syria during Abdur Rahman's period and made them part of the government.

98 The British Interference in Afghanistan

His major contribution was the founding of Habibia School on modern lines of thought to support the future development of his country. After his death, his son Amanullah became the Amir.

Notes

1 Ewans, *Afghanistan: a new history*, p. 42.
2 Fletcher, *A complete history of Afghanistan*, p. 93; ibid., p. 45.
3 Ewans, *Afghanistan: a new history*, p. 46.
4 Fletcher, *A complete history of Afghanistan*, pp. 108–109.
5 Ewans, *Afghanistan: a new history*, p. 49.
6 Fletcher, *A complete history of Afghanistan*, p. 112.
7 Fletcher, *A complete history of Afghanistan*, p.124.

Bibliography

Dunbar, S.G., *India and the Passing of Empire*. Nicholson and Watson, London, 1951.

Dupree, N.H., *An Historical Guide to Afghanistan*. Afghan Tourist Organization, Jagra Ltd., Tokyo Japan, Publication Number 5, 1970.

Ewans, M., *Afghanistan: A New History*. Curzon Press, Richmond, 2001.

Fletcher, A., *A Complete History of Afghanistan*. Cornell University Press, New York, USA, 1965.

Omrani, B., and M. Leeming, *Afghanistan: A Companion and Guide*. Airphoto International Ltd., Odyssey Books and Guide, Sheung Wan, Hong Kong, 2007.

Tharoor, Shashi, *An Era of Darkness, The British Empire in India*, Aleph Book Company, New Delhi, India, 2016.

6

STRUGGLE FOR INDEPENDENCE OF AFGHANISTAN

Amanullah was born in 1890 at Paghman. When Habibullah was killed in Laghman, Amanullah was twenty-nine years old. He was married to Souriya after the death of his first wife. His uncle Nasrullah Khan and brother Inayatullah Khan got the body of Habibullah back to Jalalabad where they expressed their claims to the throne. Amanullah's mother was the daughter of Mohammad Sarwar, a very powerful chief of the Barakzai Durrani tribe. She was very influential and convinced the tribal chiefs in favor of Amanullah. Later, Nasrullah Khan and Inayartullah Khan pledged allegiance to Amanullah. However, both of them were arrested and brought back to Kabul and put in prison. Nasrullah died naturally while in prison and Inayatullah was released.

Amanullah became Amir on March 1, 1919, and he announced his three priorities: first, he will bring the killer of his father to justice; second, he will get independence of Afghanistan; and third, he will abolish the system of forced labor (beeger).[1] On March 3, 1919, he sent a message to the British[2] viceroy of India, Lord Chelmsford, informing him that he had taken over the throne. The letter did not talk about the agreements of Abdur Rahman and Habibullah but mentioned an independent and free Afghanistan and that he will be willing to negotiate and conclude the commercial agreements with the British.

In the meantime, disturbance had broken out in India, especially by the Muslim population of Punjab and other areas against the way Muslim Turkey was forced to strike a deal and considered it to weaken Islam. According to the deal, all the non-Turkish areas had to be taken away from Turkey. This means Mecca had to be taken away from Muslim Turkey and be given to an infidel country. This was not acceptable to the Muslims of the Indian subcontinent. This is why the Muslims of India despised Habibullah, who did not support Muslim Turkey and instead indirectly supported the British who later awarded him with a bullet. Unlike Habibullah, Amanullah felt the vox populi of the

DOI: 10.4324/9781003198376-6

100 Struggle for Independence of Afghanistan

Muslims of India and gathered a meeting of the tribal chiefs on April 13, 1919, in which he said that now a holy war had become imminent. He organized three armies. The first one under the command of General Saleh Mohammed for the northern Khyber Pass; the second one under the command of Nadir Khan for the central Khost area; and the third one under the command of Abdul Quddus for the southern Kandahar area.

Under the command of general Saleh, Shinwari and Mohmand tribesmen crossed the Durand Line and occupied Bagh village in the south of Khyber Pass and announced that this was an Afghanistan area. Actually, the Bagh village was within the British-controlled area and was about 200 meters away from the border. British Brigadier General G.F. Crocker repulsed this attack and the irregular army of the tribesmen fled and took position on Khargali Nala Hill. The next day, on May 11, the Afghan tribesmen were confronted by the new British commander, Major General Fowler. The irregular army of the tribesmen fled leaving behind 66 dead. The British moved out of Khyber Pass and captured the Afghan village of Dakka which was left abandoned. There the British army was confronted by a big Lashkar of Mohmands, Safis, Khugianis, and Shinwaris. The tribesmen of this Lashkar were very expert in guerrilla war. From the top of the hills, the Lashkar fired at the British forces and injured them and then vanished. The British army, nevertheless, continued their stay at Dakka.

The Afghan central army stationed at Matun, led by Nadir Khan of the Musahiban family, advanced toward the British posts not waiting for the British to attack first and captured their post Spinwan. Nadir Khan continued his march until his army reached the Thal Fort. Nadir Khan's army did not storm into the fort but took their positions 5,000 yards away from the fort. Nadir Khan fired at the British forces which were consisted of Khyber Rifle and Zhob militia and both of these units showed a tepid response. The British got reinforcement under the command of General R.H.F Dyer and repulsed Nadir Khan's attack on Thal. Nadir Khan was forced to retreat.

On the southern front, General Abdul Quddus did not engage the British until the British, under the command of Lieutenant General Wapshare, captured the Afghan fort of Spin Baldak. At this point the Third Anglo-Afghan War ended. With the cease of the war, the British accelerated their diplomatic activities. On May 28, Amanullah Khan wrote a letter to the British stating that General Saleh's activities in Khyber Pass were misunderstood. These disturbances were from the irregular army of the tribesmen and that Afghanistan had no intention of attacking India. Amanullah suggested the British to agree upon a truce. The British agreed on a conditional truce, and the conditions of the truce were: one, irregular tribesmen will not attack the British; two, remove both the Afghan regular and irregular army of the tribesmen from the border and the British forces will stay where they are now in Afghanistan territory. Amanullah's response to both of these conditions was negative in that neither it was possible for Afghanistan to withdraw the tribes from the border nor could it prevent them

Struggle for Independence of Afghanistan **101**

from attacking the British. Instead, Amanullah Khan preached the British the spirit of freedom.

Finally, the British sent a message to Amanullah for holding peace talks that were later held at Rawalpindi. The Afghan delegation was led by Amanullah's cousin Ali Ahmad Khan and the British were represented by Sir Hamilton Grant. On August 8, 1919,[3] a treaty was concluded which called for: one, the withdrawal of the British forces from the Afghan territory; two, the cessation of the British subsidies; and three, the discontinuation of the flow of Afghan war material through India. No mention was made about the sovereignty of Afghanistan. The Afghan delegation pointed out this lacuna and the British responded that this was implied and finally added a rider to this effect.

The circumstances that compelled the British to this agreement were caused by the Muslims of India, who were very furious against the British's handling of Muslim Turkey. The Muslims of India had started a movement against the British and supported Amanullah. Moreover, the British intercepted the messages between Afghanistan and Russia for establishing cordial relations. The British had reached the nadir of their ability to manage the foreign affairs of Afghanistan and were left with no choice but to surrender the sovereignty back to Afghanistan. Amanullah was jubilant that Afghanistan had won its freedom on August 8, 1919, through a war and Nadir Khan was the hero of this war. After this, Amanullah Khan became a popular leader of an independent Afghanistan.

After becoming independent of the British, Amanullah now wanted to establish diplomatic relations with the rest of the world. Amanullah sent his representative Mohammad Wali Khan, a Tajik leader, to Germany, Italy, Russia, and the United States to discuss the establishment of diplomatic relationships. All the countries gave a positive response with the exception of the United States under the Harding administration. The US did not have enough knowledge of Afghanistan and responded that it would consider this in the future.

Afghanistan was strategically important for Russia and Russian leader Lenin tried to trap the naïve Afghans who did not have the political acumen to understand communism. In his letter to Amanullah, Lenin spoke against imperialism and said that Russia was determined to help those countries who are struggling for freedom. Lenin sent his diplomat Michael Bravine who arrived in Kabul on September 12, 1919,[4] as the first foreign ambassador to Afghanistan. The British activated their sleuths in Kabul who reported on Michael Bravine's activities in Afghanistan on a daily basis to the British. The British wanted to know whether the tribal insurgencies across the Durand Line were instigated by Russia or carried out by the tribesmen themselves. The British agents reported that these tribal insurgencies were carried out by the tribes themselves and that Amanullah was aware of this situation. Also, Amanullah considered the Indian Muslims' sedition against the British as a support and strength for him.

In 1920, the Indian Muslims who revolted against the British after the defeat of Muslim Turkey during WWI decided to migrate to the Muslim Afghanistan. About 20,000[5] Muslims from the North-West Frontier Province, Punjab, and

Sind migrated to Afghanistan, in the summer of 1920, as refugees and they arrived in the Darul-Aman area of Kabul city. Amanullah did not support them and compelled them to go back. These Muslims did not have a good feeling about Amanullah and his prestige inside Afghanistan was hurt as the Afghan Muslims did not like Amanullah's treatment toward the Muslims coming to Kabul from across the Durand Line.

With the arrival of the Russian ambassador in Kabul, the British felt that Amanullah had fallen under the influence of the Russians. Therefore, the British accelerated their diplomatic activities and sent an invitation to Amanullah to visit India. Amanullah sent his representative Mohammad Tarzai to India who held talks with the British representative Henry Dobbs. The meeting remained unproductive. In October 1920, Amanullah invited the British to visit Kabul for further discussions. The discussions between the British representative Dobbs and the Afghans' representatives Mohammad Tarzai and Nadir Khan continued for eleven months without reaching any agreement.

Most of Central Asia in the north of the Amu River was under the control of Russia with the exception of Khiva and Bokhara which though independent states were still under Russian influence. The Russian soldiers included the Tajiks, Uzbeks and Turkomen. Bokhara had been under the rule of the Uzbek Amir, Said Alim Khan, since 1911. Amir Said was also under the direction of Russia. During Said Alim Khan's rule a Jadid Party emerged whose members were influenced by the Turks. The upheaval of the Jadid Party, which was also supported by the Red Guards, was crushed by the Amir of Bokhara. The Afghans fearing that they could be the next advised the Amir of Bokhara to make peace with Russia.

Said Alim Khan clearly read and understood the Russians' intentions that this would not be their last stop but that they would go further. Reluctantly, the Amir of Bokhara made peace with Russia and Amir's reservations proved true when on August 25, 1920, Frunze, the commander of the Red Army, ordered his army to help the Jadid Party and attack Bokhara. On September 1, 1920, Bokhara fell to the Red Army. The people of Bokhara crossed the Amu River along with their flocks of karakul sheep and entered Afghanistan as refugees and narrated the horrible stories of rape and desecration. This situation alarmed Amanullah Khan. At that time, Afghanistan was the only Muslim state in the region.

The fugitive Said Alim Khan arrived in Kabul and lived here as a karakul trader. In the spring of 1921, a revolt in the Russian Turkestan by the Uzbek Muslims, supported by the Afghans, took place against the communists and the Jadid Party. The Russians called these anti-Russian activities "Basmachi". Basmachi[6] was the term the Russians used for all anti-communist activities in Central Asia and in Turkish language it means "the bandits". The Uzbek Muslims were against the communists' control and their revolt was led by Ibrahim Beg who was the commander-in-chief of the Bokhara Amir. The Afghans took part in this Basmachi movement and the Afghans' northern commander was

Struggle for Independence of Afghanistan **103**

asked to support the Basmachi movement indirectly. The Afghans supplied the arms and ammunition that crossed the Amu River to support the Uzbek Muslims in the north.

The Basmachi movement was joined by Enver Pasha who once ruled Turkey. After the defeat of Turkey during WWI, Mustafa Kemal Pasha took the control of Turkey and asked Enver Pasha to leave the country to save his life. Enver Pasha left Turkey and reached Moscow and assured the Russians that he would help in reconciling the differences between the Muslims and the communists. One day on the pretext of hunting, he left Moscow and secretly arrived in Turkestan where he joined the Basmachi movement. Ibrahim Beg and Enver Pasha posed a serious threat to the communists. On June 12, 1921, Enver Pasha led the Uzbek army and was defeated and killed by the communists.

In August 1921, Afghanistan and Russia signed a treaty which called for the restoration of the Panjdeh territory back to Afghanistan in return for allowing Russia to establish their consulate offices at Herat, Maimana, Mazar-i-Sharif, Ghazni, and Kandahar and payment of a yearly subsidy of one million rubles. The Panjdeh territory, near Herat, was an Afghan territory. By capturing Panjdeh, the Russians got an opportunity to have access to the junction of the Kushk and Murghab rivers, which were strategically important for the defense of and entry into Herat. This position was strategically important for Russia's future expansion toward Afghanistan and India. According to Omrani and Leeming,

> Russian were beginning to succeed in their long cherished aim of expanding into Central Asia, occupying Tashkent in 1867, Samarkand in 1868, and Bokhara in 1869, Kokand followed suit in 1871 and Khiva scummed in 1878. This encroachment did nothing to make the British feel easy about the safety of their Indian possessions.

The Panjdeh territory had been occupied by the Russian forces in 1885 at the battle of Kushkan between the Russians and the Afghan forces, during the rule of Abdur Rahman. When the Russians took over the Panjdeh territory, Abdur Rahman was in India having discussions with the British. Although, according to the 1921 agreement, the Russians agreed to restore Panjdeh back to Afghanistan, the Russians later reneged on their promise and never left Panjdeh.

After a review of the situation across the north of Amu River, on November 15, 1921, Afghanistan expressed its intention of signing an agreement with the British. This agreement called for establishment of a diplomatic relationship between the two countries and allowed duty-free Afghanistan shipments and unlimited transit across India. There was no mention of the Durand Line.

Now, after Russia, the other countries including Britain, Germany, France, Italy, and Turkey established diplomatic relationships with Afghanistan and opened their embassies in Kabul. Now Kabul became a center of hot diplomatic activities and the ambassadors of these countries started hiring the Afghans as their sleuths. In 1922, the tribal troubles across the Durand Line started making

104 Struggle for Independence of Afghanistan

the Anglo-Afghan relationship uneasy and a little bit sour. The British did not trust the Frontier Levy and replaced it with the Khasadar scouts who were previously managed by the local maliks. Most of the tribes after plundering, murdering, and kidnapping used to cross the border to Afghanistan where they were supported by Amanullah Khan. The British threatened Amanullah to stop this or face the breakup of the diplomatic relations and suffer military action.

Inside Afghanistan, in March 1924, Amanullah was confronted with a revolt by the Mangal and Jaji tribes of Khost and these tribes had no links with other tribes. One of the reasons behind this revolt was religious leaders, like Mullah Abdullah, who were against Amanullah's social reforms introducing the Western culture and Western dresses for the Afghan men and women. Especially the women wearing the skirts and the pants and doffing of the burqas (veils) was against the Islamic culture. The religious leaders were of the opinion that mere donning of Western dresses could not be considered as a harbinger of an advanced society without actual development through Islamic education. They further argued that the West was not developed just through demonstration of the modern dresses but that their development was a result of the education for economic development.

This group was supported by the exiled Amir Yaqub Khan's son Abdul Karim Khan who claimed his right to the throne. Amanullah thought that this movement was a result of the British bribing the Afghan tribal chiefs. Amanullah's regular army was unable to handle this revolt. So Amanullah asked the private tribal chiefs for assistance and the Mohmands, Shinwaris, Waziris, and Afridis responded positively. But all these tribes even together could not keep the Mangals, Jajis, and Abdul Karim Khan at bay. At one point, the rebels were just near Kabul. Failing to deter the rebels, Amanullah used two airplanes that were borrowed from the British and crushed the rebels at Charasyab and Mullah Abdullah was arrested and executed while Abdul Karim Khan went back to exile in India.

In India, during this period, Mohandas Karamchand Gandhi made a call for Hindu–Muslim unity and this movement was also supported by Abdul Ghaffar Khan, son of Mohammadzai Khan of Utmanzai village near Peshawar in the North-West Frontier Province. In 1927, Abdul Ghaffar Khan organized a party known as Pushtun or Afghan Jirga which later, in 1929, became Khudai Khidmatgaran. The uniform of this party comprised a red shirt and this color was chosen by chance and it had no relevance to Russia. Because of the red color, the party was labeled by the British as pro-Russia because in those days the British were suffering from Russian phobia. Moreover, the members of the party had no knowledge of communism.

The goal of Ghaffar Khan's party was achieving freedom from the infidels through the nonviolence movement. Ghaffar Khan's movement was very successful in uniting all the Pushtuns. Both these movements perturbed the British. Amanullah also supported the notion of Hindu–Muslim unity, and the Pushtuns from the British side of the Durand Line supported Amanullah. During the

Struggle for Independence of Afghanistan **105**

Mangals' revolt, the Pushtuns from the British side of the Durand Line wanted to cross the border to support Amanullah in his fight against the Mangals. To avert this support to Amanullah, the British whipped up the Shia–Sunni Orakzais' conflict to keep the tribes engaged internally rather than letting them cross the border to help Amanullah. The British announced that they would stand neutral and would not interfere in Afghanistan's affairs.

Amanullah was interested in the development of his country and for this purpose he planned a long junket of the important world capitals to learn about their development experience. On December 7, 1927, Amanullah and Queen Souriya along with a big posse and tons of luggage visited India. The British in India toured him through the various army installations, facilities, and historical places. Amanullah expressed his desire to meet with Gandhi who was in jail and the British government denied Amanullah's request. Amanullah made speeches exhorting the Hindu–Muslim unity.

After his India visit, Amanullah left for Egypt which was under British influence. The British sleuth, Thomas Edward Lawrence, whose real name was Robert Tighe Chapman and who was an archeologist by profession, was responsible for the defeat of the Ottoman Empire. The British occupied Egypt in 1882. The British built the Suez Canal to link it with the Mediterranean and Red seas for their military and commercial requirements, and then attacked the Roman Empire on the pretext of the local unrest that led to the occupation of Egypt by the British. Amanullah stayed in Egypt for ten days and his visit was not successful in that he criticized them as to why they were so beholden to the British. He also violated the protocol when he kept King Fuad waiting for 30 minutes to review a military parade.

After Egypt, Amanullah embarked on a European tour. In Italy he was decorated with an award of Collar of Annunciation by the king and President Doumergue of France, and President Hindenburg of Germany also decorated him and presented him with gifts. In England, Amanullah and Queen Souriya met King George and Queen Mary and toured the country for twenty-three days. He was toured through the military installations to give him an idea of British power. After England, Amanullah visited Britain's rival country, Russia. In Moscow, President Kalinin welcomed him with a grand reception that became the headlines of the international newspapers. After Moscow, Amanullah went to Turkey, where he was very much influenced by Mustafa Kemal's reforms and the progress that Turkey had made under his leadership. After Turkey, Amanullah visited Reza Shah Pehlvi of Iran as the last leg of his junket and then journeyed back to Kabul.

Through this junket, Amanullah was very much influenced by the development of the West that created an urge in his heart to change his country. The first change that he made was a social one in which he asked every man and woman to wear Western dresses. On the day of Istiqlal, he announced a Jirga of the tribal chiefs, and the Maliks and the Khans were asked to wear the Western dress to attend this function. They did it but were very uncomfortable. At this Jirga he

106 Struggle for Independence of Afghanistan

announced his reforms. The institutional reforms included the establishment of a legislative assembly consisting of 150 members to be elected on the basis of votes of all the adult male members. He abolished the hereditary ranks and the military service was to be extended for three years.

As far as these reforms were concerned, the members of the Jirga had no problem. But discontent arose when Amanullah began talking about doffing of the burqa by the women, compulsory education for boys and girls, and that all the government employees were to keep only one wife. On hearing these reforms, the eyebrows of Jirga members were raised that was a foreboding of the future troubles. The young boys welcomed these reforms because they were interested in modern education and the women felt comfortable too to unveil themselves as soon as Queen Souriya doffed off her burqa in public. But the conservative Afghans and religious leaders, especially the mullahs, became concerned that his junket of the Western countries brought back nothing but infidelity which would be controvertible and resisted.

Amanullah, undeterred by the opponents, continued the reforms that he had planned as a result of his long junket of the world through India, Egypt, Italy, the United Kingdom, Germany, France, Russia, Turkey, and Iran. His cultural and educational reforms included the permission, in 1922, to Oriental School of France for archaeological work and the establishment of the Istiqlal School to supplement Habibia School's efforts. The Istiqlal School was staffed by French teachers. Another school Ghazi was staffed by British-trained Indians and Nijat School was staffed by Germans. This was a good start in the education sector and these institutes played a key role in the development of a cadre of leadership. These schools were welcomed by the young Afghans who were very much interested in modern education. But the Afghan parents were suffering from a paranoid fear that these institutes manned and run by the foreign nationals may turn their kids into infidels and the mullahs were on the frontline to fan this trepidation and did their best to keep it alive.

As far as the development of the Afghan national army was concerned, Amanullah hired a technical assistance team from Turkey. The Turkish military experts were only concerned with their lucrative salaries and perks rather than developing the army. Amanullah himself was least concerned about the army. He was most interested in construction projects. He developed a tourist resort at Paghman, about 18 miles from Kabul, which included parks, playgrounds, restaurants, and residences in the pattern as seen in Germany. He also tried to develop a new city called Dar-ul-Aman (abode of peace) in the pattern of Ankara, Turkey. Unfortunately, he could not complete this project. Dar-ul-Aman exhibits debris of the royal palace that was destroyed during the Russian invasion. At Dar-ul-Aman, a new agricultural research station and a new parliament building were built.

Amanullah's reforms did not go uninterrupted. Some of the internal problems were not because of him but just happened by accident. One of the incidents happened in November 1928, when a nonsedentary Suleiman Khel Ghilzai tribe was on a winter move toward India, the caravan came across a group of Shinwaris whom they mistakenly thought that they could be the robbers. Because of the mistake and misunderstanding, the Ghilzai tribes killed several Shinwaris of the Sangu Khel clan. The Ghilzais were arrested and were later released by satisfying the avarice of the officials. The Shinwaris rose against this killing and captured the two military posts of Achin and Kai. Later, the other tribes of Shinwaris joined the Sangu Khel clan of Shinwaris and captured the forts of Torkham and Dakka and got their hands on the lot of military equipment. This capture encouraged the other tribes like the Khugianis and Safis to become part of this revolt.

At first, Amanullah did not take this revolt seriously as he was of the view that these were common tribal reactions. However, Amanullah sent a troop of 500 soldiers under the command of Col. Mahmud Khan Sarwar. Sher Ahmad Khan, the governor of Jalalabad, held discussions and the talks failed. Now Amanullah took it seriously and sent an additional force under the command of his cousin, Ali Ahmad Jan, who was influential in the east. At the same time, Amanullah sought help from the other tribes. Most of the tribes did not respond due to the cold weather, except Ghiasuddin Khan, the chief of the Ahmadzai Ghilzai tribe of Gardez. Ghiasuddin Khan came to Kabul, collected the arms, and went back home instead of going to Jalalabad.

Bacha-i-Saqao (son of Mashki, water carrier) heard the appeal of Amanullah Khan for the tribal assistance and considered this an opportunity to get a royal pardon. Bacha Saqao, whose real name was Habibullah, was from a village Kala Khan, 20 miles to the north of Kabul, in the Kohistan area. Bacha Saqao was in the Afghan army where he hurt a senior officer and he was jailed. He escaped from jail by bribing jail officials and fled to Peshawar. In Peshawar, he ran a tea shop and under the cover of this tea shop he was engaged in illegal activities and smuggling and operated as a fence.

In 1928, Bacha Saqao, on the promise of getting a pardon, came back to Kabul and Amanullah gave him rifles and enrolled him in the army. Bacha was a very crafty person. He sensed that Amanullah had run out of gas and could not defend Kabul city. He went back to Kohistan and raised a group of about 300 bandits and attacked Kabul city. The Afghan army acted quickly to stymie Bacha. Bacha was defeated and wounded and retreated to Kohistan. At this moment, the British, based on security concerns, evacuated 560 of their people out of Kabul.

The Afghan government made a mistake in that its forces pursued Bacha in the Kohistan area. When the government forces reached Kohistan, they were surprised to see the thousands of Kohistanis standing behind Bacha. The government forces were surrounded and were forced to surrender. On January 14, 1929, Bacha attacked again and captured Kabul and Amanullah and his posse were confined to the royal palace.

Amanullah held a meeting with the inner circle of his family and decided to abdicate his power in favor of his brother, Inayatullah Khan. Amanullah himself fled to Kandahar by road and Queen Souriya was evacuated by airplane.

108 Struggle for Independence of Afghanistan

Inayatullah was not virile like his brother Amanullah. He lacked the competence to defend his capital. Instead, he held negotiations with Bacha-i-Saqao and agreed to leave the country. The mugger Bacha entered the royal palace as the new Amir Habibullah Ghazi on January 27, 1929.

He started to organize his government. The treasury was empty as the same was taken away by Amanullah. But Bacha, who was an expert in extortion of money, plundered the citizens of Kabul. As Bacha himself was illiterate, so his cabinet was illiterate too with the exception of two persons who could read and write.

Although Amanullah received a tepid reception at Kandahar, the Kandaharis despised Bacha and did not like him to have ascended the throne to rule the Pushtuns. They decided to support Amanullah to take possession of power back from Bacha. With a lashkar of 5,000 tribesmen, Amanullah marched toward Kabul. While on his way Amanullah heard the rumors that there was a possibility of his being killed by some tribes. Amanullah feared that some of the tribes like the Ghilzais might switch their side to Bacha Saqao. Amanullah, therefore, decided to terminate his move and decided to return to Kandahar. In Kandahar, he collected his belongings, the treasury, and family members and left Afghanistan for good to take refuge in Italy.

During the internal strife, Amanullah Khan did not get any cooperation from the Musahiban or Yaya Khel family of Mohammadzai clan which was led by Nadir Khan. The Musahiban were the five brothers, the descendants of Dost Mohammad's brother, Sultan Mohammad. The five brothers included Nadir Khan, Shah Wali Khan, Shah Mahmud, Hashim Khan, and Shah Mohammad. Nadir Khan, Shah Wali Khan, and Shah Mahmud were generals in the Afghan army. Shah Mohammad who remained in Afghanistan was the governor of Khost Province. Nadir Khan was the commander-in-chief in the army of Amanullah.

Nadir Khan got frustrated when he felt that Amanullah Khan was influenced by the advice of the tribal chiefs and at times ignored his advice especially during the Mangal revolt. Consequently, Nadir Khan resigned from the command of the Afghan army. He was offered another post in his government which he refused. Nadir Khan exiled himself to France, where he was later joined by his brother, Hashim Khan. Because of the differences between the Musahiban and Amanullah, Nadir Khan and his brothers did not help Amanullah during the revolt against him. Amanullah depended on his inner circle and relied on the advice of Queen Souriya, Mohammad Wali Khan, and his father-in-law, Mahmud Tarzai.

During the 1920s, Amanullah received a lot of foreign assistance, which brought many technical experts such as engineers, technicians, teachers, and Russian pilots for the development of the Afghan airforce. The foreigners were treated with great respect and hospitality by the Afghans. The Afghans did not despise the infidels. During this period, no act of violence against the foreigners occurred. Unlike the Afghans, the law was broken by a couple of foreigners. In 1924, the first violation was by an Italian engineer, Piparno, who was apparently drunk and shot one police officer. He was arrested. He was sentenced to one-year imprisonment, which he escaped by satisfying the avarice of the concerned officials. He managed to get to the border where he was caught and was killed by the border police. The Italian government protested and Amanullah settled the case by paying $24,000 to the family of Piparno. The second violation was done by a German tourist who was traveling by motorbike through the countryside. The noise of the motorbike disturbed a horse and an argument between the German traveler and the Afghan sparked off. During the course of the back and forth argument, the German tourist shot the Afghan horseman. The tourist was awarded four years' sentence, but being a foreigner he was finally released by the government.

With the disappearance of Amanullah from the scene of Afghanistan, Bacha Saqao felt comfortable and raised an army of 10,000 who were paid by the money that Bacha extorted from the people. Like the previous rulers, Bacha also executed his opponents and got control of Kabul and Kandahar. Bacha was despised by the Pushtuns who were trying to dislodge him from the government. This provided an opportunity for the Musahiban brothers led by Nadir Khan.

On hearing the news of the fall of Amanullah and the occupation of Kabul by Bacha-i-Saqao, the Musahiban brothers, Nadir Khan, Hashim Khan, and Shah Wali Khan, who were in self-imposed exile in France, decided to come back to Afghanistan. Nadir Khan and his brothers arrived in Peshawar on February 25, 1929, for an onward march to the fort of Matun in Khost Province. Khost was governed by Nadir Khan's brother Shah Mohammad, who had remained in Afghanistan while Nadir Khan and his brothers exiled in France. In Khost, Col. Nur Mohammad, the commander of the Afghan army in Bacha's government, placed his army at the disposal of Nadir Khan. This support was supplemented by his brother Shah Mohammad, the governor of Khost. A big lashkar of the Mangal tribe was formed. Nadir Khan marched toward Kabul but had to stop due to the infighting among the tribes of his lashkar.

Nadir Khan tried again to build up a lashkar of the Mangal, Jaji, Ahmadzai, and Totakhel wazirs. This lashkar was supplemented with 1,000 Darwesh Khel Waziris from across the Durand Line. Bacha Saqao's army was defeated in different battles thereafter and finally Nadir Khan's lashkar reached Kabul on October 9, 1929. Bacha could not defend and fled to Kohistan. On October 16, 1929, Nadir Khan victoriously entered the city of Kabul where he was greeted by the people of Kabul who were fed up with Bacha's extortion practices. On October 17, 1929, at the age of forty-five, Nadir Khan was approved by the Afghan Jirga as the Amir of Afghanistan. Unlike his predecessors, he was a devout and conservative Muslim. Bacha Saqao surrendered on the promise of pardon. That promise, however, was broken and Bacha Saqao was executed. The ascension of Nadir Khan to the throne of Afghanistan brought back again the rule of the Durrani Mohammadzais, also called the Musahiban or Yahya Khel.

Nadir Khan, now Nadir Shah, clearly understood that Amanullah's downfall was a result of the Mullahs' radicalism. He was very careful about them.

110 Struggle for Independence of Afghanistan

As an act of reconciliation with the mullahs, Nadir Shah reversed Amanullah's policy of doffing off the burqa or the veil and now made the veil mandatory for Afghan women. Nadir Shah appointed one of the mullahs, Mohammad Siddiq, the Hazrat of Shore Bazaar, as ambassador to Egypt. Shir Agha of Jalalabad was granted a huge pension. All of his four brothers were given key positions in Nadir Khan's government.

Nadir Shah tried to strengthen his regular army to which Amanullah had paid the least attention. Nadir Shah got a gift of 10,000 rifles from British India that were given to the army. He raised the salary of the army and abolished any sort of deductions from their wages and raised the morale of the soldiers. He put his army under the command of his brother, Shah Mahmud.

Most of the Afghans who were pro-Amanullah did not consider Nadir Shah as the legitimate claimant to the throne. In 1930, the first revolt was from the Shinwaris, which was settled through bribery. The second revolt was from the Persian-speaking uncle of Tajik Bacha-i-Saqao from Kohistan. As the regular army was not well equipped to deal with such kind of unrest, a call was made to the tribal chiefs who crushed this anti-government movement. During the same year, the Red Army entered Afghanistan hunting for Ibrahim Beg who was working against Russia from the soil of Afghanistan. Both the Afghanistan and the British governments protested against the Russians' move and later the Russians went back.

On October 31, 1931, Nadir Shah promulgated a constitution with certain modifications and changes in the constitutional draft of Amanullah. The constitution provided for a cabinet, a senate, and a house of representatives. Nadir Shah reversed Amanullah's policy of abolition of the hereditary ranks and restored it in his own family. According to the constitution, the king was the head of the executive, the legislative, the judiciary, and was the commander-in-chief of the armed forces. The constitution created a despotic leader in the form of a king who could declare war, appoint the prime minister and the other key posts, and make laws not by the legislative process but simply by fiat. The country was divided into the five Wilayats (Provinces) and the four Hakumat-i-ala (minor Provinces) which were governed by the Wali and the Hakumat Naibs, respectively.

Afghanistan then was an agricultural and pastoral country without the infrastructure of communications. Trade was carried out on horses, camels, and donkeys' backs mostly by the Sikhs and the Hindu camel nomads or the Kuchis. There was no industry and the consumption goods for urban areas were imported from the neighboring countries. For economic policies, Nadir Shah had picked up Abdul Majid, a merchant from Herat, who was a successful businessman having earned his fortune through trade with Russia. Nadir Shah established the Bank-i-Milli (Shirjat-i-Ashami-i-Afghan) with a capital of 120 million Afghanis, a unit of currency that was changed from Kabuli Rupee to Afghani. For production purposes, the needed private capital was not available. To overcome this constraint, Nadir Shah granted monopoly rights to the Shirkat or holding

Struggle for Independence of Afghanistan **111**

companies whose majority of shares came from the royal family. There was no infrastructure of roads and trade was carried out on dirt roads, all potholed and crumbled. Nadir Shah started a road project from Kabul through the Hindu Kush to Mazar-i-Sharif and this project employed a large number of Afghans.

In the education area, Nadir Shah opened all schools that had been closed down by the illiterate bandit Bacha-i-Saqao. However, he reversed the policy of Amanullah by removing the foreign teachers from the schools and ordered that instructions should be carried out in the Pushtu and Persian languages. But this reversal did not work as there was no infrastructure of trained teachers, the teaching materials, and curriculum in these vernacular languages. Habibia and Ghazi schools were returned back to the English medium of instruction and employed teachers from British India. For Istiqlal School, the French teachers were hired, and for Nijat School, the German teachers were hired. Here, again two antagonistic nations, Britain and Germany, were influencing the Afghans and cropping up the loyalty for their interests through providing education and schooling in Afghanistan.

In spite of these reforms, the Afghans despised Amir Nadir Shah for being the puppet of the British as he did not support the Pushtuns across the Durand Line. Abdul Ghaffar Khan and his brother Dr. Khan Sahib requested Nadir Shah for assistance against the British. Nadir Shah gave a tepid response that it was their business to deal with the British. After breaking his exile in France, Nadir Shah had been supported by the British sleuth, Richard Maconachie, who was acting as the British minister in Afghanistan and had served in the Kurram Valley. The British gave him 10,000 rifles along with 180,000 pounds sterling. "Furthermore, because of the resumption of cordial relations with Britain, King Nadir Shah was accused by some of being puppet raised to the throne by the British to replace the too anti-British Amanullah", writes Dupree. The young Afghans did not like Nadir Shah's policies toward the British. A young Afghan, named Kemal Syed who was a graduate of Nijat College and had gone to Germany for higher education, one day entered the Afghan embassy in Germany and killed the Afghan ambassador, Mohammad Aziz Khan. Another student from Nijat College entered the British embassy in Kabul and tried to kill the British minister. Although he could not kill the British minister, he did kill one clerk and two servants. The student was executed and thirty-two of his friends were sent to prison. The Pul-e-Charkhi prison is a big prison in east of Kabul that holds upto 5,000 inmates.

The deadliest event occurred on November 8, 1933, when Nadir Shah entered a football ground to inaugurate a series of football matches among the schools. One of the participants, again from Nejat School, came forward and shot at Nadir Shah. Nadir Shah was hit at the mouth and shoulder and did not survive the attack. It is ironic that all the attacks against Nadir Shah and the British came from Nijat School, which was staffed by the Germans. In fact, Nadir Shah's murder plan was prepared at Nijat School. The seventeen-year-old assassin, Mohammad Khaliq, narrated his story that he had taken revenge for

112   Struggle for Independence of Afghanistan

the execution of Ghulam Nabi Charkhi by Nadir Shah. Ghulam Nabi Charkhi was the son of Ghulam Haider Charkhi who was the commander-in-chief of Abdur Rahman's army. Mohammad Khaliq was an adopted son of Ghulam Nabi Charkhi and Khaliq's real father was a servant of Ghulam Nabi Charkhi.

At the time of Nadir Shah's death, his elder brother Mohammad Hashim Khan was in Afghan Turkestan and the younger brother Shah Mahmud was in Kabul. Shah Mahmud immediately announced the eighteen-year-old Mohammad Zahir Shah, the son of Nadir Shah, as the new king of Afghanistan. Zahir Shah was born in Kabul on October 15, 1914, and had graduated from Habibia and Istiqlal colleges in Afghanistan. During the course of his father's self-imposed exile in France, he had attended many lycées. When Nadir Shah returned back to Afghanistan, Zahir Shah attended the military college in Kabul. At the age of 18, Zahir Shah was the minister of war and education. Enthroned at such a young age, Zahir Shah was supported by Mohammad Hashim Khan and Shah Mahmud. Hashim Khan was the prime minister with all the powers vested in him. Zahir Shah took a back seat.

Instead of despised Russia or the hostile British, Nadir Shah approached Germany for technical development assistance. From 1935 to the beginning of WWII, the German experts lived and worked in Afghanistan on the development projects in the areas of dam building, installation of a hydroelectric power plant at Chak-i-wardak. Lufthansa air flights were started between Berlin and Kabul and for the first time Kabul was accessible through the air. Similarly, Japan also established trade relations with Afghanistan. In 1934, Afghanistan joined the League of Nations sponsored by Turkey. In 1934, US President Franklin Delano Roosevelt recognized Russia. In 1936, the US established relations with Afghanistan through the British. Also, in 1936, according to Fletcher, "Afghanistan government demonstrated its confidence in American altruism by granting a 75 years' concession to the Inland Exploration Company of New York for the development of Afghanistan's presumed petroleum deposits". However, the company stopped petroleum mining operation in 1939 due to the threat of war. In 1937, Afghanistan signed a nonaggression treaty with Turkey and Iran.

In 1937, an Iraqi firebrand Syed Mohammad Saadi, known as Shami Pir, a relative of Queen Souriya, challenged the throne of Zahir Shah. Shami Pir made a call to the tribal chiefs to join him to overthrow the illegitimate king. The Waziri and Suleiman Khel tribes from the east of the Durand Line attacked the Matun Fort which made the British discomfited. The British sleuths gave Shami Pir 20,000 pounds and transportation to go back to Iraq.

During the course of WWII, Afghanistan announced its neutrality on August 17, 1940. The allied countries asked Afghanistan to expel the German Axis nationals from Afghanistan, which was against the Afghan tradition of hospitality. Many Afghan leaders expressed resistance to this demand, but Hashim Khan yielded to the pressure of the British sitting in the east of Afghanistan and, on approval by the Loya Jirga, asked the Axis nationals to leave the country. As a conclusion to WWII, the Axis powers were defeated,

Germany was dismembered, Russia survived, and the United States emerged as the world's leading nation. Now Afghanistan turned its attention toward the United States.

In 1946, Prime Minister Mohammad Hashim Khan retired due to health reasons and he was replaced by his younger brother, Shah Mahmud. At this time, the king, Zahir Shah, was thirty-two years old and started taking an active part in the state's affairs. Shah Mahmud sent his son, Zalmai Khan, to the United States for higher education. This was a reversal from the royal family's preference for France. Shah Mahmud was very tolerant and granted amnesty to all the political persons and even the killers of Nadir Shah and the attackers of the British embassy. Some were even assigned important positions in the government.

On the economic front, the development planning failed due to the lack of technical skills and poor implementation. The Shirkat program, which was initiated under the leadership of Abdul Majid Khan who had served as the minister of finance for a decade, was involved in the karakul business which was well in demand in the United States. Under this program, a credit of $20 million was built to support the development projects in irrigation and the reclamation of barren land in southern Afghanistan. The idea was that bringing additional land under irrigation would pay off the investment through the increased output, sales, government revenue, and taxation. Consequently, an Idaho-based US construction company, Morrison–Knudsen, Inc., with its headquarters at Boise, was invited to start work in Helmand Province. Soon the American engineers of the company arrived in Afghanistan and set up their camp offices at Kandahar and Girishk to implement the project.

The Helmand Valley project was started with a cost estimate of $17 million. Most of the expenses went into salaries, equipment, and supplies. Soon the entire budget was spent and the project was still incomplete. The Afghans were asked that in order to complete the project additional resources had to be obtained as a loan through the Export-Import Bank. In 1949, the Afghan government's request for the entire amount was not accepted but was granted $21 million as a tied conditional loan, which meant that this money could only be used for the Helmand project. In 1953, the Afghan government again approached the Export-Import Bank for a nonrestricted loan of $36 million, a part of which was intended to be used for road construction in Kabul. Again, a loan of $18.5 million was approved with the same conditions that this money could only be used for the Helmand project. Both of these loans with an amortization period of eighteen years carried an interest rate of 4.5%.

The project failed due to a variety of reasons. The Afghans blamed the American engineers for this failure and the American engineers blamed the Afghan government for poor planning. The American engineers of Morrison–Knudson claimed that as far as the project's execution was concerned, the Americans did a good job. The main reason for the project failure was that the land that was reclaimed was not productive due to the high salinity and alkalinity. However, Afghanistan did not fault itself on its international obligations.

114 Struggle for Independence of Afghanistan

In addition to the Helmand Valley project, the United States provided economic development assistance as a loan and not as a grant. The American aid was in the education sector. The US government provided male and female teachers who served Habibia School. The Americans' presence in Afghanistan was not liked by the Russians who protested and their protest was ignored. There appeared to be good relations developing between Afghanistan and the United States and these relations progressed to the level of the establishment of embassies and the US appointed Eli Palmer as its first ambassador to Afghanistan.

In September 1953, Shah Mahmud retired as the prime minister on the pretext of health reasons and he was replaced by his forty-three-year-old nephew, Sardar Mohammad Daud. Sardar Daud was supported by his cousin, King Zahir Shah, and his own brother, Mohammad Nahim, the foreign minister of Afghanistan. Sardar Daud was the elder son of Mohammad Aziz Khan, who was Afghanistan's ambassador in Germany. Aziz Khan was killed inside the embassy in Berlin in 1932 by an Afghan student who had attended Nijat School in Kabul. Daud graduated from Habibia College and Military School, Kabul. King Zahir Shah and Daud led a group of young Afghans. Daud was aggressively concerned about the Pushtuns to the east of the Durand Line in spite of the fact that those Pushtuns had already voted in a referendum to join Pakistan at the time of the independence of Pakistan and India from the British rule.

Afghanistan's policy during Daud's regime was to keep both the antagonistic powers of Russia and Britain at bay. Although both of these countries maintained their embassies in Kabul, the Afghan government never hired any expert from these countries with the exception of a few British. The Russian embassy was out of bounds for the Afghans and was under the Afghan police's radar. Moreover, the British had left the Indian subcontinent and there was no threat from the east by India and Pakistan. The only potential threat could be imagined from Russia, who were capable of intriguing with the tribal chiefs to overthrow the government. That's why the Russian embassy in Kabul was kept under surveillance by the Afghan government.

Similarly, the Afghans were not satisfied with the United States either. Morrison–Knudson's engineers and the US State Department's teachers who lived and worked in Afghanistan did not know much about Afghan etiquettes and traditions. The Americans committed some gaffes that were smirked at by the Afghans. The Afghans were disappointed by the failure of the Helmand Valley project. The Afghan government was more interested in procuring military equipment to modernize its army. The US refused to give military equipment to Afghanistan with an understanding that this could be used against Pakistan instead of Russia. As Afghanistan was out of the Central Treaty Organization, therefore, it could not have access to the military equipment enjoyed by Pakistan and Iran being its members. Afghanistan's army had never been a strong force as compared to an irregular army of the Afghan tribes. In 1949, Mohammad Amin, the half-brother of Amanullah, visited Waziristan, to the east of the Durand Line to hire recruits for an attack on Kabul. This attempt was foiled by the rumors spread by some tribes that this was not a faithful attack as Amins's wife was a British woman.

In 1956, Nikita Khrushchev arrived in Kabul and met King Zahir Shah and Prime Minister Mohammad Daud and "promised a $100 million credit, on the very soft terms of a 30 year repayment period and 2% interest", writes Ewans.[7] This assistance was not tied to any conditions. This unconditional assistance provided the Afghan government an opportunity to develop its first five-year plan. This money was allocated to all sectors of the economy with the major share going to agriculture, transportation and communications, industry, health, education, and mining. In addition, Nikita donated fifty buses for public transportation and an airplane. After the completion of the first five-year plan, Afghanistan prepared its second five-year plan which was also supported by Russia. The major projects funded by Russia concerned agriculture, hydroelectric power, petroleum exploration, and highways. The highway from Kushka on the Russian border through Herat to Kandahar was built with a $80-million grant from Russia. In addition, Russia constructed the roads and streets of Kabul and also assured Afghanistan of their assistance against Pakistan. This attempt was considered in Pakistan as the Russians' desire to reach the hot water. Russia also helped to modernize the Afghan army and provided necessary military equipment including jet fighters and bombers, which Afghanistan had failed to get from the US.

During this period, the US was also active in Afghanistan. The US assistance was provided in the fields of irrigation, transportation, and education with some of the resources going to the Helmand Valley project. First, the Afghan airline, Ariana, was started with the assistance of the US which operated the international flights. Kandahar airport was built by the US at a cost of $6.4 million. The US's major contribution was in the education sector where, by 1962, more than 1,000 Afghans were trained in different universities of the US. The education development projects were supported under contracts with Columbia and Wyoming Universities. These universities provided technical assistance in the form of the American faculties assigned to Kabul University, the Technical Institute, and the teacher training and the vocational schools.

As far as the constitution was concerned, Amanullah had prepared and promulgated a constitution which was later modified by Nadir Shah. Amanullah had abolished the hereditary ranks and Nadir Shah reestablished the hereditary line in his family. During this period, the Afghans felt that the power was always vested in the hands of the royal family. Amanullah doffed off the purdah (veil), which conservative Nadir Shah donned on again. Daud, later, through a decree, declared that the purdah was not required in Afghanistan.

The relationships between Afghanistan and Pakistan during the entire regime of Sardar Mohammad Daud were not cordial. As Daud was more concerned with the Pushtuns to the east of the Durand Line than with the development of Afghanistan, he kept the tensions on the border alive. During his period, the skirmishes on the border with Pakistan did occur and one was in Bajaur Agency. In Bajaur Agency, the Pakistan army captured about 300 Afghan army soldiers

116 Struggle for Independence of Afghanistan

inside Pakistan's territory. When Pakistan asked the reason for this attack, the Afghan government claimed that it did not order any attack and these soldiers went on their own will.

Pakistan used its air force and crushed the insurgents inside Afghanistan along the border. Pakistan closed its consulates in Jalalabad and Kandahar and asked Afghanistan to close its consulates in Peshawar and Quetta. The diplomatic relations were cut off and Pakistan blocked the trade route for Afghanistan from Karachi to Torkham. The border was closed and it badly hit the Afghan economy as it lost 45% of its revenue that was coming through the custom duties. This affected Afghanistan's trade with the rest of the world too. The Russians then offered that Afghanistan can use the Russian route for their trade.

However, the termination of the trade route also affected the development projects of Afghanistan which were being implemented by the United States. The United States refused to use the Russian route for the import of project supplies. With the depletion of the foreign exchange reserves, the lack of revenue resources, and the high inflation rate, the economy was in a bad shape. The bad economy led to the downfall of Daud, who was responsible for this situation due to his unwise policies toward Pakistan, which were let to continue for a long time. In 1963, Sardar Mohammad Daud resigned and his resignation was immediately accepted by the king who wanted his exit as a need of the hour. The king asked Daud that he should address in his farewell speech, on March 12, 1963, the issue of constitutional reforms apropos of the separation of powers among the different organs of the state, which he did.

King Zahir Shah set up a seven-member committee to review the separation of the powers among the state's organs and submit the draft constitution to the Loya Jirga for approval. The committee included a liberal politician Mohammad Siddique Farhang and this committee was assisted by a French constitutional expert. The committee took one year to craft a constitutional draft. The draft was reexamined by another thirty-two-member constitutional commission. The constitutional draft then was submitted to the Loya Jirga of 452 members. The Loya Jirga held detailed discussions to make sure that the constitution provided a strong watertight system to stymie the return of Daud. The Loya Jirga also had concerns about the royal family. They wanted to make sure that no member from the royal family will be the prime minister, minister, member of the parliament, or chief justice of the supreme court. Also, no member of the royal family will neither be a member of any political party nor will engage in political activities.

The new constitution provided for two legislative branches: Wolsi Jirga, a lower house of 216 members elected by a secret ballot; and an upper house of 84 members, the Meshrano Jirga, partly elected and partly nominated by the king. On September 9, 1964, the Loya Jirga approved the new constitution that separated the powers between the executive, the legislative, and the judiciary. The throne was kept hereditary in Zahir Shah's family with built-in rules for succession. The king signed the constitution that became effective on October 1, 1964. This act of separation of the powers made the king, Zahir Shah, the most

Struggle for Independence of Afghanistan **117**

popular among the Afghans. The Afghans respected Zahir Shah like the father of the nation, Ahmad Shah Durrani.

Consequent upon the resignation of Sardar Mohammad Daud, a window of opportunity was opened for improving the relations between Afghanistan and Pakistan. Afghanistan had become dependent on Russia for international trade and most Afghans feared that this dependence could hurt their freedom. The Afghans wanted to mitigate this overdependence on Russia. Afghanistan's foreign exchange was exhausted. With Daud gone, in July, the Shah of Iran offered his good offices to ease the situation for Afghanistan. He mediated to restore the diplomatic relations between the two countries and these relations were resumed late in 1963. The export–import route for Afghanistan was reopened. On March 20, 1963, the United States announced to build another alternative route by constructing a highway from Herat to Islam Qala on the Iranian border to reduce the burden on the Pakistan route.

Under the new constitution, King Zahir Shah formed a new interim cabinet which was led by a PhD in physics, Dr. Mohammad Yousaf. Dr. Yousaf belonged to an ordinary family, who was neither rich nor related to the royalty or any influential tribe. Most of the ministers were young master's degree holders coming from poor and ordinary background. In the whole cabinet there was only one minister who came from the royal family. Under the new arrangement, the country was divided into twenty-nine administrative units, each governed by a young master degree-holder Afghan governor without any family ties.

Under the new constitution, the elections were held in August and September, 1965. The rural and urban populace participated in the elections along with the religious groups led by the Mujadadi family. When Dr. Yousaf appeared before the shura to present an interim report of his government, the members of the shura criticized the interim government as well as the royal family. In the meantime, there was a demonstration of Kabul University students who marched toward the venue of shura. The students entered the chamber and occupied the seats and announced that they would not leave until their demands were met. Their demand was that the number of graduating students was increasing due to the improvements in Kabul University and other educational institutions through American aid. However, there were no jobs, and even if there were a few, they were low paid.

The demonstration spread throughout the streets of Kabul city. The army was called in and two students and one passerby were killed. Consequently, Dr. Yousaf resigned and he was replaced by a diplomat, Mohammad Hashim Maiwandwal, who had served as ambassador to the US and UK. Maiwandwal immediately rushed to the Kabul University and calmed down the students. Maiwandwal was a good administrator and dealt skillfully with the Loya Jirga and immediately got the budget approved by the Loya Jirga which had been delayed for months during Dr. Yousaf's period.

With the promulgation of the new constitution, an era of democracy began and many political parties started emerging. The first party that came into

118 Struggle for Independence of Afghanistan

existence was a communist party known as the People's Democratic Party of Afghanistan (PDPA). This was led by Nur Mohammad Taraki, Babrak Karmal, and Hafizullah Amin. All three of them came from different backgrounds. Taraki came from a poor family and after attending elementary school became a clerk in a trading company in Kandahar. Later his company sent him to Bombay, India, where he was mentored by the Communist Party of India. Taraki was a self-made person and started writing in magazines. He worked for the Radio and Press Information department. In 1953, he was sent to the US where he served as a press attaché in Washington. He used to do translation work for the Russian embassy in Afghanistan and the money he was paid for this he used for his party's participation in the 1965 elections. Taraki lost in the 1965 elections. He visited Russia on a travel invitation from Russia where he was treated like a head of the state.

On the other hand, Babrak Karmal came from the upper class. He was the son of a major general, who was also the governor of Paktya Province. Karmal received good education and was a graduate of Nijat College. It was he who had instigated the students of Kabul University for demonstration. At one time he was banned from the Kabul University. Later, he was admitted to the Faculty of Law and Political Science but was put in jail for three years. After his release, he completed his degree. It was during his three years of imprisonment that he became a communist. He was a good orator. As per rules, he completed military training and got a government job. He was elected to the shura through the 1965 elections. Babrak Karmal was a frequent visitor of the Russian embassy. He was again elected in the 1969 elections.

Much unlike Taraki and Babrak Karmal, Hafizullah Amin was a young American-educated Afghan, who received his master's and PhD education from American universities. He was the principal of Kabul Teacher Training College, which was technically and financially supported by the US. Amin joined the PDPA but continued his job with the ministry of education. He lost in his 1965 election to the shura. However, in the 1969 elections Amin was successful in getting elected to the shura.

Although the PDPA was not successful in reaching out to the masses for support, it did reach the Kabul University and other educational institutions where the communists could create unrest any time they wanted to. Under the new constitution, the parliament in 1966 passed a law for the publication of magazines and newspapers. Taraki started his party's magazine *Khalq* (the people); however, the material that was published in the magazine led to the immediate ban of the *Khalq*.

In 1966, Karmal and Taraki disassociated. Karmal started his own political party called Parcham (the banner) and Taraki formed the Khalq Party. This disassociation was evident because both of them came from different backgrounds. Taraki came from the lower classes and Karmal from the upper classes. Taraki wanted to stick to the cause of the lower-class struggle, while Karmal wanted to see the system as moving forward with loyalty to the king.

Karmal wanted to play his role in the parliament. Hafizullah Amin stayed with Taraki.

In addition to Parcham and Khalq, many other political parties also emerged. A pro-Chinese political party named Shula-i-Jawed (eternal flame) was formed by the Mahmudi family and Sitm-i-Milli (national oppression) was formed by a Tajik, Tahir Badakhshi, who was also a member of the PDPA. The right-wing party was a religious group headed by Mujadidi and was based at the Faculty of Law in Kabul University. Maiwandwal formed a socialist party called Progressive Democratic Party. Another party named Afghan Millat came into being and this party published a newspaper in its name. But none of these parties played any role in national affairs.

In 1967, because of health problems, Maiwandwal was replaced by a former diplomat Nur Ahmad Etmadi. Although Etmadi was able to get some bills passed by the Wolesi Jirga, most of the time he was obstructed by the latter. In the 1969 elections, the majority of the members were new belonging to the right wing, while only 60 members of the 1965 elections were able to get reelected in 1969. Maiwandwal and Farhang lost the election in 1969 while Babrak Karmal got reelected. Etmadi was reappointed as the prime minister and remained in office until 1971, when he was replaced by Dr. Abdul Zahir, the former speaker of the Wolesi Jirga. Zahir remained in office for a short period and was replaced in 1972 by another American-educated Musa Shafiq. Musa played a key role in the drafting and promulgation of the 1964 Constitution. He was very active and improved government performance by aggressively pursuing development projects and at the same time curbing corruption. He was also able to settle the Helmand Basin water issue with Iran.

Although King Zahir Shah promulgated the 1964 constitution, unfortunately, that constitution was never implemented. His failures in the implementation of the constitution were that: (1) he did not let pass the legislation for the establishment of the political parties, as he feared that the left wing communist parties may win the election and disturb the system of the government through extremism and factionalism; (2) he did not approve the legislation about the development of some sort of mechanism for mutual dependence of the executive and the legislative; (3) the judiciary was never reformed and functioned in the light of the constitution and the Supreme Court was never convened; and (4) although the press law was passed in 1965, censorship and closures were common. Although Musa Shafiq was making good progress and he had the full backing of the king, it was too late. Then all of a sudden on July 17, 1973, when the king had gone to Italy for his eye treatment, Musa was driven to dead end by the reemergence of Daud, who took the control of the government in a bloodless coup. Abdul Wali who was guarding the royal palace surrendered and was put under house arrest for two years. Thereafter he was allowed to join King Zahir Shah in Italy.

Daud retained complete control as he kept all the powers with him as the president, prime minister, and minister of defense. He established a central committee consisting of military officers. He was in touch with Babrak Karmal

120 Struggle for Independence of Afghanistan

and the Parchamis. A number of Parchamis were part of his coup. Karmal did not join the government and soon Daud started delegating his powers to the Parchamis. The Khalqs also favored Daud but did not take part in his coup. Both the Parchamis and the Kalqs were on Daud's side but Daud felt threatened by the religious groups who could revolt against him. As a precautionary measure, he arrested Mohammad Khan Niazi, a leader of Ikhwanul-Muslimeen (Muslim brotherhood) and about 200 of his associates and put them in jail. The rest of the religious groups fled to Pakistan where they were granted political asylum and lived in Peshawar. Two of the prominent religious leaders were Engineer Hekmatyar, a student of Kabul University, and Burhanuddin Rabbani, a teacher of Islamic law at Kabul University. Their followers in Afghanistan could not do anything with the exception of Ahmad Shah Masoud, who was able to capture a few government posts in Panjsher but later was overwhelmed by the government forces.

In 1974, both Hekmatyar and Rabbani disassociated and made their own factions. Hekmatyar established a party called Hezb-i-Islami (Islamic Party) and Rabbani established his Jamiat-i-Islami (Islamic society). To avoid foreign intervention, Daud banned contacts with the foreigners and imposed restrictions on the press. The opposition groups anonymously managed and distributed an evening newspaper called *Shab-Nama*. Daud established his own party known as Hezb-i-Inqalabi-i-Milli. In 1977, he convened a Loya Jirga and got a fresh constitution approved. The new constitution provided one-party form of government. The members of the parliament, Loya Jirga, were nominated by the president and then president was elected by the two-third majority of those nominated members. The nominees included military people, party members, and government officials. Although the constitution included social slogans like social reforms, land reforms, and nationalization, nothing really happened.

Economy was in poor shape in that it was not generating enough revenues. Consequently, the budget of the third five-year plan was cut by 40%. Daud tried to get some assistance from the oil-rich Shah of Iran whom Daud sensed as arrogant and humiliating. However, Shah approved $1.2 billion over a period of ten years. Some aid came from other oil-producing countries like Saudi Arabia, Iraq, and Kuwait. Agricultural production was also stagnant and not keeping pace with the population growth. However, unlike his previous term, the relations between Afghanistan and Pakistan improved during his second term.

Although the Russians were in touch with Daud before his coup through the Parchamis, the Parchsmis supported Daud that in return Daud will provide them assistance on their anti-Pakistan policies. Later, Daud removed some of the Parchamis from the key positions in the government and army and this offended Russia and the relations between Afghanistan and Russia started becoming cool. Now Daud looked toward Egypt and India for assistance in military training.

In 1977, when Daud visited Russia where he had a very tough discussion with Brezhnev, Brezhnev complained as to why he had removed the Parchamis from the civil government and the army services and as to why the military training was being shifted from Russia to other countries. Daud with a dour expression on his face said, it depended on his wishes, and he would do what he liked. He would not accept any dictation on this. He broke off the meeting abruptly and left the room. That was the tipping point in Daud's political career.

Notes

1 Fletcher, *A complete history of Afghanistan*, p. 187.
2 Ibid., p. 187.
3 Fletcher, *A complete history of Afghanistan*, p. 194.
4 Ibid., p. 197.
5 Ibid., pp. 197–198.
6 Ibid., p. 201.
7 Ewans, *Afghanistan: a new history*, p. 113.

Bibliography

Dupree, N.H., *An Historical Guide to Afghanistan*. Afghan Tourist Organization, Jagra Ltd., Tokyo, Japan, Publication Number 5, 1970.

Ewans, M., *Afghanistan: A New History*. Curzon Press, Richmond, UK, 2001.

Fletcher, A., *A Complete History of Afghanistan*. Cornell University Press, New York, USA, 1965.

Omrani, B., and M. Leeming, *Afghanistan: A Companion and Guide*. Odyssey Books and Guides, a division of Airphoto International Ltd., Sheung Wan, Hong Kong, 2007.

7
RISE AND FALL OF THE COMMUNIST REGIME IN AFGHANISTAN

During the period of 1955–1978, Russia had trained about a thousand armymen who were brainwashed about communism during the process of their training. To use these returned participants along with the Peoples Democratic Party of Afghanistan (PDPA) movement for subversive activities, a plan for the coup was hatched. The Russians provided the resources and Hafizullah Amin was chosen as the key strategist to recruit young Afghans in the PDPA army. Incidentally, on April 17, 1978, Mir Akbar Khyber, a Parchamist, was killed. The killers were unknown. Some blamed the Americans and the CIA. On Akbar's funeral there was a big anti-American demonstration that later spread to the streets of Kabul. Daud thought that such a big support for the Parchamis could overthrow his government. So, Daud ordered the arrest of all the key Parchami leaders and their followers on the early morning of April 26. Before the police came to arrest Hafizullah, he had got enough time to pass on instructions to his followers for staging a coup on the morning of April 27 to attack the royal palace and to take over the government. On April 27, 1978, there were tanks rolling in the streets of Kabul all destined to the royal palace.[1]

On hearing this news, Daud sent his chief of staff to the nearby army units at Kargha and Rishkore. The Kargha unit could not mobilize due to the absence of a commanding officer. Rishkore unit did mobilize but was dispersed by an air attack. Daud summoned the aircraft from Shindand airbase in Herat. The aircraft did arrive from Shindand but had run out of fuel by the time they reached Kabul. The rebel group led by Major Mohammad Aslam Watanjar reached Kabul airport and took its control from the coup leader, Col. Abdul Qadir Dagarwal. Dagarwal left by helicopter for Bagram airbase to command an air attack on the royal palace. Daud and his guards defended the royal palace through fierce fighting for the whole day and night. Finally, the presidential guards were captured and Daud along with his family was killed. The military coup by the communists

DOI: 10.4324/9781003198376-7

Rise and Fall of the Communist Regime in Afghanistan **123**

supported by Russia was successful while the PDPA's leadership was in jail. The power was handed over to a joint military and civil revolutionary council with Taraki as its head as the president and the prime minister.[2]

As soon as Nur Mohammad Taraki formed his government, it was immediately recognized by the Soviet Union and in the same breath announced that it was not involved in this coup. Taraki's cabinet included an equal number of the Parchamis and the Khalqs. However, the Khalqs had an edge over the Parchamis due to the administrative capabilities of Hafizullah Amin who was part of the Khalq camp. Babrak Karmal, Hafizullah Amin, and another army coup leader Mohammad Aslam Watanjar, served as the deputy prime ministers under Taraki. Soon differences emerged between Taraki and Babrak Karmal with regard to their policies. Taraki wanted to take radical revolutionary measures to transform the society into communism, while Babrak Karmal was in favor of gradual changes without disrupting the system. After Taraki's government was stabilized for some time, Taraki and Amin started thinking of getting rid of the Parchamis from the civil government and military services.

As a first step in this direction, Taraki gave the diplomatic assignments to Babrak Karmal and the other key Parchamis so that they could be made to leave the country. Babrak Karmal was made the ambassador to Czechoslovakia. After the departure of Babrak Karmal and his key associates, Taraki and Amin started removing the Parchamis from the civil government and the army and their positions were filled in by the Khalqs. Taraki also arrested Col. Abdul Qadir, who was in charge of the coup against Daud, along with other Parchami leaders on charges of planning a coup against the government. After in-country arrests of the Parchamis, the Taraki government sent notices to Babrak Karmal and his associates in the foreign missions to come back and face a trial. Babrak Karmal and his associates did not come back but instead got in touch with Russia.

The changes and the reforms that the Khalqs made through promulgation of the fiats were related to: land reforms by redistribution of excess land to landless people, the establishment of cooperatives, abolishing of haq-mehr and bride price, and setting a minimum age for marriage. The universal education for boys and girls was modeled on the curriculum of communism in Russian language as a medium of instruction. These reforms were criticized and objected to by the citizenry. To implement the land reforms, there was no land record available. Even the grantees of land were reluctant to accept, considering it as un-Islamic as it amounted to the extortion of one's right. The Khalqs wanted to abolish the feudal system based on the tribal chiefs, Khans, and Amirs in order to make the state the sole authority. As far as bride price was concerned, this was a part of the age-old traditions of the society to safeguard the interests of the bride. The implementation process of the reforms was very brutal that led to torturing, killing, and assassination. "The Russian were dismayed at the turn of events in Afghanistan. Fearing that communism would be seen to fail there, they tried to persuade the Afghan government to slow the pace of reform", write Omrani and Leeming.

124 Rise and Fall of the Communist Regime in Afghanistan

Another area where Taraki made a departure from traditions was that he "chose to replace the flag, with its green stripe representing Islam, with a solidly red flag which, apart from the symbols at its corner, was indistinguishable from the flags of other communist countries", writes Ewans. In December 1978, Taraki signed a treaty of friendship with Russia. Unlike Afghan's Islamic culture, he omitted the Quranic words which were supposed to be written on the top of all public documents or statements. These words in English translation were "In the name of Allah, the Beneficent, the Merciful". Both of these actions were disliked by the Afghans. Taraki had sown the seeds of hate in his own people, the crops of which he would have to harvest later on.

Taraki pursued the policy of tyranny to acquire and sustain control over his opponents. After oppressively dealing with the Parchamis, he turned to his other opponents. Anyone and everyone in the civil government, armed forces, the public including politicians and religious leaders who were opposed to Taraki's rule were tortured, killed, assassinated, or forced to flee the country. He constructed a notorious Pul-i-Charki jail devoid of facilities like sanitation, with narrow and dark space for the political prisoners. This jail was filled in by more than 12,000 of his opponents. Musa Shafiq, who was the prime minister during King Zahir Shah, was put in this jail. Moreover, no record or information about the prisoners was made available. The prisoners' relatives did not know about the whereabouts of their loved ones who went missing. Taraki, in 1978, arrested all the family members of Mujadidi, a respectable religious family group of Afghanistan. About 70 male members of Mjujadidi's family were killed. He captured all the religious prisoners who were arrested by Daud and killed them all in one night. His atrocities did not limit to the cities but were spread to the rural areas as well. In April 1979, he completely destroyed the Kerala village in Kunar Province and killed about a thousand residents. He did not want to hear any voice against him or his government.

After the expulsion of the Parchamis from the civil and military services, the gap thus created was filled in by 5,000 Russian advisors and a lot of military equipment was supplied by Russia. Russia wanted to make sure that this system does not break.

The policies of the Khalqs sowed the seeds of resistance in Afghan society. First of all, a guerrilla war started in Kunar Province. In 1979, the American ambassador, Adolph Dubs, was kidnapped and held as a hostage in Kabul Hotel. Instead of talking to the abductors, the Khalqs in connivance with the Russians attacked the hotel and killed the ambassador along with others. The American's plea of restraint was ignored and the Khalqs did not bother to consult the Americans before the attack. Consequently, the US stopped its aid to Afghanistan and this was followed by other donors as well.

The second big protest was started in March 1979 in Herat for inclusion of women in the education program and the whole garrison became part of the protestors. About 100 Russian men, women, and children were tortured and killed and their bodies pierced on spikes were paraded in the city streets. The Russians

Rise and Fall of the Communist Regime in Afghanistan   **125**

attacked Herat by ground and air forces. The city was reduced to rubble and 20,000 Heratis were killed. Such a situation of endless atrocities gave birth to a hero in the name of Ismail Khan, a former army officer. Ismail became the leader of all soldiers who defected to the protestors' side and, assisted by the Russians, started a guerrilla war against the government.

With these unrests, Taraki became weak and his weakness created an opportunity for Hafizullah Amin, who was an awesome planner and manager, to grab the power and become the prime minister. To overcome these unrests, Hafizullah Amin depended on the Russians. A big tranche of military equipment, including MI-24 helicopters, immediately arrived from Russia. Now the disturbances spread throughout the country including Jalalabad, Faizabad, and Bamian in Hazarajat. In June 1979, a major demonstration took place in Kabul which was dispersed by the army leaving many killed and wounded. The army units in Paktya and Kunar defected and joined the protesters and attacked the Chaga Serai center of Kunar Province.

A big traffic of Russian civilian and military advisors started arriving in Afghanistan on the pretext of helping the Afghan government ease the situation. In fact, their major task was to assess the situation for an invasion of Afghanistan. However, sleek Hafizullah Amin was not cooperating with the Russians by accepting their advice. Finally, in August 1979, the Russians sent their famous General Pavlovsky, who had invaded Czechoslovakia in 1968, to Afghanistan to use his expertise to bring the Russian boots to Afghanistan. General Pavlovsky was accompanied by a sixty-member military team. At the end of his junket, he recommended to the Russian government for removal of Amin and the invasion of Afghanistan. The Russian government decided to talk to Taraki who had gone to Cuba and was supposed to stop over in Moscow for three days. The Russians supported the former Afghan ambassador in Czechoslovakia, who had taken refuge in Russia, to team up with Taraki to depose Hafizullah Amin. Shah Wali, the foreign minister of Afghanistan, who was accompanying Taraki, had attended this meeting. Shah Wali was pro-Amin, he immediately alerted Amin about this plan. Amin immediately fired the four pro-Taraki ministers from his cabinet.

After his arrival back in Afghanistan, Taraki, on September 14, 1979, summoned Hafizullah Amin for discussion. Amin checked with the Russian ambassador if there was any danger in going to the palace. The Russian ambassador gave a go-ahead signal, saying there was no such danger. When Amin was entering the palace, he was ambushed by the palace guard who was killed but Amin survived. Amin immediately ordered his forces for an attack on the palace. Taraki was captured and killed but his death was kept secret. Immediately, an announcement was made on Radio Kabul that Taraki had resigned due to health reasons and that Hafizullah Amin had taken over as the president of Afghanistan on September 17, 1979.[3] On October 10, 1979, an announcement was made that Taraki had died because of illness. Amin declared the Russian ambassador as persona non grata and was made to leave the country. Nevertheless, the Russians did not budge and continued their efforts to get rid of Amin.

Now the Russian-supported protests were intensified in Kabul against the Khalqs. But these protests were not successful in removing Amin. The Russians were disappointed and thought that the final solution should be an invasion of Afghanistan. In December 1979, Amin moved to Darul-Amaan palace which was built by Amanullah and took his residence over here. The Russians started working on a plan to remove Amin using Babrak Karmal. In December 1979, a final decision was made to bring the Russian boots to Afghanistan. At this point in time, the Russians had sufficient army within Afghanistan to post at the key places. One battalion was posted at Kabul airport and three at Bagram airbase which could reach Kabul immediately. On December 24, units of the 105th Guards Airborne Division started landing at Kabul airport and round-the-clock shuttles of AN-22 and AN-24 transport aircraft started bringing advance army units into Afghanistan. With this, the Russians had enough security forces inside the country to provide protection and ensure safety for the invading army that was about to cross the Oxus River.

On December 27, before attacking Darul-Amaan, the Russian advisors disarmed all the soldiers and the officers of the Afghan army and they were locked up in their units. On the 27th night, the Russians attacked Darul Amaan and killed Amin. On December 28, 1979, the Russian forces crossed the Amu River and spread across the country by taking different routes. One route was to reach Kabul and Bagram base via Salang Pass that was built by the Russians and the second route was toward Herat in the west and from there onward through Farah to Kandahar in the south. About 50,000 troops and 1,000 vehicles took control of all the major cities within a week. Later the troop level increased to 85,000.

While the Russians were in Afghanistan, they did not tell the world how did they come over here in Afghanistan and on whose invitation. They invaded Afghanistan just like France had attacked and captured Tunisia in 1881,[4] Great Britain attacked Egypt in 1882,[5] and the Italians attacked Libya in 1911,[6] which finally resulted in the defeat of the Ottoman Empire. Now the Russians started finding reasons to justify their invasion. Amin did not invite them and Babrak Karmal was not in the country. Who else could be? The Russians made an announcement from Termez across the Amu River (in modern-day Uzbekistan) that Babrak Karmal had taken over and Amin had been deposed. Babrak Karmal was flown in from Russia after the invasion and was installed as the puppet ruler of Afghanistan. The Russians fabricated a story that they had been invited by Babrak Karmal who was not even in the country at the time of invasion. Now the Russians were in a hot soup. They had come on their own but how they would get out of there was a million-dollar question for them.

Another reason that Russia tried to craft was that they alleged Amin as an American agent and thus through him America was interfering in Afghanistan's affairs and that the Russians had come in response to that interference. The Afghans with families started leaving the country to take refuge in Pakistan and Iran. The local groups stayed in the country to resist the Russians. These small groups resisted the Russians in Kunar, Nuristan, Badakhshan, Hazara, and other

Rise and Fall of the Communist Regime in Afghanistan **127**

parts of the country. Those refugees who came to Pakistan started organizing themselves and set up their training camps in frontiers of Pakistan to prepare a Mujahidin force to go back to Afghanistan to fight Russia. Initially, they got some arms from China.

The US condemned the Russian invasion and pledged that it would not allow Russia to implement its nefarious plans. It canceled its export of 17 million tons of grains to Russia and imposed restrictions on the technology transfer to Russia. These measures were outplayed by the other countries who immediately jumped to capture these economic opportunities that were created by the American actions. Argentina offered its grains at a low price and the European filled the technology transfer gap. America, Germany, and Japan boycotted the 1980 Moscow Olympics. America threatened Russia that if it entered the Persian Gulf oil fields, then it will face America in action. Pakistan on the next door was concerned about Russia's movement toward the warm water. Pakistan welcomed the refugees and alerted the world against the menace of Russia. The Russians on the other hand thought that if they were able to stabilize communism in an Islamic country, that would be their great success for years to come.

The United Nations condemned the Russian invasion through a resolution passed on January 14, 1980. Russia found a little satisfaction from the abstention of India from this resolution as a homage to Russia for assisting India in the bifurcation of Pakistan that led to the creation of Bangladesh. Pakistan convened a meeting of the foreign ministers of the Organization of the Islamic Countries (OIC) in Islamabad that condemned the Russian invasion of a Muslim country.

Russia remained undeterred and did not bother about world opinion. The Europeans were least concerned and declared that America should not destabilize world peace for the sake of an insignificant country like Afghanistan. Russia's main concern was the stability of Babrak Karmal's regime. Karmal's government included a majority of the Parchamis with only three members of the Khalqs who too were opposed to Amin. Karmal revealed his plans for a new constitution based on the multi-party system, the review of the land reforms, the grant of amnesty to the returning refugees, and the release of the prisoners, the majority of whom were the Parchamis. However, the arrests and the executions were part of his activities. Still 15,000 prisoners were behind the bar. On January 11, many Afghan families visited Pul-i-charki jail to receive their relatives, when they were astonished to know that their loved ones were not there. The mob attacked the jail and only 120 prisoners were found. The Afghan families lost their hope of finding their relatives alive.

Karmal tried to buy off the religious leaders by allowing the freedom of religion, the establishment of the Islamic centers, and the restoration of the original red, black, and green flag of Afghanistan. He formed a National Patriotic Front, later named as National Fatherland Front. Although Karmal announced these measures, actually these measures were designed by the Russians who had control on all the matters as they were controlling all the ministries and KHAD (Afghan intelligence agency) which replaced Amin's KAM (intelligence agency).

128 Rise and Fall of the Communist Regime in Afghanistan

As the Khalqs did not like Karmal's restoration of the old flag, the divergence between the Parchamis and the Khalqs became wider and wider in the military and civil departments and the ministries. This resulted in the weakness of the government. The Russians were calling shots in all the departments and the Afghans were dependent on the Russians, even for food.

Now, the Afghan refugees who were living in Peshawar, Pakistan, started organizing themselves into a united force of Mujahidin to fight the infidel occupant of their country. There were many Mujahidin groups who wanted to fight the Russians independently. Here both the American CIA and the Pakistani ISI coalesced to organize and streamline the needed support to them. The ISI reduced the number of the groups to seven, all the Sunnis, in order to better train and support them. Of these seven groups, four were Islamists who believed in the Islamic rule of law and considered the monarchy as un-Islamic, and the other three were traditionalists, who were in favor of restoring the monarchy of King Zahir Shah. Pakistan asked all the independent fighting groups to merge into the main seven groups in order for them to qualify for food aid, medical aid, and weapons.

The first major group was the Hezb-e-Islami led by Engineer Hekmatyar Khan. Hekmatyar, a Pushtun from the north, was the guerrilla force commander of the highest order. His group was well organized and disciplined. He was intolerant to any kind of compromise on his faith. His mission was to bring Islamic rule to Afghanistan by expelling the infidels from his country and was against the monarchy. Because of his management and organizational capabilities and commitment to his cause, he was very famous and much favored by the ISI and the CIA. His group comprised the fiercest guerrilla fighters. Hekmatyar maintained the training camps at Nangarhar in the east and at Baghlan and Kunduz in the north. The second group was also a Hezb-e-Islami that split from Hekmatyar's main Hezb-e-Islami, under Mullah Yunus Khalis. This group was not a guerrilla fighter like Hekmatyar. Mullah Yunus Khalis had support from the Pushtun maulvis. His main commanders were Abdul Haq from Jalalabad and Maulvi Jalaluddin from Paktya.

The third group was the Jamiat-e-Islami led by Rabbani who was supported by the Tajiks and non-Pushtuns. His commander was a Panjsheri Ahmad Shah Masoud who was also a guerrilla commander of the order of Hekmatyar. His operations were in the north at Panjsher valley and the Salang pass, which was the main supply route of the Russians' 40th Red Army. This group did not receive much assistance from ISI and CIA, but was the biggest sole recipient of the British assistance and the equipment supplied through its MI6. The MI6 agents made Panjsher their second home and provided the international coverage of Masoud's fight against the Russians. The MI6 undercover agents acted as the journalists. The MI6 agents also provided the night vision goggles to Masoud to facilitate the night attack on the Russians. After the Russians left Afghanistan, Ahmad Shah Masoud became a victim of the conspiracy under which the two international journalists sought an audience with him which he

Rise and Fall of the Communist Regime in Afghanistan **129**

granted. At the start of the interview, the interviewers' cameras exploded and Ahmad Shah was killed instantly. His body was taken to Tajikistan and was soon returned to Panjsher as it was decaying rapidly. Ahmad Shah Masoud has been buried in Panjsher on the top of a hill where a tomb has been built by the Karzai's government. During my stay in Afghanistan I have visited the tomb of Ahmad Shah Masoud in Panjsher.

The fourth group, called Ithihad-i-Islami Bara-i-Azadi-i-Afghanistan (Islamic Union for freedom of Afghanistan), was led by Abdul Rasul-Sayyaf. Sayyaf was supported by Saudi Arabia and he recruited the Arab volunteers for Jihad. This group was not much effective for guerrilla war.

The fifth group was Harkat-i-Islami (Islamic Movement) led by the Pushtun Maulvi Nabi Mohammad. He was active in Logar and the Helmand valley. This group was also ineffective militarily. The sixth group was a religious group known as the National Islamic Front led by Syed Ahmad Gillani of Kandahar who was pro king Zahir Shah. This group did not get much attention from the ISI and the CIA. The seventh and final group was Jabha-i-Nejat-i-Milli (National Liberation Front), which was led by Sebghatullah Mujadadi whose entire family was killed by Daud's regime and he was the only one who was lucky to save his life. He fled to Denmark and then came to Peshawar, Pakistan during the Russian invasion. His group was also ineffective in the guerrilla war.

In addition to the above mentioned seven groups that were supported by the ISI and the CIA, there was another group of the Shia of Hazarajat and another Shia faction known as Sazmani-i-Nasr-i-Afghanistan were merged into a single group known as Hezb-e-Wahdat (Unity Party). Hezb-e-Wahdat was supported by Iran.

The Mujahidin were completely independent people who hate to be controlled and kowtowed. In order to make a concerted effort to fight the Russians, an attempt was made by calling a Jirga in Peshawar to organize all of the Mujahidin groups into one entity under the leadership of the former King Zahir Shah. This move was resisted by Hekmatyar and the other groups. Thus, Jirga failed to produce a unified group of the Mujahidin. Every group wanted to fight the infidel on its own. However, two major groups who made an impact on guerrilla war were led by the behemoth guerrilla commander Engineer Hekmatyar Gulbedin who was fighting on the east, the south and the north and a successful guerrilla warrior Ahmad Shah Masoud fighting in the north. Other Mujahidin groups' role was minimal.

The whole world condemned the Russian's invasion of Afghanistan and stood behind the Afghan people. First of all, Pakistan welcomed the Afghan refugees who fled to Pakistan to take refuge. More than 3.5 million Afghan refugees entered Pakistan while 1.5 million found their refuge in Iran. The world at large offered all kinds of assistance to the Afghan people. The United States and Saudi Arabia were the major donors in addition to China, the UK, the Gulf States and the European countries. Whatever the US contributed that was matched by Saudi Arabia.

130 Rise and Fall of the Communist Regime in Afghanistan

The US Senator, Charlie Wilson[7] was the key actor in the resource generation for the Afghan war through the Senate's appropriation committee. Sometimes he consulted and coordinated with the CIA while most of the time he acted independently. Charlie consulted the CIA and the ISI for the type of equipment needed by the Mujahidin and traveled to the different countries such as Egypt and Israel to identify the appropriate weapons. The main reason for finding non-US weapons was that the US did not want to use US made weapons in the war. The 40th Red Army used the Hind Helicopter, MiG fighters, T-72 tanks, and other war equipment. The Mujahidin needed those types of weapons that could bring down the Hind Helicopter and destroy their tanks, etc.

Charlie got the information about the prices of the weapons available in any country. According to his information, AK-47 was being sold at $299 in the world black market, while the same was being sold in Egypt at $139 and in China at $100. A piece of mine was sold in the black market at $500 while its cost in Egypt and China was $275 and $75 respectively. The CIA also purchased 2500 mules from Egypt at a cost of $1300 per mule and these mules were brought to Afghanistan via Pakistan. These mules were used to carry the weapons to the fighting points of the Mujahidin. While Charlie arranged the resources, the CIA provided all the types of weapons to the seven groups of the Mujahidin through the Pakistan's ISI. The British MI6 provided the weapons and the resources to the northern guerrilla commander Ahmad Shah Masoud.

Most of the weapons were Russian made that were procured from Egypt and Israel. Israel had captured these weapons from the Palestine Liberation Organization (PLO). Pakistan had established the training camps in Pakistan's Northwest Frontier now Khyber Pukhtunkhwa where the Mujahidin were trained by the ISI for the use of the weapons and the other tactics. Among the crucial weapon was a seven feet green tube Stinger which cost between $60 and $70,000 and killed the Russian Hind helicopter that cast more than $20 million and this made the Russian worrisome.

All the big cities that were under the Russians' control were being attacked by the Mujahidin. The Russian army was ambushed on the Salang pass road in the north and at Serobi on the Kabul-Jalalabad road in the east. The Afghan soldiers deserted their army and started joining the Mujahidin and the national army was reduced from 90,000 to 30,000, a level to be totally ineffective. The civil government's employees also started joining the Mujahidin. In Kabul city at the time of sunset, the Afghans used to climb on the roof of their houses and started saying Adhan, a call for prayers and distributed the evening newspaper. The Russians destroyed the villages, the crops, the livestock, the irrigation systems, poisoned wells, threw mines and toy bombs and these were the cut-throat activities they could do. The Russians realized that Babrak Karmal had become ineffective and they called him to Moscow for discussion.

The Russian decided to replace the current puppet with a new puppet Dr. Najibullah, who was the founder member of the PDPA. In November 1987, Karmal left as president and took refuge in Moscow and his relative Mohammad

Rise and Fall of the Communist Regime in Afghanistan **131**

Chamkani became the president. Najibullah who had already taken over as General Secretary of the PDPA and the head of the KHAD. Najibullah developed the KHAD on the lines of KGB and was in complete control of the country's affairs. Finally, Najibullah was elected for the position of president by the Loya Jirga in November 1987. The elections were held in April 1988, with Najibullah emerging as the powerful president.

In February 1988, Gorbachev announced the withdrawal of the Russian troops over a period of ten months starting on May 15, 1988, when the first group of 12,000 men left Jalalabad for home. The situation was very tense as the Russians had failed to negotiate an agreement for their safe exit as well as the formation of a coalition government in Afghanistan. Some of the resistance groups wanted to cut them all during their retreat while the others were of the opinion of letting them go. Finally, the Mujahidin let the Russians cross the Amu River into the Russian territory. But still the Russians brought additional weapons like MiG-27 aircraft and surface-to-service SCUD-B missiles with a range of up to 175 miles to escort the safe exit of the Red Army. The Red Army's retreat continued until the last contingent crossed Amu River with their commander General Gromov in February 1989. The Russians left behind a fragile government of Najibullah's regime at the mercy of the Mujahidin.

About 300,000 Mujahidin led by 300 commanders fought the Russians and 15,000 Russian soldiers were killed and 37,000 wounded and handicapped over a period of nine years of the Russians' occupation of Afghanistan. One million Afghan civilians were killed. The cost of war to Russia was about 90 billion dollars over the nine years of occupation. The Russian soldiers that were captured by the Mujahidin told horrible stories of their treatment in Mujahidin's captivity and that was a message that was sent to the Russian people just like the message Dr. Brydon took back to Britain in 1842. Stingers that were provided to the Mujahidin during the war stayed with them even after the withdrawal of the Russians. Those missiles were used in the subsequent civil war among the resistant groups.

Now the question was how long Najibullah could resist the Mujahidin without the support of the Russian army. The answer to this question lied in to what extent the Mujahidin were united. If they were united, then it was only a matter of days for Najibullah to remain in power. To support Najibullah, a lot of military equipment worth $3–4 billion per annum was provided by Russia. Najibullah's 55,000-men army supported by the 10,000 presidential guards and other paramilitary forces was well equipped with the Russian arms, including the SCUD-B missiles with a range of up to 175 miles, to tackle the Mujahidin. In spite of this, the Parchams and the Khalqs stayed divided and Najibullah faced opposition in the Parcham party. To strengthen himself, Najibullah declared an emergency in the country by suspending civil rights. He strengthened his Parcham-dominated cabinet and showed exit to the non-Parcham cabinet members. To bring peace he declared that the Jihad was over and it was time to build the country.

132 Rise and Fall of the Communist Regime in Afghanistan

On the other hand, an Islamic shura was convened in Peshawar which elected Mujadadi as the president of the Afghan Interim Government (AIG) and a cabinet was formed under the leadership of Professor Sayyaf as the prime minister. The recognition of this interim government by the US and Pakistan was subject to the condition of holding control of sufficient territory of Afghanistan. In this pursuit, the Mujahidin chose Jalalabad for an attack with the hope that after its capture it will become a seat of the new Afghan government. Najibullah used SCUD-B missiles to disperse the Mujahidin and this resulted in the killing of one thousand Mujahidin and wounding many times that number. The US decided to reequip the Mujahidin with arms to make another attempt at Jalalabad, which again failed. In July, Hekmatyar's group killed thirty men of Jamiat-e-Islami in a war over Panjsher. Masoud retaliated and captured and killed Hekmatyar's men who were responsible for the killing of the Jamiat-e-Islami men.

Now the Mujahidin, divided as independent groups, continued their activities against the government. The famous warlords including Uzbeck Abdur Rashid Dostam, Engineer Hekmatyar of Hezb-e-Islami, and Tajik Masoud from Panjsher in the north engaged the government in their respective areas of influence. They captured the villages and the towns in their areas and put pressure on Kabul. Masoud got control of the Salang Pass which was the main route for the supply of Russian's equipment and established his headquarters at Taloqan in Takhar Province.

On the other hand, Najibullah was becoming weaker by the day as the differences between the rival Parcham and Khalq incumbents in the government and army started emerging. Najibulla smelled conspiracy and arrested the army officers for alleged planning of a coup against his government. The trial of the army officers produced evidence that implicated the sitting defense minister, General Shah Nawaz Tanai. On hearing of his implication in the coup, the General attempted a coup the next morning that was foiled by Najibullah and the General fled to Pakistan. In Pakistan he met Engineer Hekmatyar to make concerted efforts against Najibullah. This was a strange alliance of a communist and an Islamist as according to an old adage where an enemy of an enemy becomes a friend. In April 1990, 3,000 Mujahidin who were going to surrender all of a sudden attacked the officials and killed the governor of Herat. Najibullah was lucky, he was not there.

Najibullah renamed the PDPA as the Hezb-e-Watan (Homeland Party) and avoided being looked upon as a die-hard communist and started paying lip service to Islam and liberalism and tried to buy the allegiance of the local leaders. By the end of the year, Engineer Hekmatyar attempted another attack on Kabul with the help of his Lashkar-i-Isar but that too was not successful. With the cooling down of the Cold War, the US left Afghanistan to pay attention to the invasion of Kuwait by Iraq. Russia was reevaluating its loss through the breakup of the Central Asian states. Both the US and the Russian governments lost their interests in Afghanistan. Here the Mujahidin again split into two groups: Hekmatyar and the other Islamist parties sided with Iraq, while the other traditional Afghan

Rise and Fall of the Communist Regime in Afghanistan **133**

freedom fighters sided with the Saudis. In Afghanistan all the warlords were engaged in discussion to find a solution, but they just agreed to disagree as each one of them wanted to be preeminent. Najibullah also traveled to Geneva to meet the king, Zahir Shah, and the Mujahidin to see if some workable solution was possible. Shah, however, had prepared his own plan.

Side by side these discussions, the United Nations based on the recommendations of the General Assembly was trying to bring peace to Afghanistan through its undersecretary, Benon Sevan. Benon's plan included independence and self-determination, ceasefire and stoppage of arm supplies, and creating an environment for a free and fair election for a broad-based Afghan government. This plan was evidently accepted by all the stakeholders, internal and external, who were interested in the restoration of peace in Afghanistan, with the exception of AIG which just agreed to disagree. Engineer Hekmatyar and Sayyaf did not accept it either.

Discussions were held first in Islamabad and then in Tehran among Pakistan, Iran, and the Mujahidin to reach a consensus. In the meantime, the Mujahidin captured Khost and instead of setting its base for the government, they just looted it. Then the Mujahidin tried to capture Gardez but were unsuccessful. In the meantime, Russia agreed on a cut-off date as January 1, 1992, for the supply of arms. The United States and Russia agreed to stop aid to Afghanistan. Russia dropped its demand for Najibullah to be a part of the new setup. However, aid from Saudi Arabia continued.

Concomitantly, Dostam, an Uzbek warlord, and Masoud, a Tajik warlord, teamed up in the north and took over Mazar-i-Sharif by ignoring the UN peace plan for transitional arrangements in Afghanistan. Najibullah felt no hope for survival and agreed to step down on March 18, 1992, with the request that he should be allowed for a safe exit. Najibullah took shelter in the UN compound and General Yaqubi of KHAD (Government Intelligence Agency) committed suicide. Najibullah tried to flee Kabul on April 15, but his attempt was foiled by the Mujahidin who blocked the road to the airport to stop his exit. That was the end of the communists' regime.

Now, without Najibullah, under the transition arrangements, a fifteen-member council of top Afghan leaders was formed to work until the interim government was in place. The forces from the north and the south started moving toward Kabul for the possession. Masoud and Dostam marched from the north toward Kabul and Hekmatyar started his journey from the south toward Kabul. The battle for the control of Kabul started on April 15, on the outskirts of Kabul between the Masoud and the Hekmatyar forces. Hekmatyar was well equipped but Masoud was also a good strategist. Hekmatyar's forces fought from the building of the Ministry of Interior and later decided to move to the south of the city, while Masoud kept the possession of Kabul.

In the midst of these confrontations, a thirty-member Islamic Jihad Council (IJC) headed by Mujadadi arrived in Kabul on April 28, 1992, and announced the formation of the Islamic Republic of Afghanistan (IRA) government with

Masoud as the defense minister, Gillani as the foreign minister, Sayyaf as the interior minister, and Hekmatyar was asked to become the prime minister, who declined to work with Masoud.

Notes

1 Ewans, *Afghanistan: A New History*, p. 136.
2 Ibid., p. 137.
3 Ibid., p. 145.
4 Anderson, *Lawrence in Arabia*, p. 34.
5 Ibid., p. 35.
6 Ibid., p. 40.
7 Crile, *Charlie Wilson's War*.

Bibliography

Anderson, L., *Arabia*. Doubleday, a Division of Random House, New York, 2013.
Ewans, M., *Afghanistan: A New History*. Curzon Press, Richmond, 2001.
Omrani, B., and M. Leeming, *Afghanistan: A Companion and Guide*. Odyssey Books and Guides, a division of Airphoto International Ltd., Sheung Wan, Hong Kong, 2007.

8

RISE AND FALL OF TALIBAN

The Islamic Republic of Afghanistan (IRA) government headed by Mujadadi had failed in uniting the Mujahidin during the first three years of its rule. Hekmatyar was not on the same page with the IRA as he wanted to be the prominent one in the new setup. Hekmatyar and the other Pushtuns were against Rabbani and Masoud (both Tajik) and Dostam (Uzbek) and their government. At the same time, there was a rift in the Jamiat-i-Islami where both Rabbani and the Badakhshi groups opposed Masoud. Hekmatyar was supported by Pakistan, Sayyaf by Saudi Arabia, and Hezb-e-Wahdat, a Shiite group under Abdul Karim Khalili by Iran.

Finally, the Mujahidin, when they took over, agreed on the formation of the 51-member Islamic Jihad Council (IJC) with Sebghatullah Mujadidi as its president. The IJC included thirty commanders, ten mullahs, and ten intellectuals for a period of two months. According to the plan, after two months, the IJC would be replaced by an interim government for a period of four months, after which the elections would be held for a permanent government. But all of a sudden, Mujadadi announced that he would remain the president for two years and this destroyed the whole already fragile arrangement and provided an opportunity for the Mujahidin leaders to gear up for action.

Immediately, Hekmatyar demanded that Dostum should withdraw from Kabul. When Dostum did not do this, Hekmatyar bombarded Kabul resulting in heavy casualties. As a result of the discussions between Masoud and Hekmatyar, both of them agreed to bring peace to Kabul. As a part of the deal, Dostum would leave Kabul, and Hekmatyar would join the government to form a council under the leadership of Rabbani to hold the elections within six months. This plan too was not implemented as Dostum refused to leave Kabul and Hekmatyar refused to join the government. At the same time, the two Islamic factions, Hezb-e-Wahdat and Sayyaf's Itihadi-Islami, started fighting resulting in many

DOI: 10.4324/9781003198376-8

136 Rise and fall of Taliban

casualties. Consequently, Mujadadi who had dreamed of being the president for two years had to step down for Rabbani to become the president.

As a part of a deal, Hekmatyar nominated Abdul Sabour Fareed for the slot of Prime Minister. A few weeks later, Rabbani fired Abdul Sabour Fareed and Hekmatyar started shelling Kabul again and killed 1,800 civilians. Rabbani expelled Hekmatyar from the Council. Rabbani got reelected from the Council of Resolution and Settlement for a period of two years and Hekmatyar and Hezb-e-Wahdat boycotted this election. Hekmatyar blocked the supplies to Kabul coming from Pakistan and this made the winter time of Kabul's populace a miserable one.

In Islamabad, a new peace plan was brokered by Pakistan, Saudi Arabia, and Iran under which Hekmatyar would work as the prime minister and all the Mujahidin groups would work together as one force to create an environment of stability required for holding the elections. This plan was rejected by Masoud and Dostum as they had boycotted this meeting. When Hekmatyar was heading toward Kabul, his entry into Kabul city was not allowed by Masoud's forces. Now, in early 1994, Hekmatyar and Dostum, who were controlling Mazar-i-Sharif and Kunduz, joined together to enter Kabul. Masoud's forces repulsed both of them and even took Kunduz back from Dostum. Dostum retreated back to the north. Hekmatyar got into partnership with Hezb-e-Wahdat and continued fighting for the possession of Kabul. Things were not settling and the UN now appointed another representative, Mahmoud Mestiri, to work for bringing a peaceful settlement in Afghanistan. That was not an easy job for Mestiri and after some time in 1995 he had to resign as his plan was rejected by a new force called the Taliban.

"Talib" means the seeker of knowledge and all the Taliban were refugees in Pakistan, where they got religious education in the different Islamic madrassas (schools) in the Balochistan and Khyber Pukhtunkhwa provinces. How and where the Taliban were originated, there is a story behind this movement. A guerilla leader in Kandahar raped and killed three women. The local people approached a maulvi named Mohammad Omar in the area and strongly protested this heinous crime by a guerilla leader and asked him if something could be done to redress it. If this was not prevented, then the respect and honor of the Pushtun women would be at stake and then anything could happen. This was a question of life and death for the Pushtun tribes. Mullah Omar asked a few religious students (Taliban) to hunt and execute the guerilla leader. They did it.

Now Mullah Omar convened a meeting of the elders and decided that they should prepare themselves and dispense justice to the people who suffered for any injustices or cruel acts done by anybody, no matter how big or small the culprit was. Then the Taliban took control of the Quetta–Kandahar road and removed all the blockades that were established by criminals and guerilla leaders for the purposes of ransom and loot. The Taliban made the criminals flee from the road and the traffic was peacefully restored without any fear and danger. The Taliban captured Spin Baldak with a big supply of arms.

Soon Kandahar was captured by the Taliban. The crime rate in Kandahar was brought down to almost zero. The Islamic sharia was imposed and the Department of Promotion of the Virtue and Prevention of the Vice was established. Criminals' hands were amputated and women were barred from outside work. Burqa (veil) for the women was declared compulsory. The girls stopped going to school. Later, Mullah Omar allowed the women to work in special circumstances under the control of the women, separate from the men. Music and television were not allowed. The shops remained open and unattended at the time of the prayer. The people of the area were happy and they started joining the Taliban. The Taliban movement started against the people who betrayed their country. This movement started in the 1980s from the south in Kandahar and spread all over the country. The Taliban had also participated in the jihad along with Hezb-e-Islami (khalis) and Mohammadi's Harakat-e-Inqilabi; they acted independently too.

A shura under the leadership of Mullah Omar was established that laid the foundation for the Islamic government. After conquering Shindand, Herat, and Girishk, the commander, Ismail, fled to Iran. The Taliban imposed sharia in Herat making the women and the girls stay at home instead of going to work and school. The capture of Herat by the Taliban infuriated Kabul and driven by this anger they burned down Pakistan's embassy in Kabul. One staff member was killed and the ambassador was humiliated. Then after capturing Hekmatyar's headquarters and routing out Hezb-e-Wahdat after killing their leader Abdul Ali Waziri, the Taliban now stood in front of the Kabul government. After a severe fight with the government forces, the Taliban had to retreat to Charasyab but continued bombarding Kabul, resulting in heavy civilian causalities.

Another problem was that Rabbani, according to Mestiri's plan, refused to stand down and the Taliban claimed that power should be handed over to them instead of an interim council. The Taliban had blocked the Jalalabad–Kabul road resulting in the stoppage of food supplies that aggravated the food scarcity situation in Kabul. Later, the UN arranged some food supplies to mitigate the difficulties of Kabul's populace.

In the summer of 1996, Engineer Hekmatyar connived with his old enemy Rabbani to become the prime minister of Afghanistan. The Taliban bombarded Kabul as a welcome note to Hekmatyar. The Taliban started their move from the east and captured the Paktya, Jalalabad, Kunar, and Laghman provinces and marched toward Sarobi where they routed out Hekmatyar's forces. In September 1996, the government forces withdrew to the north and there was no hurdle for the Taliban to enter Kabul city.

The first thing that the Taliban did was to surround the UN compound where the deposed Najibullah was hiding. Najibullah wanted to flee the country but the road to the Kabul airport was blocked by the Taliban to foil his effort. Finally, the Taliban got hold of Najibullah and his brother and shot them both and hanged their bodies on the square on the Kabul–Jalalabad road. Kabul was ruled by a six-man shura but the final directions came from Mullah Omar's shura

138 Rise and fall of Taliban

based in Kandahar. The Taliban abolished all the laws and regulations that were formulated and put into effect by the communist regimes. However, the Taliban restored King Zahir Shah's 1964 constitution with certain modifications with respect to the monarchy and gender issues. King Zahir Shah's 1964 constitution contained a provision that permitted the kingship to stay in Zahir Shah's family. The Taliban rejected it. Similarly, the 1964 constitution provided equal rights between men and women. The Taliban kept women at home by disallowing them the right to employment and schooling for the girls. The Taliban introduced the hijab, covering the body from head to toe to restore respect and honor to the women. The Taliban also banned the women from wearing white socks as these were considered to solicit unwanted attention from the men. And, the final decision-making power vested with the ulema. In October 1997, the Taliban renamed the country as Islamic Emirate of Afghanistan with Mullah Omar as its head. After Dost Mohammad, Mullah Omar was the second Amir-ul-Mominin.

After Kabul, the Taliban moved to the north and reached the Salang Pass, but were soon driven back by Masoud's forces. In the west, the Taliban captured Shindand and Herat and from there they advanced further and captured the Shiberghan and Faryab provinces. In the meantime, Abdur Rashid Dostam's general, Abdul Malik, defected to the Taliban and Dostam fled to Tashkent in Uzbekistan and from there he proceeded to Ankara, Turkey. In May 1997, the Taliban took over Mazar-i-Sharif. After capturing Mazar-i-Sharif, the Taliban were now the master of most of the country. Pakistan, Saudi Arabia, and UAE recognized their government. As the Taliban did not share power with General Abdul Malik, he defected again and attacked the Taliban from the rear just after three days of their taking control of Mazar-i-Sharif. Hezb-e-Wahdat, in collaboration with General Malik, slaughtered more than 2,000 Taliban, whose bodies were later found in a mass grave in Shiberghan. The Taliban lost control of the city and their commander, Abdul Razak, and the foreign minister, Ghaus, were taken as prisoners. The Taliban were also forced to leave Pul-i-Khumri in Baghlan Province.

Rashid Dostam came back and ousted General Malik in September 1997 and occupied many of the central north provinces. The Hezb-e-Wahdat under the leadership of Ustad Karim Khalili controlled Hazarajat. In July 1998, after capturing Faryab, the Taliban marched toward Shiberghan and hearing the news of Taliban's arrival, Dostam left the country. In August 1998, the Taliban retook Mazar-i-Sharif. After Mazar-i-Sharif, the Taliban captured Taloqan, which was used by Masoud as his main supply route from the Central Asian states. In order to take revenge for the slaughtering of more than 2,000 Taliban by Hezb-e-Wahdat, the Taliban killed 6,000 Hazara people. In September 1998, the Taliban occupied Bamian Province, the main center of the Hazara people. The peace talks that were held in Ashkhabad, the capital of Turkmenistan, in 1999, decided that both the parties – the Mujahidin under Rabbani and the Taliban – would work together through a broad-based government and that both the parties would continue talks. Mullah Omar announced that the Taliban would not share the power with those who have destroyed the country. Until 2000, the talks between the warring groups remained indecisive. In the meantime, the former king, Zahir Shah, called a Loya Jirga in Italy for settlement of peace in Afghanistan, which was rejected by the Taliban.

The West and the neighboring countries had concerns about the Taliban government in Kabul. The West was concerned that it could be a source of religious extremism that could engulf the whole world, thus destabilizing the peace in the region as well as in the rest of the world. Among the neighboring countries in the north, Tajikistan had problems. After the independence of the Central Asian states, an Islamic Renaissance Party was formed in Tajikistan, which later shifted to northern Afghanistan and set up a government in exile. From northern Afghanistan, the terrorists crossed the border into Tajikistan and carried out terrorist activities. This situation was viewed by Russia seriously and feared that Islamic fundamentalism could be spread through the whole of Russia.

Stalin's policy of forced settlement of the different ethnic groups in the different regions of the Central Asian states had created an environment which was not conducive to the Taliban's creed. However, the Central Asian states, namely Tajikistan, Kirgizstan, Kazakhstan, and Russia, were badly affected by the opium and heroin supply from Afghanistan. Russia immediately decided to help Tajikistan and sent 20,000 troops to Tajikistan to handle the cross-border terrorism.

Similarly, Uzbekistan complained that Uzbeki Islamic fundamentalists were being supported and trained by the Taliban. The leadership of the Islamic Movement of Uzbekistan has been provided shelter in Afghanistan. Russia was also concerned in that the Taliban were providing training and support to the Chechnyan rebels. In addition to aiding Tajikistan, Russia was also supporting the Northern Alliance to take the Taliban down a peg. One country in the north, Turkmenistan, stayed away from contributing to these allegations to maintain good relations with the Taliban, so that they could be able to win the Taliban's support to implement their potential oil and gas pipeline project to Pakistan through Afghanistan to revive their economy.

However, Russia was very careful because of its currently weak and demoralized army and more than that there was no guarantee that by supporting the Uzbek commander, Abdur Rashid Dostam, in the north, the Taliban movement will be controlled. Russia decided not to support Dostam.

In the west, Iran had historically experienced inconvenience in its relationship with Afghanistan. Iran wanted to hegemonize its imperial Persian culture in Afghanistan, which had its own cultural, territorial, and linguistic ethos and took pride in its Dari and Pushtu languages. Apart from this, Iran was afraid of the Taliban's successes and had concerns about the killing of its Shia people (Hazara). The Taliban had killed eight Iranian diplomats and one Iranian journalist at the time of the Taliban's capture of Mazar -i-Sharif in August 1998. In June 1994, the bomb explosion at the shrine of Imam Raza at Mashhad alerted Iran about the spread of Taliban movement across the Afghan borders. Moreover, Iran was

140 Rise and fall of Taliban

also affected by the copious supplies of opium and heroin from Afghanistan. The Taliban had made it clear that it had no intention of exporting its creed beyond the Afghan borders.

Iran backed the minority Shia Hizb-e-Wahdat party in support of its creed. The furious Iran sent its troops to the border for military exercises but did not dare attack Afghanistan. Iran knew that it was no win–win situation for both Afghanistan and Iran. It was worried about the safe return of the Afghan refugees sitting in Iran. The other concern that Iran had was the spread of Islamic fundamentalism through the support of Saudi Arabia. Soon after the takeover of Kabul by the Taliban, Iran organized a regional conference in Tehran on October 29–30, 1996. Russia, India, Pakistan, China, Saudi Arabia, Central Asian republics, the European Union, the UN, and the Organization of the Islamic Countries (OIC) were invited to attend to discuss the Afghanistan situation. Pakistan, Saudi Arabia, and Uzbekistan did not attend this conference. Iran did not recognize the Taliban government and instead supported the President Rabbani government. Iran provided military support to the opponents of the Taliban and granted refuge to Herat's governor, Ismail Khan.

In the east, Pakistan had a different viewpoint altogether. Pakistan's viewpoint was that as the Pushtuns are in majority in Afghanistan, therefore a Pushtun-dominated government should be in Afghanistan. The Taliban are Pushtuns who are linked to the Pushtuns on both sides of the border. For Pakistan, it will be easy to deal with them. And, most importantly, with the support of the Taliban or the Pushtun government, Pakistan would be able to implement its oil and gas pipeline projects from the Central Asian states, Turkmenistan, Tajikistan, Uzbekistan, and Kazakhstan. The opening of the trade route to the Central Asian states through Afghanistan will boost up Pakistan's economy. That's why Pakistan was the first to recognize the Taliban's government.

The United States and the West were wary about the Taliban's handling of state affairs. The West alleged that the Taliban were involved in human rights violation, drug production and trading, and international terrorism. That's why the US and the West denied recognition to the Taliban government and their seat at the United Nations was not handed over to them in spite of the fact that they were holding the majority of the areas under their control. The UN seat stayed with Rabbani which did not make any sense.

On September 9, 2001, two days before the 9/11 incident, the guerrilla leader of the Northern Alliance, Ahmad Shah Masoud, was blown up in Takhar Province by two Tunisians who posed themselves as the journalists. Masoud was buried on September 15 on the hill of Saricha, Panjsher. A tomb has been built on his grave. Mohammad Omar, the Northern Alliance commander, who was with Masoud at that moment said, Masoud immediately died. Masoud's dead body was taken to Tajikistan. The Northern Alliance did not announce his death as it was a big shock for them. The Northern soldiers, who were not good soldiers, were motivated by the leadership and command of Masoud and now felt dejected and lost hope against the Taliban. The Northern Alliance soldiers were already driven to the north by the Taliban, away from Kabul.

International problems for the Taliban started with the attack on the World Trade Center in New York, and the Pentagon, Washington DC, on Tuesday, September 11, 2001. The four planes that were hijacked by the terrorists just smashed into the twin towers of the World Trade Center and killed and wounded numerous people. The US government started looking at the reasons for this attack. The preliminary thoughts that were floating, inter-alia, included: the US support to Israel to oppress the Palestinians; the US attack of Iraq; and the US presence on the Saudi soil. These were the probable issues that could lead to the reasons for the attack. The American investigations, however, revealed Osama bin Laden as the prime suspect. Osama had lived in Khost, Kunar, Laghman, and Jalalabad in Afghanistan and had fought in the war against Russia.

After the completion of the withdrawal of the Russian army in February 1989, Osama bin Laden went to Sudan and carried out terrorist activities from there. Under the pressure of the US, the Sudanese Government asked Osama to leave the country. In 1996, Osama bin Laden was invited back to Afghanistan by Abdur Rasul Sayyaf, a Northern Alliance leader. On August 7, 1998, the American embassies in Nairobi in Kenya and Dar es Salaam in Tanzania were attacked. According to the US authorities, these attacks were led by the group of Osama bin Laden where 250 people were killed and around 5,000 wounded. On September 11, 2001, the World Trade Center in New York was attacked, which, the US agencies found out, was also an act of Osama's followers. The US attacked Osama's bases in the border areas of Afghanistan, but neither was he killed nor was captured.

The 9/11 attack was so sophisticated that it could not be imagined that it could be the work of the Taliban. Then who else? None but Osama bin Laden, who had access to modern communication technology and had links with North Korea for training on chemical weapons. Moreover, the previous attacks on the American embassies in Africa were the acts of Osama's people. The US government established its firm position that this was an act of Al-Qaeda, a terrorist organization run by Osama bin Laden and Aymen Al-Zawahri who rung number two in this organization. Osama became the most wanted person by the U.S.

The US asked the Taliban to hand over Osama bin Laden for trial for the terrorism activities that were carried out at the World Trade Center in New York and the American embassies in Tanzania and Kenya. The Taliban gave two reasons for not handing over Osama to the US. The first argument was that there was no evidence of the involvement of Osama neither in the World Trade Center nor in the American embassies. The Taliban further argued that they would make sure that Osama did not use Afghan soil for activities in other countries. The second argument was that according to the Islamic hospitality ethos, no guest under their protection would be expelled. At the same time, Saudi Arabia demanded Osama who was committed to the removal of American forces from the soil of Saudi Arabia. That too was not allowed on the same basis. Saudi

142 Rise and fall of Taliban

Arabia, in September 1998, closed its mission in Kabul and threatened to cut off aid to Afghanistan. Mullah Omar was under pressure by the US and announced that Osama bin Laden had disappeared. He was no more in Afghanistan and that Afghanistan did not know Osama's whereabouts.

In October 1999, the UN Security Council demanded the handing over of Osama within one month's notice for the trial on the terrorism charges. The Taliban still did not yield. At the expiry of the one month's notice, owing to the noncompliance by the Taliban, the UN imposed sanctions by freezing Afghanistan's assets abroad and banning flights of Ariana out of Kabul. These sanctions too did not budge the Taliban. Now additional sanctions were imposed on the Taliban according to which a unilateral, Taliban-specific arms embargo was imposed on the Taliban. There was no such embargo on the Taliban's opponents such as the Northern Alliance. In addition to this, travel restrictions on the Taliban leadership were also imposed. Interestingly, the UN Secretary General did not appreciate these restrictions on the plea that these would neither bring peace nor would facilitate humanitarian assistance in the rural area where hunger and malnutrition were widespread. The world at large did not recognize the Taliban administration because of their involvement in human rights violation, drug production and trading, and international terrorism.

According to Marsden, "The humanitarian assistance organizations worked largely through Mujahidin commanders, providing cash and wheat to them for distribution to communities within Afghanistan". The Taliban who were critical of the foreigners in their country, on August 5, 2001, captured eight Christian aid workers belonging to Shelter Now International, which included four Germans and two Americans named Heather Mercer and Danya Curryon, on the charges of proselytizing the local Afghans.[1] The charges carried the death penalty. "The trial of the eight foreigners which include four Germans, began on 4 September at the Supreme Court in Kabul under Sharia or Islamic law", writes Rashid. The Supreme Court indicted them. But both these American girls were later rescued by the US Special Forces when the Taliban left Kabul after the fall of their government.

Finally, before the attack on Afghanistan, the US, through the courtesy of Pakistan, gave Taliban leader Mullah Omar a choice of two options: either hand over Osama and the Al-Qaeda network or get ready to fight. Consequently, Pakistan's ISI DG, General Mahmood, accompanied by some religious leaders of the Khyber Pakhtunkhwa visited Kandahar. The group met Mullah Omar in Kandahar and delivered the US message and tried to convince him to make a decision that was best in the interest of Afghanistan. Mullah Omar said that Osama was their guest and, according to the Islamic ethos, the Taliban could not hand over Osama. He demanded proof of Osama's involvement in the 9/11 event. The Taliban's foreign minister, Muttawakil, said that we cannot hand over Osama, but we can try him over here if the proofs of his involvement are given to us. Most of the Afghans were feeling that now the American knee-jerk attack was looming large.

On September 13, the US ordered the evacuation of its staff in Afghanistan. The Arabs living in Kabul moved to Logar and all the Westerners were ordered to leave Afghanistan. The United Nations evacuated all of its staff. Pakistan closed its borders with Afghanistan on September 14.

The US finally attacked Afghanistan on October 7, 2001, with a small number of troops on the ground. Most of the Afghan and international defense strategists were surprised to see a small number of troops on the ground for such a big strike. The US depended on the air bombardment. On the ground, it depended on the Northern Alliance soldiers. The Northern Alliance soldiers were very poor fighters as compared to the Taliban fighters. Another reason for sending a small number of troops was that the US had another plan of attack on Iraq after finishing with Afghanistan. It was very strange that here the US allied with the Northern Alliance, whose important leader, the number two after Ahmad Shah Masoud, was Abdur Rasul Sayyaf, who was a close friend of Osama. Abdur Rasul Syyaf had invited Osama to Afghanistan when he was expelled from Sudan by the Sudanese government. Now here, the US was trying to hunt down Osama with the help of Osama's friend. That had never happened before. Another important aide of Osama was Jaluluddin Haqqani, who was running the Al-Qaeda network in Khost, which was the base camp of Osama bin Laden. Haqqani remained steadfast and did not hand over the Al-Qaeda network to the US.

Soon after this attack, the Taliban's foreign minister, Wakil Ahmad Muttawakil, in a hurriedly called press conference, condemned the attack and said that the Taliban had nothing to do with the attack on the World Trade Center in New York. Muttawakil ignored the questions about Osama's presence in Afghanistan.

The American and the British fighter jets carried out a very intense bombardment on the Taliban headquarters, army offices, ammunition depots, and the Taliban's antiaircraft guns mounted on the hills. The bombardment was administered during the night and during the day there was no attack. Other than the use of antiaircraft guns, the Taliban were seen nowhere. In this intense bombardment, innocent children, men, and women were killed. The Taliban had lost Mazar-i-Sharif in the north, though Kunduz and Kandahar were still in their possession. No Taliban resistance was left in Kabul. The Wazir Akbar Khan area, where most of the Arab, Chechan, and Uzbeki Mujahidin were living, was targeted. The Taliban's prime minister, Mullah Hassan, held a meeting, outside of Kabul, to develop a strategy for the encounter. By November 12, the fall of Kabul was visible and in order to avoid the chaos, the looting, and the lawlessness, the US asked the Northern Alliance to keep their people out of Kabul, which was rejected by Abdur Rasul Sayyaf. Mullah Omar was not in Kabul. Prime Minister Mullah Hassan, Police Chief Mullah Dadullah, Information Minister Qadratullah Jamal, Health Minister Mullah Mohammad Abbas, Deputy Health Sher Mohammad Stanikzai, Interior Minister Abdul Razak, and Foreign Minister Wakil Ahmad Muttawakil, all left Kabul and escaped. "The

144 Rise and fall of Taliban

Taliban had taken the aid workers when they fled", writes Gannon. November 13, 2001, was the day when Kabul became free of the Taliban and the fall of the city was only due to the American and British bombardment without any contribution from the Northern Alliance. The Northern Alliance could not even get Mazar-i-Sharif from the Taliban until the American and British bombardment made the Taliban flee the city. The Taliban's rule that extended from September 1996, through November 13, 2001, came to an end with the fall of Kabul. The city was left ravaged with its buildings shattered and jutted by shrapnel.

Note

1 Gannon, *I Is for Infidel, J Is for Jihad, K Is for Kalashnikov*, p. 84; Rashid, *Taliban, Militant Islam, Oil and Fundamentalism in Central Asia*, p. xii.

Bibliography

Gannon, K., *I Is for Infidel, J Is for Jihad, K Is for Kalashnikov: From Holy War to Holy Terror in Afghanistan*. Public Affairs, a member of Perseus Group, New York, USA, 2005.

Rashid, A., *Taliban, Militant Islam, Oil and Fundamentalism in Central Asia*. Tauris and Co, UK and Yale University Press, USA, 2000.

Marsden, P., *The Taliban: War and Religion in Afghanistan*. Zed Books, London, 2000.

9

LAND AND PEOPLE

The Land

Afghanistan, a corridor for the invaders, existed as a semi-independent and independent country for two centuries. It is a land of Afghans, a name applied to the Pushtun tribes, with an area of 250,000 square miles. Afghanistan, a landlocked country, shares borders with many countries. About 60 percent of its area is mountainous. It includes the treeless Hindu Kush range, which extends to the Pamir mountain ranges in the northeast of Tajikistan and along the Wakhan corridor in Afghanistan and Gilgit-Baltistan, Pakistan, to the world's highest ranges of Karakoram and Himalayas in the east that touches China.

The range to the north of Kabul is known as Koh-i-Baba (father mountain) with the highest peak of Shah Foladi rising 16,240 feet, or about 4,951 meters, and a source of three rivers.[1] The first river originating from Koh-i-Baba is the Kabul River that flows into Pakistan and falls into the mighty Indus River at Attock. The second river that originates from Koh-i-Baba is Helmand-Arghandab which irrigates the Kandahar, Lashkargah, and Sistan areas and falls into the lake of Hamun-i-Helmand in Iran. The third river originating from Koh-i-Baba is Hari Rud or Herat river which flows in the west of Herat until it reaches Turkmenistan. The range in the northeast is known as Safed Koh and the western range is known as Parapomisus that extends to the Iranian frontiers and the Suleiman range along the eastern frontiers which open the gates through the passes such as the Bolan, Shorawak, Gomal, Tochi, Paiwan, and Khyber.

Afghanistan and its aggressive warriors have ruled Iran and India. Its population is about 33 million. The bridge between Tajikistan and Afghanistan built on the Punj River shows a natural boundary between the two countries. The Oxus River forms the boundary between Afghanistan and Uzbekistan. In the north it shares a border of 1,206 kilometers with Tajikistan, 137 kilometers with

DOI: 10.4324/9781003198376-9

146 Land and people

Uzbekistan, 744 kilometers with Turkmenistan in the northwest, 936 kilometers with Iran in the west and southwest, 76 kilometers in the northeast with China, and a long and porous border of 2,430 kilometers with Pakistan in the east and southeast of Afghanistan.

In the past, Afghanistan has been a buffer state between the two big powers of the world, viz. British India and the Russian Czars. Afghanistan served as a route for foreign visitors and invaders who crossed this land through the Khyber, Paiwan Kotal, and Bolan passes to reach the Indian subcontinent and thus helped shape the political structure of Asia.

The People

The Afghans are the most independent people that one could think of in this world. More than 80% of the Afghans are Sunni Muslims and the remaining are Shia and other minorities including Sikhs, Hindus, Christians, and Jews. The four largest ethnic groups are the Pushtuns, the Tajiks, the Uzbeks, and the Hazaras, while the minor groups include the Turkmen, Nuri or Nuristani, and Chahar Aimak.

The Pushtuns

Originally, the word "Afghan" refers to the Pushtuns or alternatively referred to as the Pukhtuns or the Pathan tribes of Afghanistan. Later every citizen of Afghanistan called himself Afghan and its currency is called Afghani. The word "Afghan" was referred to in the writings of Mohammad Ibn-Ahmad-Al-Beruni[2] who served in the court of Sultan Mahmud of Ghaznavi, the first Muslim ruler of Afghanistan. According to Al-Beruni, the Pushtuns lived in the northwestern part of modern-day Pakistan. Ghaznavi's army largely consisted of the Pushtuns. The Pushtuns speak the Pushto language, also called Pukhto. The Pushto is considered to be the original version and the Pukhto is a colloquial version based on day-to-day use.

According to the Pushtuns' own traditions, they think of themselves to have been originated in Palestine and Israel and were later driven out to Syria. From Syria they migrated to the western mountains of Ghor in Afghanistan where they got settled and worshiped one God. The Pushtuns also believe that they are the descendants of King Saul's grandson, whose name was Afghana. While they were in Israel, they were taught the Pushtu language by Soloman, the master of the jinns, and this language has been alleged to be a language of the hell. According to another tradition, the Pushtuns claim to be the descendants of Qais,[3] a companion of the Holy Prophet Mohammed, peace be upon him, who was from Ghor and went to Mecca and learned Islam and came back to Ghor to teach the same. Later his Pushto-speaking descendants moved to the south, east, and northwest of modern-day Pakistan. However, there is no complete agreement about the origins of the Pushtuns. Some call them Suleimani, assuming that they entered and lived in the Suleiman Range. Some Afghan scholars trace their origins to the people of Bactria, now known as Balkh Province in the north of Afghanistan.

According to an unofficial estimate, the Pushtuns are in the majority representing a little more than 40% of the total population[4] of Afghanistan, albeit, no official census has taken place. Afghanistan was created by a Pushtun warrior named Ahmad Shah Abdali after the death of the Persian warrior Nadir Shah. Ahmad Shah had served in Nadir Shah's army. When Ahmad Shah became the king of Afghanistan, he changed the name of his tribe from Abdali to Durrani and established the Durrani dynasty. Afghanistan was always ruled by the Pushtun leaders with the exception of Habibullah, also known as Bach-i-Saqao, and Burhanuddin Rabbani, the two Tajik leaders from the Parwan and Badakhshan provinces, respectively. The majority of the Pushtuns in Afghanistan live in the northeast to the southeast bordering Pakistan. Some Pushtuns also live in other parts of Afghanistan such as Baghlan, Kunduz, Balkh, Parwan in the north, and Herat in the west.

The Pushtuns are divided into many tribes and subtribes[5] bearing the names of their ancestors and the degree of the loyalty they command. These include the Waziris, Afridis, Mahsuds, Khattaks, Shinwaris, Mohammedzais, Suleimankhels, Yusufzais, Durranis, and Ghilzais. The Durranis and Ghilzais are the two big tribes of Afghanistan and most of the Afghanistan Pushtuns have descended from these two tribes. The Durranis live in the west and the south and the Ghilzais live in the south and the east.[6] The degree of loyalty is very strong within a tribe and is only weakened when rivalries exist within a tribe. The leaders of the tribe are known as the Khans or the Maliks, the titles they inherit, or some exceptional persons may get these titles regardless of their family ties. However, the Khan or the Malik cannot impose his decision on his tribe without the approval of the majority of the population of the tribe, known as Jirga. The collective decision of the Jirga is final and binding. However, in some cases the decision may be defied by a powerful group of the tribe.

People living in the neighborhood of a tribe and not members of the tribe are called Hamsaya or "neighbor". These non-tribal people have low status in the area and do not take part in the decision-making activities of a tribe. However, these people are protected by the tribe from any external threat or intervention from the government and other agencies.

The Pushtuns have some traditions or code of customs called Pushtunwali[7] according to which they govern themselves. The Pushtuns' code of customs generally includes three rules. First, nanawati (sanctuary or hiding place), which means a person is protected if he enters the tribal area, or hamlet of a tribe, and takes refuge for protection or mediation to resolve and settle peacefully an offense that he has committed somewhere else. Under the nanawati code of conduct, the person is protected by the tribe and granted immunity from punishment, even if he is an enemy or belongs to an enemy or a hostile tribe or non-tribal area. As an example, if a woman wants to protect herself and or her family,

148 Land and people

she will send her veil to the head of the tribe asking for assistance and according to the Pushtuns' tradition, this request is never denied. Second, badal (Qisas),[8] meaning to return like for like, or (Diyat)[9] to return in kind any injury, wrong, or insult to oneself or member of one's family, a sort of revenge or retaliation. The settlement varies from tribe to tribe, some can settle the issue on payment of money and some may take personal vengeance, such as murder for murder, injury for injury (Qisas). And this vengeance may continue for generations and this fact is the main cause of the lack of unity among the Pushtuns. Although this custom is fading out among the educated Pushtuns to some extent in the urban areas, in the rural areas it is still common. It is a well-established fact that a Pushtun cannot take an insult or injury and is not satisfied until personal vengeance is taken. Third, melmastia, which refers to hospitality. If a person becomes a guest of a Pushtun, the person and the property of the guest, his comfort and pleasure become the sacred responsibility of the host Pushtun and he will protect it no matter what it costs him.

The majority of the Pushtuns are Sunni Muslims, based on the Islamic system of Abu Hanifa and a few tribes such as Turi, some clans of Orakzai and Qizilbash are Shiite Muslims, followers of the fourth Caliph, Hezrat Ali, son-in-law of the Holy Prophet Mohammad, peace be upon him. Mythical Sufism, through the two orders, namely Qadiriyya and Naqashbandiyya, has inspired spiritualism through the interconnection of the Pirs or the Mursheds (spiritual leaders) with their followers.

Many historians have characterized the Pushtuns as warlike, proud, and aggressive individualistic with predatory habits, uncertain tampers, uncompromising on their independence, ruthless, contentious, revengeful but most hospitable. A story about the tribal Pushtuns goes like this. The British Indian government discussed and completed an agreement with the Jirga of the tribes of the Pushtuns on the east side of the Durand Line for laying a railway track from Peshawar to Torkham border at a certain amount agreed to be given to the Jirga. When the railway track was completed, the British informed the Jirga that now they are going to run a train. The Jirga rejected this plan on the plea that the agreement was just for laying a railway track and not for running a train. For running a train, a new agreement with additional money is needed. The British had to pay more money to run the train.

The Tajiks

The Tajiks are the second largest ethnic group representing 33% of the total population. They are scattered throughout the country, especially in the north and the west of Afghanistan. The Tajiks live in Afghanistan, Iran, Tajikistan, and Sinkiang province of China. The Tajiks in Afghanistan speak Dari (Farsi). Those who live in the west are sometimes called Herati and have the same ancestors as that of the people of eastern Iran. Those who live in the north of Hindu Kush are called the Farsiwans (Persian speakers). They are the descendants of the

Aryans and Alexander and other settlers who lived and married in Afghanistan and influenced the local culture. However, Tajik is an Arabic term, which refers to a non-Arab Muslim, which in the 14th century was considered a Persian-speaking Moslem.

The Tajiks have lived under the Pushtun hegemony for two centuries. In the history of Afghanistan, the Tajiks ruled twice, first under Bacha-i-Saqao, who became the head of Afghanistan by overthrowing Amanullah in January 1929. The stage for the overthrow of Amanullah was set by a Tajik religious leader, Habibullah Kalakani, known as Bacha-i-Saqao, with the support of the ulema. Bacha-i-Saqao reversed the Western-based education system that was established by Amanullah and, instead, introduced the Sharia law and the education system was brought under the management of the ulema. The Pushtuns did not like the rule of the Tajik and with the support of the Pushtun ulema, the revolt was organized against Bacha-i-Saqao. Bacha-i-Saqao was unable to maintain his control and was finally overthrown in October 1929, by Mohammad Nadir Khan, a third cousin of Amanullah. The first rule of the Tajiks in Afghanistan was just for a brief period of about nine months.

The second rule of the Tajiks was under Burhannudin Rabbani from Badakhshan Province of northern Afghanistan. Rabbani was a leader of an Islamist party known as Jamiat-i-Islami founded in 1972. He was a lecturer in Islamic theology at Kabul University. He was influenced by the Egyptian Islamic Brotherhood movement. Rabbani was considered to be a moderate and pragmatic. He fled to Pakistan during Daud's regime to escape arrest. Rabbani became the president after the fall of the Najibullah regime in July 1992. A major rocket attack on Kabul was executed in August 1992, which killed more than 18,000 civilians. In December 1992, Rabbani got himself reelected as the president by a handpicked national assembly. The continuation of the heavy fighting during January–February 1993 compelled Rabbani to share power with Hekmatyar, the Pushtun leader from Baghlan Province, as prime minister. Although Hekmatyar became the prime minister, he could not nominate his cabinet at a meeting scheduled at his base at Charasyab in the south of the capital, as President Rabbani failed to attend that meeting due to an attack on him on his way to Charasyab and he had to return back to Kabul. Thus because of fighting among the different Afghan groups, Hekmatyar could not exercise his power. In January 1994, both the Pushtun leader Hekmatyar and the Uzbek leader Rashid Dostam from Shiberghan Province joined forces to accelerate attack on Kabul to unseat Rabbani. Although this attempt failed, Hekmatyar continued the attacks on Kabul during 1994 forcing 300,000 civilians to leave the capital. Rabbani's regime ended when the Taliban entered Kabul in September 1996.

The Tajiks are mainly agriculturalists, often working as tenant farmers or laborers. They are also well-educated people, very social and not conservative, hold public offices, and some are engaged in trade and handicrafts. They are very peaceful and hardworking people, not inclined to warlike activities, with the exception of the Tajiks of Kohistan who live in the north of Kabul and are considered to be as aggressive as the Pushtuns. The Tajiks are brunettes with slender figures, deep-set eyes, and oval faces.

The Pushtuns and the Tajiks have lived together in harmony for several centuries and have engaged in intermarriages. The Tajiks have served in the past at high-level government positions and are currently holding various ministries and departments under President Ashraf Ghani's government.

The Uzbeks

The Uzbeks, of Turko-Mongol origin, are the follower of Uzbek Khan, a descendant of Genghis Khan who had entered Afghanistan in the 15th century. The Uzbeks entered Afghanistan from Central Asia during the 1920 and 1930s due to the religious persecution committed by the Soviets against them. Unrealistically, laziness and procrastination are attributed to them.

The Uzbeks live in the north, centered in Mazar-i-Sharif and Shiberghan, and are about 9% of the total population of Afghanistan. Their leader is General Abdur Rashid Dostam, the head of ethnic Uzbek party Jumbush-i-Milli and a former general and militia leader who mostly controlled the north of the Salang Pass. Dostam fought against the Soviets as part of the Mujahidin. His army is famous for looting and raping. One time, Dostam even printed

FIGURE 9.1 Agricultural market in Mazar-i-Sharif, Balkh.

his own currency. After the Russians left Afghanistan, there was a big fight between the Taliban and Dostam's forces. Dostam's general, Abdul Malik, defected to the Taliban and helped them capture Mazar-i-Sharif. Dostam fled to Uzbekistan.

The Uzbeks speak Uzbeki[10] language, a form of Turkish, and intermarry with the Tajiks but not with the Pushtuns. The Uzbeks are primarily agriculturalists and expert breeders of horses and karakul sheep.[11] Their other activities included trading, handicrafts, and carpet making. Buzkashi (goat killing) is their favorite sport (Figure 9.1).

The Hazara

Genghis Khan's forces arrived in Bamiyan, a valley of Buddha statues carved in the mountains in Afghanistan, where Buddhists from all over the world visited on pilgrimage. Genghis Khan's forces were confronted by the local army. He killed the whole population of the valley and no man, woman, child, livestock, crops, irrigation infrastructure, trees or anything was left behind. The valley was resettled by the Hazara people who are the descendants of Genghis Khan's regiment. The Hazaras comprise 11% of the total population.

Ninety percent of the Hazaras are followers of the Shia version of the Islamic religion and do not intermarry with other ethnic groups. The majority of Hazaras live in Bamian, Ghazni, Parwan, Baghlan, Balkh, Kabul, and Uruzgan. The educated Hazaras hold public offices. Hazara women are engaged in carpet-making business. Illiterate Hazaras are engaged as home workers. The major activities of Hazaras involve agriculture and livestock (sheep breeding), carpet making, and business. The Hazara people speak Hazaragi, a form of Persian but enriched by Turkic and Mongol languages.[12] The Hazaras are divided into different tribes, the most important of which are the Besud, Dai Kundi, Polada, Dai Zangi, Jaghuri, and Uruzgani.[13]

The other minor communities include the Turkoman (2%), Nuris or Nuristanis (1%), and Chahar Aimak (1%). The Turkoman population live in Badghis Province and relate to Turkmenistan. The Turkoman migrated from Central Asia during the 1920s and 1930s and are good karakul sheep breeders and carpet makers. The Nuris or Nuristanis live in Nuristan bordering Chitral. Alexander the Great passed through Nuristan and the people were so brave that they even resisted him. Alexander liked them and took them into his army that attacked the Indian subcontinent. Before their conversion to Islam during Abdur Rahman's period, they were known as kafirs (infidels).[14] They are known as the descendants of Alexander's army.

The other minor community is Chahar Aimak (four tribes). Their population is very small (1%) and is divided into tribes Jamshidi, Firozkohi, Timuri, and Taimani.[15] They practice Sunni Islam and speak Persian of Herati type. They are nomadic or seminomadic. They live in Badghis, Ghor, and Herat.[16]

152 Land and people

Political Parties of Afghanistan

Hezb-e-Islami

Hezb-e-Islami was founded in 1969 and since then it has been headed by the former Afghan Prime Minister Gulbeddin Hekmatyar from the north. Gulbeddin Hekmatyar was born on June 26, 1947, in Imam Sahib District of Kunduz Province. Hekmatyar first joined the Military Academy and later in 1968 joined Kabul University's Engineering Department as a student of engineering. Hezb-e-Islami (Hekmatyar) has influence in Nuristan, Zabul, Wardak, Parwan, Kapisa, Baghlan, and Badghis. Its philosophy is to develop a revolutionary movement that could gain power to establish an Islamic state based on the Quran and the Hadith. It has its own educational institutions and camps.

In the 1960s, when Hekmatyar was a student at Kabul University, he along with Rabbani, Masoud, and Sayyaf was an active member of the Islamic Movement and was critical of Sardar Mohammad Daud. The Islamic Movement was started against Daud at Kabul University and it was inspired by the Egypt's Al-Ikhwan-al-Muslimin (Muslim Brotherhood) – which was created by Hasan al Banna in 1928.[17] Later all of these Islamic movement leaders became Mujahidin leaders during the course of war against Russia. Daud with the assistance of communist Babrak Karmal's Percham Party wanted to crush the Islamic Movement.

Daud became very antagonistic toward Pakistan as soon as he came into power. When Daud and Babrak Karmal took action against the Islamic Movement, their leaders took refuge in Pakistan and the Pakistan government supported them against Daud. Daud sought assistance from Russia which provided more than a billion dollars in the form of economic and military aid.

During the course of war against Russia, Hekmatyar, among other leaders, was supported by the US and Pakistan and he also visited the White House. Hekmatyar told the US administration that Mujahidin need military equipment and that it did not matter where it came from, be it even Israel or elsewhere. During the war against Russia, Hekmatyar turned out to be a behemoth guerrilla leader. With his base camp at Charasyab in the south of Kabul, he used to attack Kabul. Later, differences between Hekmatyar and the US developed and as a result of these differences Hekmatyar was tried to be assassinated with a missile attack but he survived. Later, during the Iraq war, Hekmatyar sided with Iraq. The US declared him a "global terrorist". Finally, the US and the Afghan government allowed him to be part of the efforts of bringing peace and stability to Afghanistan.

Gulbeddin Hekmatyar has been the prime minister of Afghanistan for two terms: first, from March 1993 through January 1994, and the second time from June 1996 until August 1996 when the Taliban drove Hekmatyar and Rabbani out of Kabul. After that Hekmatyar took refuge in Iran. After the US attack on Afghanistan in 2001, Iran expelled him from Iran and he took refuge in his own country, Afghanistan.

Hezb-e-Islami (Khalis)

Maulvi Yunus Khalis was born in 1919 in Khugiani District of Nangarhar Province. Khalis had studied at Madrassa Haqqania, at Akora Khattak, Nowshera, Khyber Pakhtunkhwa, Pakistan. When Sardar Mohammad Daud ousted King Zahir Shah in 1973, Maulvi Khalis fled to Pakistan and joined Gulbeddin Hekmatyar's Hezb-e-Islami. When the Soviet invaded Afghanistan, Maulvi Khalis split away from Hekmatyar's Hezb-e-Islami considering him a rigid hardliner and established his own party known as Hezb-e-Islami (Khalis) in 1979. Its purpose was the same as the Hekmatyar's party but the modus operandi to accomplish that purpose was different. Maulvi Khalis was a conservative fundamentalist and was anti-Shia. Unlike Hekmatyar, his party depended more on the ulema.

Mullah Omar, later the leader of the Taliban, had joined his party for jihad against the Soviets. Many famous Mujahidin commanders were associated with his party, including Haji Abdul Qadeer, the former governor of Nangarhar Province; Abdul Haq of Kabul, the younger brother of Haji Abdul Qadeer; and Jamaluddin Haqqani from the Paktya Province. Haji Abdul Qadeer was assassinated in 2002. His party played an important role in fighting the Soviet forces and compelling them to withdraw from Afghanistan.

After the withdrawal of the Russian forces from Afghanistan, Maulvi Yunus Khalis supported the Taliban in fighting against the NATO forces. After the fall of Najibullah, the Taliban with Khalis' support got control of Nangarhar in September 1996. While Khalis' forces were fighting the NATO forces, he died on July 19, 2006. After his death, his son Anwar-ul-Haq Mujahid took the command of Hezb-e-Islami (Khalis) and pledged for the rule of God in Afghanistan and jihad against the NATO forces until they leave Afghanistan. Anwar-ul-Haq had a strong hold in Khugiani and Tora Bora mountains where allegedly Osama bin Laden was hiding. The US drones attacked Tora Bora mountains but Osama escaped.

Jamiat-i-Islami

Jamiat-i-Islami wanted to accomplish the same goal of changing the society through building up support and guidance from ulema. In 1946, a Sharia faculty was established at Kabul University to conduct research and teach Islamic law and try to integrate it with traditional civil law. In the 1960s, Burahanuddin Rabbani, Gulbeddin Hekmatyar, and Ahmad Shah Masoud were all members of the Islamic movement. During the rule of Daud, these Islamists launched a movement at Kabul University to overthrow Daud. Daud took immediate action to crush this movement by arresting its leaders. Rabbani, Hekmatyar, and Masoud all fled to Pakistan to escape arrest.

Both Hekmatyar and Maulvi Yunus Khalis led their own factions of Hezb-e-Islami. Rabbani and Masoud retained their faction as Jamiat-i-Islami (Islamic Society of Afghanistan). Rabbani was born in 1940 in Badakhshan.

154 Land and people

He studied at Darul-Alum-e-Sharia (Abu Hanifa), Kabul University, and Al-Azhar University, Cairo, Egypt. Rabbani studied Islamic law and theology and later served as professor at the Faculty of Sharia at Kabul University. In 1972, Rabbani became the head of Jamiat-i-Islami. Other members included Ahmad Shah Masoud; Mohammad Ismail Khan, the former governor of Herat; and Ata Mohammad, the governor of Balkh. At Kabul University, the government raided his department to arrest him but the students resisted and foiled the government's move and Rabbani was able to escape from the university and later flee to Pakistan. Later, all factions of the Islamists became involved in war against each other. The fierce fight occurred between the forces of Hekmatyar and those of Masoud until the Taliban drove them all out and took control of Kabul in September 1996. Rabbani, the head of the Jamiat-i-Islami, remained the president of Afghanistan from 1992 through 1996 until the Taliban's takeover.

Ittehad-i-Islami

Ittehad-i-Islami (Islamic Union) was headed by Professor Abdul Rab Rasul Sayyaf. Sayyaf was born in 1946 in Paghman District near Kabul. Sayyaf studied Islamic studies at Kabul University and Al-Azhar University in Cairo, Egypt. The atrocities carried out by Sayyaf's men had been a concern of the human rights organizations.

Sayyaf was the only Pushtun leader who had aligned with the Tajik-dominated Northern Alliance, which was opposed to the Pushtun-dominated Taliban. During the 1960s, Sayyaf was part of the Al-Ikhwan-al-Muslimin that was founded and run by Rabbani, Hekmatyar, and Masoud. This organization was inspired by the Egypt's Al-Ikhwan-al-Muslimin. The purpose of this movement was to overthrow Daud, failing which all four of them had to flee to Pakistan. However, when Sayyaf came back, he was arrested. He was released by the PDPA government of Hafizullah Amin, who had some family ties with Sayyaf. Sayyaf's party, Ittehad-i-Islami, was recognized by the CIA–ISI as part of the seven parties of the Mujahidin which received the CIA–ISI assistance in the form of arms and money for fighting the Russians.

Sayyaf was also supported by Saudi Arabia to promote Wahhabism in Afghanistan, but that was not successful as Afghanistan was influenced by Sufism from Central Asia which opposed Wahhabism. Although Sayyaf failed in his attempt to win the presidentship of Afghanistan, he became member of the parliament (Wolesi Jirga member). In addition, he ran a private university, a radio and TV channel in the name of Dawat, and made quite a good fortune.

Harkat-e-Inqalabi-i-Islami

Harkat-e-Inqalabi-i-Islami (Islamic Revolutionary Party) was founded by Maulvi Mohammad Nabi Mohammadi in Quetta in 1978. His party included hardcore madrassa students. Maulvi Mohammad Nabi received religious education at Darul Uloom Haqqania, Nowshera, Khyber Pakhtunkhwa (KPK), Pakistan. When he came back to Afghanistan, he started his own madrassa. Madrassa Haqqania was established by Maulana Abdul Haq, father of Maulana Samiul Haq, who was a student and also teacher at Deoband India. When Abdul Haq came back from Deoband, he established the first Deoband madrassa at Haqqania in northwestern Pakistan in 1947. Initially, Mufti Mahmood was a part of Haqqania but later split from it and formed his own faction as Jamiat Ulema-e-Islam and set up his own schools. Madrassa Haqqania had become a major center of religious education in the region and reserved seats for students from Afghanistan, Tajikistan, Uzbekistan, and Kazakhstan. When these students went back to their countries, they formed their own religious parties against their respective governments.

In addition to the religious education that Maulvi Mohammad Nabi received at Haqqania, he was also influenced by Sufism through his association with the Qadirayya and the Naqshbandi orders. Mohammadi's party was based on a loose structure of the tribal chiefs' alliance to bring the Islamic revolution to the country. His party had influence in Logar and Helmand. Mullah Hassan had joined his party. At one time, Ismail Khan, the former governor of Herat, was also associated with his party. Mohammadi's party was recognized by the CIA and ISI for the supply of weapons and resources to fight against the Russians. His operations were in Ghazni, Herat, and Kabul. Nabi was also part of the Mujahidin leaders' group who had visited the White House, Washington DC, and met with President Reagan. Muhammadi died in a hospital in Pakistan on April 21, 2002.

Mahaz-i-Milli Islami (National Islamic Front)

Syed Pir Gillani of Kandahar, a spiritual leader of the Qadariyya Sufi order, had Pushtun followers from southern Afghanistan. He led his Mahaz-i-Milli, a moderate, liberal, and traditional party of Afghanistan. Because of his links through marriage and his family's close relationship with the former rulers of the Durrani dynasty, Pir Gillani was in favor of the former king, Zahir Shah, to lead the opposition parties against the Russian invasion. The United States and Pakistan denied this request. However, his party was a smaller part of the Mujahidin. Unlike the other Islamist parties, his party pledged to defend the tradition of Afghanistan and was considered more nationalist rather than being a radical Islamist party. King Zahir Shah was very much popular among the Kandaharis, who wanted to see the return of the Durrani dynasty to power in Afghanistan. Kandahar is the second biggest city after Kabul and is located on the old historical trade route that served both the East and the West. In the East, it served India and Pakistan through the Bolan Pass, and the West through Herat and Iran. Kandahar is very famous for its pomegranate known as Kandahari anaar (pomegranate). When Gillani could not win support for King Zahir Shah, they both supported Hamid Karzai for the president of Afghanistan.

156 Land and people

Jabba-e-Najat-e-Milli Afghanistan

The Jabba-e-Najat-e-Milli Afghanistan (Afghanistan National Liberation Front) was set up by Sibghatullah Mujaddadi in Peshawar in 1980.[18] Mujaddadi was the sole survivor after the communists killed seventy-nine members of his family in Kabul in January 1979.[19] Mujaddadi, a Pushtun, was the leader of the Naqshbandi Sufi order. In 1959, Mujaddadi was jailed by Daud for protesting against the visit of Khrushchev.[20] In the 1950s and 1960s, Mujaddadi had maintained links with Egypt's Muslim Brotherhood.[21] His party was also a traditional party in that it did not have an ideology. His group operated in the Kandahar, Farah, and Baghlan provinces. Mujaddadi had links with the former rulers and was a strong supporter of King Zahir Shah and wanted to bring him back from Rome, but his idea was opposed by Hekmatyar.

Mujaddadi was appointed the president of Afghan Interim Government (AIG) in 1989 and then became the first president of Afghanistan in 1992. In April 1992, an agreement was reached in Islamabad in the presence of representatives of Pakistan, Iran, Saudi Arabia, and the UN that a fifty-person commission will be headed by Mujaddadi to take the control of Kabul. The commission will plan formation of an interim government to be headed by Rabbani for further planning to restore democratic government in Afghanistan through formation of an assembly to elect the president.

Hezb-e-Wahdat

Hezb-e-Wahdat is the only Shia party of the Hazara people in Afghanistan. Hazarajat became part of Afghanistan during the rule of Abdur Rehman in 1893.[22] The Hezb-e-Wahdat party wanted to establish an Islamic state on the model of Ayatullah Khomeini. This party was not part of the group of the seven parties that received military aid from the CIA and the ISI. This was the only party which had women as its members and these women were engaged in social activities at the community level. The Hezb-e-Wahdat took control of Hazarajat in 1987 under the leadership of Abdul Ali Mazari.

The Hezb-e-Wahdat and Ittehad-i-Islami parties had a long history of faith differences that led to hostilities. Based on these differences, a heavy street fight took place in Kabul between the Iran-backed Hezb-e-Wahdat and the Saudi-backed Sayyaf's Ittehad-i-Islami. Hezb-e-Wahdat occupied the western part of Kabul. Masoud joined Sayyaf and attacked western Kabul in February 1993.[23] The logic that made sense for Masoud to join the Pushtun Sayyaf was that Masoud remembered the removal of the first Tajik ruler Bacha Saqao, or Habbibullah, in 1929, by the Pushtuns. Thus, for Masoud ignoring the Pushtuns was not an option. Therefore, opposing the Hazaras was considered appropriate. As a result of the joint efforts of this alliance, the Hezb-e-Wahdat had to retreat from Kabul.

Unnatural alliances based on self-interests rather than one common goal have been a common practice among the Afghan warlords. At one time, the

Tajik–Uzbek–Hazara–Ismail alliance was formed against the Taliban. This northern alliance gave a tough time to the Taliban who were confronted by Uzbek Abdul Malik from the west, Ismail from the south, Masoud's forces from the east, and the Hezb-e-Wahdat from the north and central Afghanistan. Later, Dostam aligned with Hekmatyar to oust Rabbani. Hekmatyar rocketed Kabul, killed 1,800 people, and made 300,000 people flee the country. Then Rabbani, Masoud, and Hekmatyar formed an alliance in order to form a broad-based government ignoring Uzbek Dostam and Hezb-e-Wahdat. Under this arrangement, Rabbani remained the president and Hekmatyar became the prime minister of Afghanistan. However, this alliance did not last very long as they were driven out by the Taliban.

In 1997, when the Salang Pass was blocked by the alliance of Dostam and Ismail, the Taliban wanted to take a detour via the Shibar Pass to reach the north. But this effort was resisted by Hezb-i-Wahdat.

After the withdrawal of the Russians from Afghanistan, Iran felt the need to strengthen the Shia community of Afghanistan as its Revolutionary Guards were doing in Pakistan and many other Sunni Muslim countries. Iran thus encouraged the eight Shiite groups who were living in Iran to unite under an umbrella of one party and that was the Hezb-e-Wahdat party. This party was supported by Iran but that support was not enough. Therefore, Hezb-e-Wahdat leader Karim Khalili visited India, Iran, Russia, and Turkey for more military aid. Due to the dwindling supply of military aid from Iran, the role of Hezb-i-Wahdat became marginal.

Iran continued the military supplies to Hezb-e-Wahdat to fight against the Taliban in Mazar-i-Sharif. The defeat of the Taliban in Mazar-i-Sharif by Hezb-e-Wahdat in May 1997 could not have been possible without the assistance of General Abdul Malik. Malik was the general of Dostam's army who had developed differences with Dostam because Dostam had killed Malik's brother General Rasul Pehlwan in June 1996. Dostam had invited General Rasul Pehlwan for a dinner and after the dinner, Dostam came out along to see him off. When General Pehlwan was going toward his vehicle, Dostam beckoned his guards to let him go. Dostam's guards attacked Pehlwan and killed him along with his fifteen guards. Because of this feud, General Malik finally defected to the Taliban and helped the Taliban enter the city of Mazar-i-Sharif and Dostam fled to Uzbekistan. The irony is that Dostam had to bribe his own soldiers at the border in dollars to let his cavalcade pass through the Oxus bridge.

General Malik had expected to have complete autonomy and control of Mazar-i-Sharif but the Taliban gave this position to Mullah Abdul Razak and offered Malik the position of deputy foreign minister in Kabul. Malik did not like this and again defected to Hezb-e-Wahdat and encouraged them to attack the Taliban. Hezb-e-Wahdat through his support sealed all the streets of Mazar-i-Sharif to thwart the Taliban's exit and 600[24] Taliban were butchered in the streets. The Taliban's bodies were cut into pieces, eyes gouged out from the

158 Land and people

sockets, noses cut and one member of Hezb-e-Wahdat was seen flaunting a bloodied knife in the air and saying this is what they did to the outsiders.[25] More than 2,000 Taliban were captured by Abdul Malik's forces and put in a truck container and taken to the Dash-te-Laili near Sheberghan in the Jowzjan Province and slaughtered and buried in mass graves. Of these about 1,350 prisoners died in the container itself due to suffocation and when their bodies were pulled out from the containers, they were decomposed owing to the heat and lack of oxygen. This was a cruel method of killing the prisoners. Dostam's forces identified at least twenty mass graves. In order to make good relations with the Taliban, Dostam offered them assistance in recovering the bodies of the Taliban and as a gesture of goodwill he released 200 Taliban prisoners.

The Taliban took it seriously that the May 1997 massacre of Mazar-i-Sharif was the result of Iranian military supplies to Hezb-e-Wahdat, which was aligned with Abdul Malik. Later in February 1998, a fight between the Hazaras of Hezb-e-Wahdat and the Uzbek forces broke out in Mazar-i-Sharif. Knowing that the internal fight among its opponents has weakened them, the Taliban again attacked Mazar and retook Mazar in August 1998. To take revenge for the killing of the Taliban in Mazar-i-Sharif by the Hazaras, the Taliban killed thousands of Hazaras along with eight diplomats of Iran and one Iranian journalist based in Mazar. In order to take revenge from Abdul Malik, the Taliban attacked Faryab Province, the base of General Abdul Malik. In 1998, the Taliban sealed 600 Uzbek villages[26] in Faryab Province in the west and pulled out the civilians from their houses and lined up and shot them all.

A big fight between the Taliban and Hezb-e-Wahdat took place in Bamian. The Taliban defeated Hezb-e-Wahdat and captured Bamian, but it was ruined and reduced to rubbles and the civilians left Bamian and reached Kabul for a living. In January 2001, when the Taliban defeated Hezb-e-Wahdat and captured Yakawlang of central Afghanistan, about one hundred civilians were killed, which became a cause of concern for the UN and Amnesty International.

Notes

1 Dupree, *An Historical Guide to Afghanistan*, p. 13.
2 Fletcher, *A Complete History of Afghanistan*, p. 11.
3 Ewans, *Afghanistan: A New History*, p. 5.
4 Asia Foundation, *Kabul: A Survey of the Afghan People*, pp. 181–182, Appendix I.
5 Ewans, *Afghanistan: A New History*, p. 5.
6 Ibid., p. 5.
7 Ibid.
8 Qisas means justice for murder, law of equality in Islam such as life for life, eye for eye, tooth for tooth, and wounds equal for equal.
9 Diyat (blood money) is the payment in the form of money if one faithful kills another faithful unlawfully.
10 Fletcher, *A Complete History of Afghanistan*, p. 16.
11 Ewans, *Afghanistan: A New History*, p. 7.
12 Ibid., p. 8.
13 Fletcher, *A Complete History of Afghanistan*, p. 18.

Land and people **159**

14 Ewans, *Afghanistan: A New History*, p. 8.
15 Fletcher, *A Complete History of Afghanistan*, p. 18.
16 Sing, *Drugs Production and Trafficking in Afghanistan*, p. 39.
17 Rashid, *Taliban, Militant Islam, Oil and Fundamentalism in Central Asia*, p. 86.
18 Marsden, *The Taliban, War and Religion in Afghanistan*, p. 31.
19 Rashid, *Taliban, Militant Islam, Oil and Fundamentalism in Central Asia*, p. 84.
20 Marsden, *The Taliban, War and Religion in Afghanistan*, p. 31.
21 Ibid., p. 31.
22 Rashid, *Taliban, Militant Islam, Oil and Fundamentalism in Central Asia*, p. 68.
23 Marsden, *The Taliban, War and Religion in Afghanistan*, p. 38.
24 Rashid, *Taliban, Militant Islam, Oil and Fundamentalism in Central Asia*, p. 58.
25 Gannon, *I Is for Infidel, J Is for Jihad, K Is for Kalashnikov*, p. 72.
26 Rashid, *Taliban, Militant Islam, Oil and Fundamentalism in Central Asia*, p. 70.

Bibliography

The Asia Foundation, Kabul, *Afghanistan in 2012: A Survey of the Afghan People*. Asia Foundation, Kabul, 2012.

Ewans, M., *Afghanistan: A New History*. Curzon Press, Richmond, 2001.

Fletcher, A., *A Complete History of Afghanistan*. Cornell University Press, New York, 1965.

Gannon, K., *I Is for Infidel, J Is for Jihad, K Is for Kalashnikov*. Public Affairs, a member of Perseus Group, USA, 2005.

Rashid, A., *Taliban, Militant Islam, Oil and Fundamentalism in Central Asia*. B. Tauris and Co Ltd, UK and Yale University Press, USA, 2000.

Marsden, P., *The Taliban, War and Religion in Afghanistan*. Zed Books, London, 2000.

10

THE GORGES CROSSED BY THE FOREIGN INVADERS

The foreign invaders entered Afghanistan from the north (Oxus River), the east (Khyber Pass and Paiwan Kotal Pass), the south (Bolan Pass), and the west (from Iran to Herat). These gorges are part of the geography and history of Afghanistan and are briefly discussed below for the information of those who have an interest in Afghanistan.

Khyber Pass

The Khyber Pass was first crossed by Cyrus the Great of the Achaemenid Empire in the 6th century BC. After defeating Darius, the king of Achaemenid Empire at the Battle of Gaugamela, Alexander the Great entered Afghanistan in 330 BC. Alexander's army crossed the Khyber Pass in 326 BC while he himself took another trajectory from Nuristan to Bajaur and Swat, and met with his army at Jhelum where he defeated the local Raja Poros and then went back. Later the Kushans and the Sassanians crossed the Khyber Pass during their control of the area.

At the advent of Islam in Central Asia, the first Muslim conqueror of Somnath, the great Sultan Mahmud of Ghaznavi (998–1030) used the Khyber Pass to carry the banner of Islam to India. Mahmud of Gazni launched seventeen expeditions, captured vast swathes of India, destroyed temple of Somnath and retured with a lot of booty. The Ghaznavids were vanquished by the Ghorids who crossed the Khyber Pass in 1191 and established Ghorid empire by defeating Prithviraj Chauhan.

Genghis Khan (1206–1227) crossed the Khyber Pass to chase Jamaluddin, who stood against the Mongols at Ghazni, as far as Indus. Genghis Khan captured Multan but ended his conquest at Multan in modern-day Pakistan in the summer of 1222[1] due to the hot weather and went back.

DOI: 10.4324/9781003198376-10

The Gorges crossed by the foreign invaders **161**

Temur (Tamerlane), born in Shakhrisabz (Kesh) near Samarkand in 1336, was a very brilliant young boy who was able to secure the governorship of Mongolistan from Tughlaq Temur Khan in 1361. After capturing, Samarkand, Bokhara, Balkh, and Herat, Temur added the entire of Afghanistan to his dominion. He crossed the Khyber Pass in September 1398 and reached Indus[2] for expansion of his empire as far as Delhi.

Mohammad Zahir-ud-din Babar, a descendant of both Genghis Khan and Temur and the founder of the Moghul dynasty took over Kabul in October 1504. Babar left Kabul for India in 1525 via the Khyber Pass and defeated the Lodi kings. Both Babar and Humayun used this route. In 1527, Babur defeated the Rajputs of Khanwa in the west of Agra and established the dynasty of the Great Moghuls. Babur died in Agra in 1530 and was buried in Kabul at Bagh-i-Babur.

In 1739, Nadir Shah of the Persian Safavid dynasty, who was also known as Nadir Quli Beg, invaded India using the Khyber Pass.

Ahmad Shah Abdali, later known as Ahmad Shah Durrani or Ahmad Shah Baba, the founder of modern Afghanistan (1747–1772), led his campaign against the Moghuls of Lahore and Delhi via the Khyber Pass (1747–1769). Ahmad Shah conquered Lahore and Delhi which became part of Afghanistan. The Khyber Pass was the most commonly used pass by the invaders who invaded the Indian subcontinent to extend their rule as far as Delhi.

General Samuel Browne[3] led a column of 15,000-strong British army through the Khyber Pass and on its way the British army attacked a fort at Ali Masjid. After repulsing the Afghans, the British army crossed the Torkham border and entered Jalalabad on December 20, 1879. This column of 15,000 men were sent in support of the British army that had already reached Kandahar via the Bolan Pass during the Second Anglo-Afghan War.

Bolan Pass

The Bolan Pass was first crossed by the Aryans (Indo-Iranian tribes) who came from Central Asia and occupied the region of Indus Valley in the 6th century BC. During 550–529 BC, Cyrus the Great,[4] king of the Persian Empire, crossed the Bolan Pass to reach Gandhara in the Indian subcontinent. Cyrus's successor Darius (521–485 BC) also crossed the Bolan Pass to strengthen the Persian Empire, also called the Achaemenid Empire.

The Bolan Pass is about 104 kilometers (65 miles) from Kandahar to Spin Baldak, Afghanistan's border with Pakistan. The British planned to dethrone Dost Mohammad who was under the influence of the then Soviet Union to install the British-favored puppet ruler Shah Shuja. The conspiracy plan that the British Governor General of India, Lord Auckland, prepared in the form of an Act in 1838 known as Shimla Manifesto was designed to establish Shah Shuja as the puppet ruler of Afghanistan by replacing Dost Mohammad. To implement this plan, the British planned an invasion of Afghanistan and thus its

162 The gorges crossed by the foreign invaders

20,000-strong Indian army under General Donald Stewart passed through the Bolan Pass and entered Kandahar.[5]

Paiwan Kotal Pass in the Kurram Valley

To reinforce the British army that crossed the Bolan Pass to enter Kandahar, the British arranged another column of 6,500 men under the command of General Roberts that passed through the Paiwan Kotal Pass in the Kurram Valley.[6] The Paiwan Kotal Pass connects Paktya Province of Afghanistan. This pass was the site of the battle in late November 1876, between the British forces led by General Roberts and the Afghan forces of Sher Ali Khan Sadozai, son of the former Amir, Dost Mohammad Khan. Roberts' forces defeated the Afghan forces and the British army entered Paktya Province for onward journey to Kabul.

Khawak Pass

To chase Bessos, the murderer of Darius, king of Achaemenid Empire, Alexander in 329 BC started from Bagram and crossed a very difficult mountainous 11,600[7] feet long Khawak Pass in the Hindu Kush range. Alexander passed through the Panjsher Valley, Andarab, and Baghlan and reached Kunduz[8] in seventeen days. Bessos's forces were surprised to see Alexander's forces behind them and deserted Bessos. Bessos fled toward the north and crossed the Oxus River to get refuge in modern-day Uzbekistan but was chased by Alexander and the local chief of Termez handed over Bessos to Alexander who later executed him.

Temur (Tamerlane) (1336–1405), who had entered Afghanistan through the Oxus River, had also crossed the Khawak Pass. Other than the invaders, the traveler from Morocco, Ibn-i-Battuta, also passed through this passage.

Salang Pass

The 2.7 kilometers or 1.7 miles long with an additional 4,972-meter gallery Salang Pass sits at a height of 3,400 m (11,200 ft.) in the Hindu Kush range (Figure 10.1). It connects Kabul and Charikar to Baghlan, Samangan, Khulm, Balkh, the Oxus River, and Termez in modern-day Uzbekistan. The 3-km tunnel of Salang Pass was constructed by the Soviets in 1964 as a part of a $100 million credit on the very soft terms of a thirty-year repayment period with a 2% interest rate. The all-weather road from Kabul to the Oxus River at the Russian border was strategically very important for the Soviets as a transit route. This route provided an alternative to the difficult mountainous Khawak Pass route. The Russian 40th Army after crossing the Oxus River on December 27, 1979, crossed the Salang Pass for their invasion of Afghanistan and this pass was the main source of their uninterrupted supplies. The unsuccessful Soviet 40th army left Afghanistan via the Salang Pass and the Oxus River on February 15, 1989, after getting its 28,000 soldiers killed by the Mujahidin. Like the British, the

FIGURE 10.1 Salang Pass.

Russians got a similar lesson by getting the "Russian soldiers in the burlap bags with their heads tied with the skin cut from their stomach".[9]

Oxus River

All the invaders from Central Asia entered Afghanistan through the Oxus River called the Bridge of Friendship forming the border between Afghanistan and Uzbekistan. Invaders who used the Oxus River, inter alia, include the Aryans, Genghis Khan, Temur (Tamerlane), Babar, and the former Soviet Union. However, Alexander the Great entered Afghanistan's Herat Province through Iran.

Notes

1. Weatherford, *Genghis Khan and the Making of the Modern World*, p. 125.
2. Marozzi, *Tamerlane, Sword of Islam, Conqueror of the World*, p. 263.
3. Fletcher, *A Complete History of Afghanistan*, p. 133; Ewans, *Afghanistan: A New History*, p. 62.
4. Omrani, *Afghanistan: A Companion and Guide*, p. 32.
5. Fletcher, *A Complete History of Afghanistan*, p. 133.
6. Ibid., 133.
7. Omrani, p. 38; Justin Marozzi cited 12,600 ft, p. 253; Romm, *The Campaigns of Alexander*, p. 144.
8. Omrani, *Afghanistan: A Companion and Guide*, p. 38.
9. Crile, *Charlie Wilson's War*, 2003.

Bibliography

Crile, G., *Charlie Wilson's War*. Grove Press, New York, NY: USA, 2003.

Dupree, N.H., *An Historical Guide to Afghanistan*. Afghan Tourist Organization, Publication Number 5, Jagra Ltd., Tokyo, Japan, 1970.

Ewans, M., *Afghanistan: A New History*. Curzon Press, Richmond, 2001.

Fletcher, A., *A Complete History of Afghanistan*. Cornell University Press, Ithaca, New York, 1965.

Marozzi, J., *Tamerlane: Sword of Islam, Conqueror of the World*. Harper Perennial, Hammersmith, London, UK, 2005.

Omrani, B., and M. Leeming, *Afghanistan: A Companion and Guide*. Odyssey Books and Guides, a division of Airphoto International Ltd., Sheung Wan, Hong Konng, 2007.

Romm, J., and R.B. Strassler, *The Campaigns of Alexander*. Anchor Books, a division of Random House, Inc., New York, 2010.

Weatherford, J., *Genghis Khan and the Making of the Modern World*. Crown Publishing Group of Random House, Inc., New York, 2004.

11

WEDDING RING TOSSED IN THE OXUS RIVER

Of the total population of 33 million in Afghanistan, 16.22 million or 48.3% are female. The female adult literacy rate (15 years and above) is 24.15% as compared to 51.99% for adult men. However, the life expectancy of women is 45.3 years as compared to 44.8 years for men. The majority of the women stay inside the house, and a small minority is engaged in public services such as education, health, and women's development. The female population is dominated by the male population with regard to economic and social decision-making. Although intermarriages between the Pushtun and the Tajik communities have been encouraged by the government in the past to integrate the society, still both these communities have taken their gloves off to take control of the power center as much as possible. The Pushtuns being in majority and the founder of Afghanistan have ruled the country throughout its history with the exception of two instances of Bacha-i-Saqao (son of the water carrier), whose real name was Habibullah, from the north of Kabul, who ruled just for nine months (January 27–October 15, 1929) and Burhanuddin Rabbani (1992–1996) ruled with the support of the US and the Mujahidin warlords.

Being a male-dominated society, the role of women is very limited. When it comes to polygamy, an Afghan can have more than one wife, all living in the same house subject to equal treatment of all of them. However, each wife is given one room and breaks bread together with the family in the same kitchen. Rivalry among the ruling elites stemmed from polygamy under which the ruler had many children from the different wives. These half-brothers had taken their gloves off against each other to have control of the government through conspiracies leading to fratricides or exile of the weakest competitor(s).

The Afghan women are very brave, let alone Malalai,[1] who had participated in the Battle of Maiwand against the British. Malalai carried the flag of Afghanistan and provided logistical support and treatment to the wounded Afghan soldiers.

DOI: 10.4324/9781003198376-11

The Afghan women were considered to be very dangerous by the foreign soldiers, as the ones who became wounded and remained in the plains, became victims of the knives and the stones of the Afghan women. This had happened to the British soldiers in the Battle of Maiwand and also to the Russian soldiers during the Russian occupation of Afghanistan. The literate women occupied key positions in the government as parliamentarians, professors, teachers, doctors, and social workers. However, majority of the women confront miserable conditions from their childhood to marriage and finally as housewives.

Marriage encapsulates very painful circumstances to be experienced by the women. The relatives and female friends in the boy's family search for a suitable bride. Once identified, the boy's family decides on sending a proposal. The process for the marriage starts with the proposal by a male. According to the practice, a boy's family sends a proposal to the girl's family; this practice is called Khawstgaari. This proposal is carried by two to three representatives of the boy to the girl's family. If the girl's family accepts the proposal, it is called in local languages Lafzgiri (acceptance of the proposal). The rural and illiterate families look for a girl who has talent in cooking, sewing or embroidery, is pious, humble, submissive, and cooperative to work and will be adaptable to the new family.[2] Then the next step is to make arrangements for the engagement which is called Namzadgi. After the Namzadgi, there is a small function arranged by the girl's family at a hotel or home called Sheernikhori (engagement feast).

When the marriage date is fixed, then a few functions start. The first one is Shab-e-Hina and the day next is the marriage ceremony called Arusi. Before Arusi, a condition is imposed by the family of the girl and that is, a certain amount of money called Walvar or Shirbaha (bride price) has to be paid by the bridegroom's family to the bride's family. The system of paying bride price is the root cause of the marriage problem that the Afghan society is facing today. Even though this system is un-Islamic, it is still very much prevalent in Afghanistan. The Walvar or Shirbaha is used for the arrangement of the dowry for the bride and is also used in the arrangement of the wedding meal for the whole village in rural areas or about a thousand people in an urban area.

After finalization of the terms and conditions of the marriage contract (Nikah-nama) between the two families, the marriage ceremony is celebrated on a fixed day. The marriage contract is respected as a sacred bond. It is executed by a religious cleric in the presence of witnesses and other older and respected people. The marriage ceremony takes place at the house of the bride in the village or at a hotel or wedding hall in urban areas. On the wedding day, the first and foremost function is Ainamassaf, which is the first meeting of the bride and the bridegroom at the mirror. The bride and the bridegroom are seated side by side attired in the Arusi dresses. The bridegroom is attired in a suit while the bride is attired in the flashing Arusi garment with a thin veil over her face. This is the first time for both of them to see each other as before the marriage they did not have this opportunity. Still they will not be directly seeing each other, but will see each other's faces through the mirror. The girls belonging to the bridegroom's family would encircle the raised platform where the bride and the bridegroom are seated. After the recitation of the Holy Quran, the bridegroom will offer a sweet to the bride who is very shy and dares to raise her shivering hands covered with henna and gold jewelry to receive the sweet. As soon as the bride receives the sweet, the girls around them start singing the traditional wedding songs praising the bride and the bridegroom.

However, nowadays in urban areas the boys and girls might have an opportunity to see each other before the marriage, but most marriages in Afghanistan are arranged by the parents of the ones to be married. After the completion of the wedding ceremony, the bride is taken in a marriage cavalcade marked with gunfire and led by a musical band to the bridegroom's house. On arrival at the bridegroom's house, the first function is to offer the bride a traditional sweet dish prepared for the occasion and after tasting the sweet she formally becomes a member of the family. The bride is seated at a prominent place surrounded by friends and relatives who offer her gifts and this is called the function of the Runomai (face showing). The next morning after the wedding day, the girl's family brings breakfast for twenty to twenty-five people and this is called Nashtai. After the third day of the marriage another feast is arranged to cement the ties between the two families, which is called Takhtijami.

Now to hark back to the status of the women in Afghanistan. The life of the new female entrant in the joint family is not a rosy one. In a joint family, all the married sons live together in a system that is managed by the elders. All the resources are pooled and the entire family breaks the bread from the same kitchen. The daughters-in-law and the children are at the command of the joint family's head, who plays the host to the old customs and traditions with which the new generations are not comfortable. The newly wed daughter-in-law is at the command of the powerful mother-in-law (khushoo) and is dictated by her in all matters. Her tyranny has become a proverb in the traditional joint family. According to the traditions in the rural areas, the wife is responsible for all the needs of her husband. If the husband and the wife are walking together, she will be walking behind her husband. She will not eat with her husband. She will eat when her husband is finished with his meal. In the urban areas, this tradition is gradually disappearing as the newly wed boys are opting for a separate residence away from the joint family. Although the joint family system offers economic security for all the family members, it comes at the cost of sacrificing personal independence.

If a boy is born in the family, the celebrations start with all the members of the village pulling up their rifles to visit the house where the boy is born. Everybody congratulates the family. On the seventh day of birth of the boy, the tradition of Sarkali (head shaving) and circumcision takes place. Two sheep or goats are slaughtered and distributed among the poor. According to the weight of the hairs of the shaved head of the boy, gold or silver's equivalent amount is given as alms to the poor. Big feasts are held. On the other hand, if a girl is born, the family does not receive any congratulations. The father of the girl is shattered as he needs a son to succeed him. He even feels humiliated as he has failed to produce

168 Wedding ring tossed in the Oxus River

a son. Similarly, the family receives greetings at the wedding of their son but does not get the same at the wedding of their daughter. Boys are preferred over girls because the boys provide a helping hand and serve as strength to the family which is needed in times of conflict with the other tribes.

The fallout of thirty years of a devastating war on the life of the people of Afghanistan is horrifying in that it has affected the fabric of their culture and socioeconomics. The people became poor and were buried under debt. The people settled their debt by raising cash using the Afghan girls. A daily newspaper, *The News*, dated May 16, 2007, published the story of an Afghan girl. According to the story, the twelve-year-old Shabana of Mazar-i-Sharif of Balkh Province of northern Afghanistan was coerced to marry a fifty-two-year-old farmer, Mohammad Asif, to settle her father's $600 gambling debt. Asif's and Shabana's fathers were friends and raised poppy and wheat crops together on a plot of land in Jawzjan Province. Asif went to Mazar-i-Sharif to meet his family. When he came back, he found that the entire harvest was lost in the gamble by Shabana's father. The payment due to Asif was $600. Asif knew that he was a poor farmer and will not be able to pay him the due sum. Consequently, Asif got married to the twelve-year-old Shabana as the settlement of the gambling debt. Shabana, who wanted to wear jeans, read books, novels, and newspapers, was taken out of school. She was very unhappy and angry. She said, her fifty-two-year-old husband was wild and had destroyed her hopes. She did not get along with her husband's first wife, who was forty-two years old.

The Express Tribune, dated August 6, 2016, reported a story where an Afghan bartered his six-year-old daughter for a goat. The father of six-year-old Gharibgul bartered his daughter for a goat, rice, oil, tea, and sugar for her to become the wife of fifty-five-year-old Syed Abdul Karim with the promise that he will not have sex with her until she was eighteen years old. The marriageable age for a girl in Afghanistan is sixteen years, while the same for a boy is eighteen. Both the alleged husband and the father of the girl have been arrested. Abdul Karim said that she was his wife, while the father reported that he had bartered his daughter in exchange for a goat in order to have one mouth less to feed as he was living in abject poverty. The illegal practice of exchanging girls in abject poverty to settle debts of opium farmers, or to settle disputes between the clans, remains pervasive throughout the country.

In Afghanistan, as in many Asian and African cultures, men pay the family of their wife-to-be an agreed sum, sometimes called the bride price, as well as the cost of the wedding which can also run in thousands of dollars – the average in Kabul was $4000. But this price varies from area to area and also person to person – say between $8000 and $14000. According to the Afghan Independent Human Rights Commission, about 57% of girls are married before the legal age of 16 years and between 60% and 80% of all the marriages are forced –without the consent or will of the girls which is required from the Islamic point of view. The women are kept so submissive that they are not supposed to talk loudly or argue with their husbands. Even in case of incompatibility, the women cannot ask for a divorce. If they do, they are likely to be killed by their parents. If a woman becomes widow, she cannot get remarried outside of the family of the husband. In case of being a widow, the woman will have to remarry any adult person available in the family of her husband. However, if a woman has become a widow with small children, she may not get remarried. Unlike women, a man can marry more than one without the consent of the first wife. The reason for this practice of polygamy is that the male cannot deny his parents' first arranged marriage. Therefore, the first wife is the choice of the parents of the boy and the second one is his own choice as a love marriage.

During the Russian invasion of Afghanistan, millions of Afghan families migrated to Pakistan, Iran, and other neighboring countries and some took asylum in European countries, the USA, Canada, and even Russia. Most of the families went to Russia where they stayed during the course of the war. When the war ended with the exit of the Red Army, many male members of the Afghan refugee families opted to stay in Russia to enjoy the lustful life they had become addicted to. Their female members, especially the wives, who hated the Russian culture opted to return back with their children. This return without their husbands compelled them to face a new challenge of their difficult, struggling life ahead.

One beautiful Tajik lady with deep-set eyes, Najiba, accompanied by her three children came back from Russia without her husband. She took a job with an educational institution to sustain her family. She started selling her jewelry to send her kids to school but kept the wedding ring on her finger. One day she was enjoying a fish dish with her colleagues at the kiosk at the embankment of the Oxus River. While chewing the fish, she paused for a while, looked at her left hand, lost in the train of thoughts inside her, and then pulled off her wedding ring from the finger and tossed it in the Oxus River. Surprisingly, one of her colleagues asked her why she did this. It was a golden ring and, most importantly, it was her wedding ring. She responded that this golden wedding ring did not do her any good and that it had lost its value to her. She said she had thrown her wedding ring in the Oxus River because the gold is good for the river, not for her. This was a miserable story of a female teacher who had returned to Afghanistan from Russia without her husband to accept a new challenge of her life. She survived and educated her kids by herself and now she feels pride.

Notes

1 Armstrong, *Veiled Threat: The Hidden Power of the Women of Afghanistan*, p. 49.
2 Doubleday, *Three Women of Herat*, p. 76.

Bibliography

Armstrong, S., *Veiled Threat: The Hidden Power of the Women of Afghanistan*. Four Walls Eight Windows, New York, 2002.
Doubleday, V., *Three Women of Herat*. Tauris Parke Paperbacks, New York, 2006.
Shakib, S., *Samira and Samir*. Arrow, London, UK, 2005.

12

THE CROSSING OF THE OXUS RIVER

On June 18, 2010, I and a friend of mine, Mr. Asif Rishi, left Kabul at 4 am for the Heratan border between Afghanistan and Uzbekistan. Our driver, Babrak left us at the gate of the border police office. We entered and got checked in with the Afghan passport control officer who took ten minutes to stamp our passport and entered our names in the exit register maintained in the Dari language. We left the passport control office and started walking toward the bridge over the Oxus River, also known as the Amu Darya, which runs all the way from the Pamir to the Aral Sea. We were very excited to cross the border bridge that was about 1.5–2 kilometers distance between the two checkposts, which we had to walk by rolling our suitcases.

When we entered Uzbekistan, we showed our passports to the first checking point, who looked at our passports and informed the next office that two foreigners were entering Uzbekistan as tourists. They asked us to continue walking until we reached the passport control office at the other end. It was a hot and humid day and we were drenched in sweat. We entered the passport control office. The passport control officers did not speak English, and we did not speak Uzebki or the Russian language either. We had to communicate with each other through signs and signals. The first customs officer looked at our passports, looked at our visa, and entered it into the computer and stamped it.

The next stage was the custom check, when the officer gave us two forms to fill in. The forms included information about the money we were taking along and any other items that we were carrying in. I entered $3,575 as the cash that I was carrying and one camera. The customs officers looked at our forms and stamped them and gave us one copy and he retained the other one. After that they passed our luggage through the detecting machine. After the machine check, the customs officer asked us to open the suitcases which we did. He pulled out everything and then asked us to put our stuff back in the boxes. We did that

DOI: 10.4324/9781003198376-12

The Crossing of the Oxus River **171**

and thought that it was over now. But it was not. He then beckoned me to a room. I followed him to the room. He closed the door and asked me to put everything on the table. I put out my purse and anything that I had in my pockets. He searched my body to make sure that I was not hiding anything. He pulled out the money from my wallet and started counting the currency notes. He wanted to verify that I had entered the right figure of $3,575 in the customs declaration form. He counted it and said that there are $150 bills which are extra. I told him, no, I have entered the right amount, please check it again. He had counted three to four times and said that there is a difference of $50. Actually, he was trying to show a difference that he wanted to keep with himself. I told him, no, it can't be, please check again, and I helped him in counting. And, finally, he got it right as $3,575 and then asked me to go forward.

When we crossed the border, we met an Uzbek driver, Fazil. He was a very crafty person and wanted to rip us off. He was speaking in broken English and asked us where we would like to go. We informed him that we were planning to go to Samarkand. He said that he could not take us to Samarkand. However, he could take us to downtown Termez, from where his friend could take us to Samarkand. He said, as you are good people, I can arrange a good driver for you who will take about $130 or the equivalent Som written as CYM 221,000. CYM, pronounced as Som, is the official currency of Uzbekistan. We asked Fazal that we needed to exchange our dollars into Uzbekistan's CYM. Fazal responded that he had a friend who dealt in money exchange and that he could get us a good exchange rate. He drove us downtown and stopped his taxi in the street and asked me to follow him. My friend was sick of his maneuvres and opted to stay in the car. I followed him and he took me to a house. I was scared to enter the house as I was expecting the money changer in a commercial office. I saw women walking inside the house and I stayed at the door. He asked me, come on, and follow me. I reluctantly followed Fazal. Inside the room there was a person sitting with his wife. I did not enter the room again as in Muslim society, no one can enter a house without permission as it is deemed an invasion of privacy. At the door, I gave $200 bills to Fazal and in return the person sitting inside the room gave Fazal CYM 340,000, which means an exchange rate of dollar equivalent to CYM1,700.

As we were doubtful of Fazal's handling of us, we asked him to take us to the market where we could get a vehicle for Samarkand. He informed us that no one other than his friend was willing to go to Samarkand. My friend who was sick of him lost his patience and asked him to leave us there and that we would take another taxi to the bus stand. He understood our seriousness and finally took us to the vehicle stand. There we negotiated with another driver who agreed to take us to Samarkand for CYM 100,000, equivalent to $54 for two persons. Samarkand was about 480 kilometers from Termez and it took us about six hours to reach Samarkand. We landed at Afrosyab hotel and checked in. As we have had our dinner on the way, we just unpacked and went to sleep because we were exhausted from a sixteen-hour road journey from Kabul to Samarkand.

172 The Crossing of the Oxus River

On June 19, we visited historical places like the tomb of Amir Temur, the conqueror of the world, Registan Square, Bibi Khanum mosque which were near to our hotel. Then we took a taxi to visit the tomb of Imam al-Bukhari, the writer of the Hadiths of the Holy Prophet, peace be upon him. The tomb of Imam al-Bukhari was outside the city with a sprawling garden area spread around it. Upon our arrival at Imam al-Bukhari's tomb, we prayed at the grave and took some photographs. The real grave was in the lower ground accessible through a door downstairs which was mostly locked and visitors seldom get a chance to visit the grave. Well, while we were standing there, an official delegation came, for whom the door was opened and I immediately beckoned my friend toward door downstairs. I immediately pulled off my shoes and ran down through the stairs leading to the door to the grave of Imam al-Bukhari and my friend followed me and the door was closed. We were inside, at the grave, in the company of the official delegation and the in-charge of the mosque led the prayer for the delegation. After visiting the tomb, we took a taxi and left for Tashkent, which was about 300 kilometers away and it took us three hours to cover this distance.

Tashkent looked like a European city with huge and tall buildings. The subway train extended its services throughout the city area. Dance clubs were common and most of them started their business at midnight. There were two types of women roaming in the market shopping for their families. Some women were having black hair, these were the Uzbeks. Some women with blond hair were the Russians who settled in Uzbekistan before its independence. Although they claimed themselves as Muslims, they were far away from Islamic traditions and culture. The society was still under the influence of Russian traditions and culture. There was one big museum that displayed information from the Temur era to the Moghal dynasty established by Zahiruddin Babar.

There was only one big mosque known as Hazrati Imam mosque, also known as Khast-Imam mosque. We entered the mosque and prayed two rakat namaz tahiatul-masjid (prayer). After this, we moved to the back of the mosque where there was a library with copies of the Holy Quran with translations in different languages, including the one in Urdu donated by the Pakistan embassy in Tashkent. Above all, at the center of the library, there was the original large Quran from which Hazrat Uthman, the third Muslim Caliph, recited. This was the oldest Quran in the world, more than thirteen hundred years old, placed on the Rahieel (book holder), which was placed inside a climate-controlled glass box. This Quran was organized in the form of a book in the city of Medina by Hazrat Uthman in 646. Hazrat Uthman was the son-in-law of the Holy Prophet Muhammad, peace be upon him. The Quran was written by hand without the superscripts. This Quran was used by Hazrat Uthman as his personal Quran. During the period of Hazrat Uthman, Islam spread from Morocco in the west to Afghanistan in the east and in the north as far as Armenia and Azerbaijan.

The librarian told us that the blood stains were not on the opened middle pages of the Quran as it stands now, but on the pages of Sura (chapter) Baqra that Hazrat Uthman was reciting at the time of his martyrdom in his house in Medina on June 17, 656. Uthman died at the age of eighty-two. After the martyrdom of Hazrat Uthman, Hazrat Ali took this Quran to Kufa in Iraq where it remained for several hundred years. In the 14th century, the Tatar, Amir Temur, during his conquests, brought this Quran from the Middle East and placed it in Nur Madrassa in Samarkand. It remained there for many years. Later it was transferred to Tashkent.

13

THE TRIO

The trio – Dr. Oval Myers, Dr. John Santas, and I – were engaged in the development efforts in Pakistan and Afghanistan for the last twenty years working as a coherent, dedicated, and motivated group. The group interlinked through the great esprit de corps of the common values of helping and enabling the downtrodden people of Afghanistan to earn their livelihood with respect, dignity, and religious freedom. The people of Afghanistan had suffered a lot during the wars with the Western invaders who considered the Afghans no more than a flock of sheep that they thought they could tame and herd. That was their mistake. History does not forget or miss any event but leaves behind the lessons to be learned. However, the adventurous part of the trip occurred on November 13, 2004, and became a signature point in our lives, as it was dreadful, painful, and uncomfortable.

It was a pleasant sunny morning of November 13, 2004, in Kabul when the three of us finished breakfast at the ASSA II guesthouse and packed our luggage for the 3 pm PIA flight from Kabul to Islamabad. In Islamabad, the group was scheduled to meet Mr. Peter Duffy, a USAID representative of Islamabad Mission, at a dinner meeting at Serena Hotel, Islamabad. After packing, having a leisurely day, the group engaged in a discussion of details of a project that it was seeking assistance from USAID Islamabad. During the course of the discussion, the group was leisurely sipping coffee, unaware of what was about to happen next.

At 9:30 am I received a sudden call from my wife who informed me that the PIA Kabul–Islamabad flight scheduled for November 13 has been cancelled due to Eid. Eid is an Islamic event celebrated after the completion of the holy month of Ramadhan. The Eid was expected to be in Pakistan the next day as per the moonsighting by the rueti-hilal committee of religious scholars, according to a normal sharia practice. When I finished the telephone call, I informed the group

DOI: 10.4324/9781003198376-13

The trio **175**

that I had disturbing bad news for them. They immediately put their coffee mugs back on the table and surprisingly asked what was happening. I became placid, cool, calm, and polite, as I was not just a member of the group, I was also their escort. As I informed them that the scheduled PIA flight from Kabul to Islamabad had been canceled due to Eid, they were astonished, nervous, and were speechless for a while as this news meant for them that today they could not reach Islamabad to attend the meeting with the USAID. Moreover, they would not be able to take their onward British Airlines flight the next morning at six for London and that their whole travel plan now stood nowhere.

To break the silence, I gazed in awe at them. What to do? I immediately said, let us talk about a plan B. Their eyes became wide open and were wondering what was going to happen. I suggested that in order to keep our travel plan intact we had no other alternative but to travel by road and this was not recommended for Americans to travel by road between Afghanistan and Pakistan. It needed for each of the trio to be intrepid and have trust in God, which we did. Trust in god is our faith and the intrepidity comes from the courage which is not inherited but has to be earned. The courage comes from self-confidence which is said to be the very father and mother of courage. And self-confidence comes after conquering the fear of failures and here the group's failure was that there was no alternative to get out of Kabul and reach Islamabad.

Their momentarily speechless condition made their mind to swim in the fear of the much heard and read tales about the Taliban's ambushes, kidnapping and killing of high-value targets such as Americans. There might be a train of thoughts running inside them. They might be thinking that this could well be the last journey of their life. They might be thinking of never seeing their families again. This was the fear that needed to be conquered in order to have the courage. Each member of the group morally and emotionally supported each other to acquire the courage. Oval and John became quiet for some moments and then reciprocated Hmmm. The group got courage by conquering fear to demonstrate itself as an intrepid esprit de corps. Oval agreed and John reluctantly seconded it.

Oval and John asked how it was going to happen. I informed the group that today is Eid in Afghanistan as Afghanistan's decision about which day to observe Eid on is based on Saudi Arabia's decision on this. Afghanistan does not follow the tradition of moonsighting per se but instead follows Saudi Arabia. Consequent upon an agreement among the three of us to travel by road, I called my friend Ahmad Shah who was celebrating Eid with his brother Babrak and family. I explained the whole situation to Ahmad Shah who immediately reacted and said, "Doctor Sahib, don't worry. I am coming with my brother Babrak who will drive us to Torkham border".

Babrak drove the car and Ahmad Shah escorted us. Normally, the Afghan people, like other Muslims, do not work on Eid day, but here they were expressing their loyalty and respect to me and my group. I thanked Ahmad Shah for his gesture and accepted his offer. I informed the group that Ahmad Shah and

176 The trio

Babrak had canceled their Eid celebrations and were coming to our place to drive us to the Torkham border. We immediately checked out of the ASSA II guesthouse and got ready for the SUV.

At 10:15 am, we left the ASSA II guesthouse for an unplanned, unexpected, and dangerous journey to the Torkham border. I prayed in Arabic for our safe journey according to our Islamic tradition, and I saw Oval's lips moving too, looks like he was also praying from the Bible for our safe journey. We crossed Ahmad Shah Masood Square near the American embassy and reached Kabul town square where the former communist leader Najibullah and his brother Shahpur were hanged by the Taliban in September 1996. From this square we turned left on the Kabul–Jalalabad road.

As we passed through the ISAF headquarters, the name of Dr. Brydon started floating in the minds of the petrified group. Dr. Brydon was part of the British Indian army about 150 years ago, when all the members of the army were slaughtered by the Afghans and he was the only survivor who reached Jalalabad without his horse, which too was dead. When Dr. Brydon asked the Afghans why he was not killed along with others, the Afghans told him that he was left alive so that he could go back and tell the world as to what Afghanistan is all about. Afghanistan, as David, successfully fought with the two Goliaths, the first was the British and the second was Russia.

To break the group's silence, I tried to engage the group that we are now on the Jalalabad road and now we are passing through the ISAF headquarters. Oval and John nodded. Oval was very fond of taking pictures while traveling. He pulled out his camera but by then we had passed the ISAF building. I asked Oval should we reverse, he said, no, go ahead. After that Oval kept his camera handy to capture the fields, crops, people, and the sites on the Jalalabad road. Being a soybean breeder by profession, Oval was very interested in taking pictures of the crops in the fields or when the farmers were working in the field. Whenever he saw such an opportunity, he would ask to stop the SUV and he would get out to capture the scene forgetting the fear of ambushes by the Taliban.

John, who was very patient, cooperative, and a good group traveler was not encouraging Oval to do that. John would ask, Qayyum, don't you think that we should continue our journey without interruption so that we are able to reach Torkham border before the sunset? I would nod yes and Oval would do the same. But Oval had interrupted the journey six or seven times and this made John nervous. John would change sides in his seat with tension. I was understanding John's concern but Oval was Oval and like any other breeder he would never miss taking a picture of any crop on the way. On an average, it used to take about six hours from Kabul to Torkham border on a crumbled road in 2004. On the way there were many checkposts where every vehicle was stopped, and so we were stopped many times. Each time Babrak expressed to the security people that he was carrying university professors and he got through as the Afghans respect people like professors and teachers.

Throughout our journey from Kabul to Jalalabad we did not stop other than for security checks. As we entered Jalalabad, I asked if anybody was feeling the call of nature. Everybody said no and kept on moving, as we were getting late. When we reached Torkham, the sun was setting and the border gates between Afghanistan and Pakistan were closed. Babrak stopped the vehicle on the Afghanistan side and we hurriedly took our luggage and jumped out of the vehicle to cross the border which we saw was closed.

When we reached the gate which was closed, our Pakistani driver Afzal Sher saw us from the Pakistani side of the border and requested the customs officials to open the gate. Afzal Sher had arrived in Torkhum from Peshawar well before our arrival and had made arrangements with the custom authorities about our arrival. The Pakistani custom officials opened the gate and five of us including John, Oval, Qayyum, Babrak, and Ahmadshah entered Pakistan. Babrak and Ahmad Shah did not have Pakistani visa but this was not a problem as Afghans were always entering and leaving Pakistan without showing any passport. This was a signature border between Afghanistan and Pakistan.

When we entered Pakistan, all the Pakistani custom officials and staff were sitting around a table alfresco which was decorated with samosas, pakoras, dates, and fruits and were ready to break the last fasting day of Ramadhan. They stood up to receive us. We shook hands and exchanged greetings. In the meantime, adhan, a call for prayer was announced from the mosque and everybody started breaking the fast and asked us to joint them and we did. We enjoyed a few pakoras. After breaking the fast one staff member took our passports and opened the custom office which was closed according to its regular working hours. He stamped our passports and gave us back. That was a special good gesture and honor for the Americans entering Pakistan.

It was past sunset and nobody can dare to travel at night on the Torkham–Peshawar road as it passes through tribal areas where kidnapping and killing is common at night. Interestingly, Ali Masjid falls on the way in the tribal area where the British and the Afghans fought their first war. The in-charge of the custom office arranged for an armed security guard to escort us from Torkham border to the Michni post, a post which was established by the then British Indian army. We jumped into our car along with the armed security guard and Babrak and Ahmad Shah took another private vehicle to reach Landi Kotal in Khyber Agency where their mother lived.

Our vehicle moved and hit the Torkham–Peshawar road and the travelers in the vehicle were filled with the fear of being kidnapped and/or killed and this fear made them quiet. We were in the danger zone now. While traveling in the Khyber Pass valley at night, there were a lot of gunfires and bonfire in the open places as this was the traditional way of celebrating the beginning of Eid, after sighting of the moon in the tribal areas. Still the group was quiet. When we reached the Michni post, the security guard was changed as we were still in the danger zone. The new guard accompanied us until we entered the settlement area in the vicinity of Peshawar. When we reached Peshawar, we stopped for a

178 The trio

quick bite at KFC on the University Road. We got our food for the road and reached the Islamabad Serena Hotel. As we were about to enter the gate of the hotel, our guest Peter Duffy was just leaving the hotel without a meeting with us. When we saw each other, we surprisingly exchanged greetings as Peter was not expecting us that late at night. After the greetings, we narrated the anecdote and Peter was stunned. Anyhow, we had a causerie for a few minutes about the development project of the Agriculture University, Peshawar, at the hotel's lobby. After that Peter left and we went to our rooms at the Serena Hotel. Thus ended the remarkable, frightening, and dreadful journey of the Afghanistan trio.

14

NAUROZ

Traditions have it that Nauroz was first celebrated during the Aryan period. It is not a religious event, rather it is a traditional and cultural event. The ancient Aryan people, the ancestors of the Achaemenids (from Cyrus' to Darius' period), celebrated Nauroz with different traditions such as wearing new dresses, playing sports, and preparing special foods. Since then Nauroz has been celebrated annually in Iran, Uzbekistan, Tajikistan, and Kazakhstan. Following that tradition, the Muslim kings of Afghanistan also continued celebrating Nauroz with different traditions. Sultan Hussain Baiqara introduced the celebration of Nauroz with the raising of the jhanda (religious banner) that flies for forty days and people from all over the country come to Mazar-i-Sharif to celebrate and touch the jhanda for blessings.

The Nauroz function is organized throughout Afghanistan with a major event at the tomb of Hazrat Ali, the fourth Caliph of Islam, at Mazar-i-Sharif. According to Afghan traditions, due to the threats of enemies, the body of Hazrat Ali was secretly brought to Mazar-i-Sharif from Najaf in Iraq where Ali was buried when murdered in AD 661. The Seljuk Sultan Sanjar constructed a tomb at the site which was later demolished by Genghis Khan. During the Temurid period in the 15th century, Sultan Hussain Baiqara rebuilt the shrine which stands as of today. Now the Afghans from all parts of Afghanistan visit Mazar-i-Sharif for the celebration of Nauroz. The first day of each solar year is celebrated as Nauroz (new day) – March 21 – in Afghanistan. Thus Nauroz is the beginning of the new year that falls at the start of spring.

The food eaten on this day includes seven meals (Haft Seen) or seven S (7-S). The Haft Seen (7-S) includes garlic, apple, spinach, sorb, vinegar, wild rye, and Samanak (sweet pudding – a kind of cream, made with germinated wheat (malt) mixed with flour). This meal is served to welcome the relatives at home. In addition to 7-S meals, Haft Mewa beverages, or seven-fruit beverages, are also added

DOI: 10.4324/9781003198376-14

180 Nauroz

to the meal. Haft Mewa fruit beverage includes green raisins, peanuts, almonds, pistachios, dry apricots, red raisins, and sorb. These fruits are mixed with water and sugar to prepare Haft Mewa beverages. Some families, in addition to Haft Seen and Heft Mewa beverage, also prepare other delicious dishes for visitors which include, inter alia, rice, spinach, chicken, sauces, salads, cookies (Kulchae Naurozi), and yogurts for lunch. Some families also cook the Samanak and while cooking the Samanak the women and girls sing a special song: "Samanak nazr-e-bahar ast, Samanak dar josh ma kapcha zanem, degran dar khawab ma dafcha zanim". This song is translated as "Samanak is a vow of the spring. We are stirring the boiling pot of the Samanak. Even if others are sleeping, we are playing the drum". The dish when cooked is placed with the 7-S meal and Heft Mewa beverage. A week before Nauroz, people clean their household effects such as carpets, sofas, curtains, etc. They wear new clothes and visit their relatives to wish each other Nauroz Tabrek Bashed (Nauroz greeting). The different kinds of dishes are served during the first, second, and third day of the new year.

Although Nauroz is celebrated in Kabul and other cities, the biggest function takes place at the Blue Mosque or Shrine of Hazrat Ali at Mazar-i-Sharif. After the Jhanda Bala (flag hoisting) ceremony, other sports are also held. In Mazar-i-Sharif, in the afternoon of the first day of Nauroz, a famous sport called Buzkashi (killing of goat) is organized in the plains. The other festivals that are celebrated by the Afghans are: Mela-e-Gul-e-Surkh or Red Tulip (red flower) celebrated in Mazar-i-Sharif and continues for forty days (mela is an outdoor picnic where men and women gather separately for the day in a park or the shrine gardens); Mela Arghawan (cercis festival) to enjoy cercis grown in the fields and deserts in northern Afghanistan including Parwan Province; Mela-Dehqan (farmer festival), which is another traditional festival celebrated on the first day of Nauroz in big cities to encourage the farmers to grow more food for their people and the country. Orange Blossom Festival is held in Nangarhar on April 13, in which poets read or sing their poems in the presence of the mandarins and the people. Baba festival in Kandahar, Mela-Sakhi in Kabul, Apple Blossom festival in Wardak, Pomegranate Blossom in Kandahar, and Sorb Blossom festival in Paktya are the other festivals held in different provinces of Afghanistan. All of these festivals fall in the first two weeks of the new year.

Naurozi traditions: In Afghanistan, it is a common tradition among the affianced families that the fiancé's family presents gifts (clothes, gold bracelet) and dishes including fried fish, jalebi (a kind of fried sweet), and dry fruits as Naurozi to the family of the fiancée on the special occasion of Nauroz or the first day of the solar year. This Naurozi costs from 30,000 to 100,000 Afghanis. Some engaged couples travel to Mazar-i-Sharif to celebrate the Mela-e-Gul-i-Surkh. Some engaged couples go for picnics to different parts of the country. But this tradition of Naurozi has created economic problems for young boys, especially those who are unemployed and are forced by the fiancée's family to present the Naurozi to them. Most religious scholars are against the practice of forced or even free presentation of the Naurozi, as it is not required in Islam.

15
THE OPIATES ECONOMY
OF AFGHANISTAN

Before the Russians invaded Afghanistan on December 27, 1979, opium production in Afghanistan was less than 200 tons per annum in 1978. The Afghans who are independent people revolted against the Russian occupation. The different Afghan groups organized themselves as the Mujahidin to fight the war that had been imposed on them. To equip themselves, they needed the indigenous resources to finance the war and the production of opium poppy was one such source that helped them to buy the arms and ammunition for the war. The opium poppy production was encouraged in the Pushtun areas of Helmond, Jalalabad, and minor pockets of north Afghanistan, Balkh and Badakhshan, and northwest Afghanistan, which were under the control of the Pushtun Mujahidin. During the war. the cultivation of poppy was neither a concern of the international community nor the United Nations as their focus was the humiliating exit of the Russians from Afghanistan.

The cultivation of poppy in Afghanistan continued after the war even during the Mujahidin's civil government. When the Taliban took control in 1996, the total area under poppy cultivation was 57,000[1] hectares with the opium production of 2,248[2] tons. The Taliban's only source of revenue was the taxes on opium export trade and this fetched as much as $3 billion in 1998. Unlike the warlords of Afghanistan, this money did not go into the Taliban's pockets but instead was spent on the salaries, food, uniforms of the soldiers, fighters, and the military equipment.[3] In July 2000, Mullah Omar issued a decree[4] banning poppy cultivation in Afghanistan, which became effective in poppy crop year 2001. The United Nations Drug Control Program (UNDCP) and the US government verified and confirmed that in 2001 there was no poppy crop cultivated. The U.S. Secretary of State in Bush administration, General Colin Powell, welcomed this ban through a statement issued in May 2001.[5] The ban on poppy cultivation led to the reduction of the area under poppy crop from

DOI: 10.4324/9781003198376-15

182 The opiates economy of Afghanistan

57,000 hectares to 8,000[6] hectares and the production of opium declined to the negligible level of 185[7] tons in 2001 when the Taliban were ousted by the US attack.

After the fall of the Taliban, Hamid Karzai was installed with the support of the US who, against the wishes of the US government, did not take any action against the cultivation of the poppy crop. Poppy cultivation became a lucrative business for corrupt warlords, drug leaders, and government officials who enjoyed complete protection from the government. When Karzai left the government in 2014, the area under poppy cultivation had increased from 8,000 hectares in 2001 to 224,000[8] hectares in 2014 and the production of opium increased during the same corresponding period from 185 tons to 6,400[9] tons representing the highest peak point in the history of Afghanistan. In 2017, the area under poppy cultivation increased to 328,000 hectares, which was the highest level ever achieved and production of opium was 9,000 tons. In 2018, the area under poppy cultivation declined, due to drought, to 263,000 hectares, which was 76% of the world's cultivation. The opium production in 2018 was 6,400 tons which accounted for 82% of the world opium production of 7,790.[10]

In 2015, during the sway of President Mohammad Ashraf Ghani, the area under poppy cultivation decreased to 183,000 hectares with the corresponding decline in opium production to the level of 3,300 tons. The yield of opium also decreased from 28.7 kilograms per hectare in 2014 to 18.3 kilograms per hectare in 2015 registering a decline of 36%. The decline in yield confirms that the decline in the area under poppy crop and the production of opium was due to climatic and security conditions. The possible reasons included bad weather, lack of water, poor density of the poppy plants, soil degradation, and, most importantly, the security situation prevailing in the different provinces. The areas that were classified as highly insecure were proved to be ideal for the cultivation of the poppy crop. These circumstances led the provinces in and out of the poppy club. For example, Balkh Province was poppy free in 2012 and resumed poppy cultivation in 2013. Again in 2014, it became poppy free and in 2015 it entered the club as a poppy grower. A similar trend was observed in the case of other provinces such as Faryab and Sar-i-Pul. The drug enforcement measures taken by the government at the governor levels to destroy the poppy crops were very negligible and amounted to 1–2% of the poppy cropped area.

Afghanistan's twenty provinces out of a total of thirty-four are engaged in poppy cultivation, which means 59% of the provinces are in the poppy and opium production business. These twenty provinces include Badakhshan, Baghlan, Kunar, Kapisa, Laghman, Kabul, Nangarhar, Balkh, Sari Pul, Faryab, Ghor, Day Kundi, Zabul, Uruzgan, Kandahar, Helmand, Badghis, Herat, Farah, and Nimroze. These provinces were part of all the six regions of Afghanistan, namely southern, western, eastern, northeastern, central, and northern regions. However, the major poppy cultivating regions are the southern, western, eastern, and northeastern. The central and northern regions are minor cultivating areas.

The southern region includes the five provinces, namely Helmand, Zabul, Kandahar, Daykundi, and Uruzgan. The largest cultivation area with 119,765 hectares under the poppy crop was the southern region, which accounted for 66% of the national cultivation of 183,000 hectares. Helmand Province alone with 86,443 hectares under the poppy crop accounted for 47% of the national cultivation in 2015. The major districts in Helmand Province that cultivate poppy are Nad Ali, Nehar-i-Saraj, Garmser, Regi-i-Khan Nishin, Musa Qala, Nawzad, Sangin Qala, Dishu, Nawa-i-Barakzary, and Baghran. The second largest province in the south was Kandahar with an area of 21,020 hectares under the poppy crop, cultivated in the districts of Maiwand, Zhire and Panjway. The cultivation of the poppy crop in Uruzgan Province was carried out in Tirin, Kot, Shahidi, Hassas, and Derawud districts. In Zabul Province, Tarank wa Jaldak, Kakar, and Mizan districts were the major cultivators. The two districts, Kajran and Mir Amor, in Daykundi Province were engaged in poppy cultivation.

The governors-led eradication of the poppy crop was just 2% of the southern region's total cultivated area. This region produced 1928 tons of opium during 2015, which was 58% of the national production. The yield in the southern region in 2015 was reported as 16.1 kilograms per hectare, which was below the national weighted average yield of 18.3 kilograms per hectare.

The second largest poppy cultivator was the western region which had 44,308 hectares under the poppy crop in 2015, which accounted for 24% of the national area. Three major producers in the western region were Farah, Badghis, and Nimroz provinces, which accounted for 96% of the western region's total cultivation. Farah Province, with 21,106 hectares of poppy cultivated in Bala Buluk, Bakwah, Khaki-Safed, Push-Rod, and Gulistan districts, was the largest grower. Badghis was the second largest province with 12,391 hectares of poppy grown in Pul-i-Hissar and Deh Salah districts. Nimroz Province with 8,805 hectares cultivated poppy crop in Kash-Rod district. The western region produced 721 tons of opium, which was 22% of the national production in 2015. The average yield in 2015 in the western region was 16.3 kilograms per hectare, which was slightly below the national average. Herat was a minor producer as its poppy activities were confined only in one district called Shindand. Shindand District was a Taliban-controlled highly insecure area governed by Mr. Lal Muhammad Omarzai as the district governor. Omarzai was a former Taliban commander, who now has been working with the NATO forces based at Shindand air base.

I and Roger Beck, while working on a USAID project in Afghanistan, visited the governor of Shindand district and for the first time met and saw eye to eye the Taliban commander, who now was discussing the development projects with the donors. He was now cooperating with NATO, specifically the Italian forces based in Herat. Mr. Bazed, who was working with the Americans at Shindand air base and comes of Iranian origin, facilitated our meeting with the governor. The governor welcomed us and said that the war had destroyed their irrigation infrastructure which was based mostly on the karezes (underground water

184 The opiates economy of Afghanistan

channels) and turned the land into barren. The farmers of this area grew the poppy crop to sustain themselves.

In order to engage the farmers into the licit crops, the rehabilitation of the karezes was essential and asked us for help in this effort. We offered to help with the caveat of the security concerns. The governor assured the security to our project. We had rehabilitated six canals and four karezes benefiting all the six buluks of Shindand District, namely Zerkoh, Qasaba, Poshteh, Koh, Zawal, and Koh-e-zoor. About 120,000 farmers in the forty villages increased the production capacity of their land. Buluk is a sub-administrative unit in the district. The governor wrote a letter of appreciation to us for assisting the Shindand farmers.

The eastern region was the third largest producer of opium with 12,242 hectares of land under the poppy crop in 2015. Nangarhar Province stands first with 10,016 hectares, Kunar Province stands second with 987 hectares followed by Laghman Province with 779 hectares and Kapisa Province 460 hectares. Nuristan Province did not cultivate poppy at all. The main contributing districts in Nangarhar Province include Khugiani, Charakar, Achin, Pachir-wagan, and Sherzad. In Kunar Province, Sarkhan, Watapoor, and Khas Kunar districts were the main growers of the poppy crop. Alingar and Dawlat Shah districts in Laghman Province were the main contributors. In Kapisa Province, Tagab District was the main producer of the poppy crop. The production of opium in the eastern region in 2015 was 446 tons, which was just 14% of the national production. However, the average yield of opium in the eastern region during 2015 was 36.5 kilograms per hectare, which was double the national average yield of 18.3 kilograms per hectare.

The northeastern, northern, and central regions are the minor producers of opium as their combined area of 6,252 hectares under the poppy crop was just 3% of the national area and their combined production of 246 tons was just 7% of the national production of opium in Afghanistan in 2015.

The milky sap extracted by lancinating the rounded capsule of the poppy plant becomes reddish brown raw opium when dried. The raw opium contains morphine. Morphine is manufactured from opium which can further be used for manufacturing heroin through the use of a precursor known as the acetic anhydride. In addition to the manufacture of heroin, the acetic anhydride is used as a precursor in the manufacture of aspirin, synthetic fibers, production of brake fluid oil, dyes, and explosives.

The acetic anhydride has been placed on the international control list under the United Nations Convention against Illicit Traffic in Narcotic Drugs and Psychotropic Substances, 1988. The annual global production of acetic anhydride is 1.5 million tons. The licit international trade is carried out by 118 importing and 45 exporting countries. The major exporters of acetic anhydride in Asia are China and Japan, in North America, the United States and Mexico, and in Europe, Belgium and Netherland.

In Asia, during the period 2007–2012, large annual imports of acetic anhydride, were reported by China (24,400 tons) the Republic of Korea (10,600

The opiates economy of Afghanistan **185**

tons), Singapore (6,700 tons), Thailand (4,000 tons), and India (12,000 tons). Turkey in southeastern Europe annually imported 1,400 tons. During the same period, Saudi Arabia annually exported 17,100 tons, UAE 15,800 tons, China 11,400, Japan 8,200, Singapore 5,700, and India 2,300 tons per year. These are the countries which could be the source of smuggling of acetic anhydride.

According to the United Nations COMTRADE data, and the International Narcotics Control Board, international licit trade wholesale prices of acetic anhydride have been reported in the range of $1–$1.5 per liter. However, during the period 2007–2012, some countries reported prices below $5 per liter, while on the Balkan route the prices were reported a little higher than $5 per liter.

Afghanistan neither produces nor officially imports acetic anhydride but is successfully processing opium and morphine into manufacturing heroin. Heroin cannot be manufactured without using the reagent acetic anhydride. This means the entire requirement of acetic anhydride in Afghanistan is met through smuggling. Neighboring Pakistan does not produce acetic anhydride and its imports have declined from 149 kilograms in 2008 to 14 kilograms in 2012. This amount is not sufficient for Afghanistan. Similarly, Iran and other countries bordering Afghanistan are not importing acetic anhydride with the exception of China. However, Uzbekistan, China, India, and Iran manufacture acetic anhydride that could be a source of smuggling for the Afghan smugglers. Clearly, the Afghan smugglers are exploiting the Pakistan and Iran routes as transit countries as was evidenced by the seizures of acetic anhydride in Pakistan and Iran. The seizures in Afghanistan were 22% of the world seizure of 131,000 liters. This shows the significantly sizeable amounts of acetic anhydride being smuggled into Afghanistan.

The large amounts of seizures of acetic anhydride in Europe, Eastern Europe, East and West Asia put pressure on the movement of acetic anhydride which resulted in an increase in its prices in the Afghanistan market. The prices in the Afghan market ranged between $300 and $430 per liter as compared to the world prices of $1 to $1.50 per liter. This shows a lucrative business for the acetic anhydride smugglers. According to Afghan narcotics officials, the Afghan smuggler whose consignment was seized in 2008 admitted that the seized consignment of 12 tons of acetic anhydride was procured from the Republic of Korea at the price of $4 per liter that was to be sold in Jalalabad market at the price of $300 per liter. The increase in the price of acetic anhydride was not of any concern for the operators of the clandestine opium processing laboratories in Afghanistan as the same price was translated into the price of the final product of heroin.

The prices of acetic anhydride depended on the sources of supply. During the 2007–2012 period, acetic anhydride's prices from the illicit sources in Asia were $4–$6 per liter in the Republic of Korea, $12 per liter in China, $60 per liter in India, and between $200 and $300 per liter in Pakistan, and from the illicit sources in Europe were $25 per liter in Slovakia, $100 per liter in Bulgaria, and between $200 and $225 in Turkey.

In addition to the sources of illicit supply, the prices also depended on the quality of acetic anhydride. There were about six levels to the quality that were

186 The opiates economy of Afghanistan

being marketed in Afghanistan. For A level quality, the prices ranged between $76 per liter and $247 per liter in 2013, which increased to $514 per liter in 2017.[11] In August 2017, the price of 'A' type quality of acetic anhydride used in the manufacture of high-quality heroin for exports to Europe and other developed countries was further increased to $700 per liter. The level of quality was related to the origin of the supplier and the general perception about its product. The major seizure of acetic anhydride had occurred in the eastern province of Nangarhar, in the southern provinces of Kandahar and Helmand, in the western provinces of Farah, Herat, and Nimroz, and in small amounts in the provinces of Baghlan and Badakhshan in the north and northeast. These seizures point to the existence of clandestine factories in these areas.

According to the UNODC study,[12] the overall market size of acetic anhydride in 2002 was $5 million which increased to about $166 million in 2009. The amount of smuggled acetic anhydride was around 475 tons and the average price was $350 per liter. For manufacturing 1 kilogram of heroin, 1.5 liters of acetic anhydride is needed. According to the UNODC's 2013 survey,[13] the average manufacturing of heroin had been estimated at 420 tons in 2013. For 420 tons of heroin production, 630 tons of acetic anhydride were needed, which at a price of $221 per liter amounted to about $139 million. Being an important factor in production of heroin, its share in the total cost of production of heroin was 2% in 2002.[14] In 2010, the total cost of production of heroin was $1600 per kilogram. This total cost was made up of 73% as the cost of opium, and 26% as the cost of acetic anhydride and 1% was attributed to other minor chemical inputs such as activated carbon (charcoal), ammonium chloride, calcium oxide, hydrochloride acid, etc. However, in 2013, due to the decline in the prices of acetic anhydride, its share in total cost of production of heroin declined to 20%.[15]

Initially, Afghanistan exported opium in its raw form and the heroin from this opium was manufactured outside Afghanistan before reaching the Europeans, Indian subcontinent, and the Middle East customers. Now, according to Christina Oguz of the UNODC, complex laboratories have been set up in the mountains of Afghanistan and about 90% of the opium is being processed in these laboratories to add value in the form of heroin and morphine before it reaches its increasing numbers of domestic and foreign customers. Oguz estimated that the annual income from the drug trade was more than $3 billion which was used for insurgency.[16] The transportation and trade of drugs were in the hands of the Pushtun Mujahidin. Therefore, the opium's movement to the bordering countries was no problem. One major trading partner was Kurdistan Working Party (PKK), a separatist party established in the Kurdish area of Turkey. This organization had its own processing factories and trading arrangements to reach out to international consumers.[17]

The production of opium and its conversion into morphine and heroin has been increasing every year with the exception of 2001 when poppy cultivation was banned by the Taliban in Afghanistan. However, there were fluctuations in the area under poppy crop and production due to variations in the yield as a result of the bad weather and drought. In 2004, poppy was cultivated in all the thirty-four provinces of Afghanistan with 131,000 hectares, which was 67% of the world cultivation of poppy (195,940 ha) and the production of 4,200 metric tons amounted to 87% of the world's production.[18] Heroin manufacturing in Afghanistan in 2004 was 500 metric tons, which was about 89% of the world's production. The farm gate value of the opium produced during 2004 was about $600 million.[19] This trend continued with slight variations in the cultivation of poppy crops and the production of opium.

In 2014, the cultivation of the poppy crop in Afghanistan reached the record level of 224,000 hectares, which was 72% of the world cultivation, the highest level that was ever recorded in the history of world poppy cultivation. The production of opium in Afghanistan in 2014 was 6,400 tons, the amount that was never produced by any single largest producer of the world, accounting alone for 85% of the world's production. The heroin production in Afghanistan in 2014 was 410 tons, which accounted for 78% of the world's production. So, Afghanistan has continuously occupied a unique position as the trendsetter for the world for poppy cultivation and production of heroin. The farm gate value of the opium production in 2014 reached $0.85 billion which contributed to 4% of the GDP of Afghanistan.[20] In 2018, the opiate economy of Afghanistan ranged between 6% and 11% of its GDP of $19,630 million.[21]

Afghanistan, the single largest producer of heroin, uniquely determines the size of the world's opium/heroin market. Its product reaches out to all regions of the world, East, North, South, West, and Central Africa; North America; Central Asia; East and Southeast Asia; Southwest Asia; South Asia; Near and Middle East; Eastern Europe; Southeastern Europe; Western and Central Europe; and Oceania.

The trafficking of Afghanistan opiates is carried out through various variable international routes. The main routes thus far used are the Balkan route, the northern route, and the southern route, and transit routes have been created, such as through Africa, for onward reaching out to the other destinations in Asia and Europe. The mechanism for trafficking and adopting of specific route is dependent upon the strength of the law enforcement and seizures carried out in the recipient countries.

The Balkan route through Iran and Turkey reaches out to Southeastern, Western, and Central Europe. The strengthening of law enforcement by Iran, Turkey, Armenia, and Georgia resulted in big seizures that compelled the smugglers to divert their trafficking of heroin to new trajectories on the Pakistan and Iran coasts in the south. In addition to Iran, Turkey also reported to have seized the sea containers coming from Iraq. Likewise, the supply of Afghanistan's opiates to Western and Central Europe via Iran and Turkey has declined due to the strict law enforcement measures taken by those countries as well as a fall in the demand for heroin.

The northern route leads through the Central Asian states to the Russian Federation for onward transit toward Europe. In the north, Tajikistan,

188 The opiates economy of Afghanistan

Uzbekistan, Turkmenistan, Kazakhstan, Kirgizstan, and the Russian Federation are the transit countries for Afghanistan opiates to Europe. Shipments along its north route have decreased.

The southern route originates from Pakistan and Iran and leads southward to Asia, Europe via the African countries. The Afghan opiates destined southward use Pakistan as a transit country.[22] Pakistan has a long porous border of 2,430 kilometers with Afghanistan and a long coastal area along the Indian Ocean that provides an opportunity for smuggling the Afghan opiates southward. Pakistan's Anti-Narcotics Force seized almost 1.2 tons of heroin at sea ports in 2013. The other transit countries are India, Kazakhstan, Kirgizstan, Netherlands. Tajikistan, Turkey, and the United Arab Emirates (UAE). The southern routes that were identified through the seizures of the big containers in Belgium and the Netherlands originating from Pakistan, Mozambique, and Iran were: Pakistan–Belgium–the Netherlands route; Mozambique–Belgium–the Netherlands route; and Iran–UAE–the Netherlands route. The seizures in Belgium and the Netherlands reflect that these two countries have become the transit countries for Afghan opiates to the UK and other European countries through heavy goods vehicles and ferries. The routes originating from Pakistan are under law enforcement targets. Pakistan is the only country that was reported with the largest number of the seizures. Most of the small shipments are carried out by road, rail, and air, but the largest shipments are through the sea.

The southern route has been a big channel for the Afghan opiates destined to East and Southeast Asia, where Myanmar, because of its limited supply, was unable to meet the demand of the area. Therefore, Afghanistan opiates targeted and captured the East and South Asian market to meet their demand. Myanmar has been the main supplier of heroin to China, but at the same time Afghanistan opiates also entered the Chinese market as Myanmar's supply was not sufficient.

The sea shipments of heroin via the Indian Ocean from Pakistan and Iran reach out to Europe either directly or through the conduit of East and West Africa. The smugglers' vessels have been reported moving in the Indian Ocean and the Red Sea carrying Afghanistan opiates to Kenya and the United Republic of Tanzania.[23] The shipment originated from Iran, of 377 kilograms and 33,200 liters of liquid heroin, that was destined for Mombasa and Kenya, was seized in Kenya. Another large shipment of 1,032 kilograms originated from Pakistan[24] was seized in Tanzania. This shipment was being smuggled into Tanzania by Dhowl shipping vessels that operated in the Indian Ocean. Some seizures were also reported in Nigeria (25 kg) in West Africa of shipments that were destined for Western and Central Europe and North America. The Indian Ocean is being monitored by the Combined Maritime Forces, a multinational naval partnership that operates in the international waters; the Forces had captured 2,200 kilograms of heroin in the Indian Ocean in 2014. These seizures reflect that Africa has become a very important transit route for the Afghan opiates destined for Europe and North America. Also, being a hub for Afghanistan opiates bound for

Europe and North America, the local consumption of heroin has also increased in Africa.

Afghan opiates trafficked through the southern route, via the African transit countries, have been seized in a number of European countries including Austria, Belgium, the Czech Republic, Denmark, Finland, France, Germany, Greece, Ireland, Italy, Lithuania, the Netherlands, Portugal, Serbia, Slovenia. Spain, Sweden, Switzerland, Ukraine, and the United Kingdom. Strict law enforcement in the European countries has restricted heroin supply via Balkan and the northern routes. On the other hand, weak law enforcement on the southern route[25] has encouraged the diversion of drug trafficking from the Balkan and northern routes to the southern routes which is a vast route by land, air, and the sea. The northern route across the Indian Ocean for shipment of heroin to East and Southern Africa for onward transit to Europe has become more common for trafficking of the Afghan opiates.[26]

Heroin in the United States is mainly supplied by the Latin American countries such as Colombia and Mexico. However, a small seizure of the Afghan opiates in the United States reflects that Afghanistan is also competing with Colombia and Mexico to capture the heroin market in the US. However, 90% of Canada's demand[27] of heroin is being satisfied by the heroin supplied from Afghanistan.

Elimination of the drug problem is a very serious issue for the world as it is taking many lives on account of drug-related deaths. To solve the drug problem of the world necessitates solving the problem of the Afghan opiates, which amount to around 90% of the world's production. No such concerted efforts from the international communities have been made so far. In 1979 when Russia invaded Afghanistan, its opium production was less than 200 tons. Then during the war and thereafter in the post-Taliban era, the production of opium skyrocketed to 6,400 tons, of which 410 tons of heroin were manufactured during 2014. The illicit trafficking of the Afghan opiates has affected all the regions of the world from Asia to Africa, Europe, and North America. Still, the world has failed to find a silver bullet solution to the drug menace.

The US Drug Enforcement Administration (DEA) made a serious effort to convince the top-level leadership of the country about the seriousness of the drug issue. President Hamid Karzai made a political statement that he was against the drug trade.[28] However, during the course of his two terms of presidency, Karzai did not do much about drug eradication. Based on its experience in Colombia, the DEA proposed the aerial eradication of poppy crops by using glyphosate herbicides which is a weed killer.[29]

Karzai rejected the proposal of aerial eradication of poppy crop, fearing a strong backlash from the poppy growers, drug traffickers, and drug lords that could destabilize his government. Karzai suggested the ground-based eradication of the poppy crop, knowing it would go nowhere. The plan of forced aerial eradication was not even endorsed by the US Army deployed in Afghanistan. Likewise, the British Army and other allies in Afghanistan were against this plan.

190 The opiates economy of Afghanistan

The British and Swedish governments even put words in the mouth of Karzai to reject the US plan of aerial eradication. Which he did.

Interestingly, the Taliban had banned the cultivation of the poppy crop in 2000, and in 2001 there was no cultivation of opium poppy in Afghanistan. This was confirmed by the UNODC and the United States. The United Nations Drug Control Program (UNDCP) had reached an agreement[30] with the Taliban in October 1997 for the eradication of opium poppy. The Taliban promised that they would eradicate the cultivation of opium poppy if the international donors provided money for alternative development of the poppy-growing areas by focusing on the introduction of alternative cash crops, rehabilitation of the irrigation infrastructure, devising income-generating schemes, and maintenance of law and order. The UNDCP asked for $25 million from the international community but failed to raise that money and this opportunity passed by.

Thomas Schweich, a counter-narcotics official of the DEA, alleged that many influential people were involved in the drug trade.[31] Finally, the DEA had to live with the ground-based eradication which remained highly ineffective due to the backlash from the poppy growers and their corrupt partners and hardly 1% of the poppy crop was eradicated. In 2014, the cultivation of poppy crops reached the world record of 224,000 hectares in the twenty provinces of Afghanistan. In 2018, the cultivation of the poppy crop reached the level of 263,000 hectares.

In 2014,[32] the production of opium was 6,400 tons with a weighted national average of 28.7 kilograms per hectare. The farm gate value of the opium production was about $0.85 billion, and 46% of this amount equivalent to $391 million was earned by the farmers of Helmand Province alone. The potential gross value of opium in 2014 was $2.84 billion, which was 13.4% of Afghanistan's GDP of $21.2 billion the same year. Of this gross value of the opium, $0.16 billion were spent on the smuggling of acetic anhydride into Afghanistan, the only input that is used to convert morphine into heroin. The net value of opium production after subtracting the cost of acetic anhydride was $2.68 billion, which was 12.6% of the GDP. The value of the opiates added by the traffickers, processors of morphine, and heroin and exporters was estimated to be about $1.81 billion in 2014, which increased to $28 billion 2018 through value added by onward trafficking to European consumer markets through the Balkan routes. The value added by the European countries was more than the GDP of Afghanistan. In 2018, the income of the poppy growers was $604 million which was lower than the 2014 level of $853 million.[33] This was due to a decrease in farm gate price of dry opium from $133 per kilogram in 2014 to $94 per kilogram in 2018 and a decrease in yield due to drought.

The farmers' gross income from opium poppy was $3,800[34] per hectare as compared to $1,000 per hectare from the wheat crop in the irrigated area. The ratio between the gross income from poppy and that from wheat was about 4:1. The production cost of opium was $860 per hectare in 2014, while during the same period the cost of wheat production was $456 per hectare. The net per hectare income from poppy was $2940 as compared to $544 from wheat.

The viewpoint of the Afghan government under President Karzai, the US and the British forces, and other international communities engaged in Afghanistan in the post-Russian era was that there was no other choice for the farming community but to grow poppy for their survival. Interestingly, according to the *Afghanistan Opium Survey 2014: Socio-economic Analysis*, women were also interviewed to get their viewpoint on poppy cultivation. The women gave interesting reasons for endorsing poppy cultivation in Afghanistan. The women are reported to have been engaged in the weeding, lancing, extraction of oil from the poppy seeds, preparation of opium gum for sale, and preparation of tea from parts of the poppy plants.

The women respondents[35] from Badakhshan Province in the northeast reported that "we grow poppy because we had poppy seeds. We did not have seeds of other crops nor did we have money to buy those seeds". Another response was that "all the residents of our village grow poppy, that's why we grow poppy". With regard to the decision-making process, the women replied that, "when our men ask us what to grow on their land, we suggest them to grow poppy". On the use of the income, one respondent said that "I have full authority to spend money for our daily needs". One woman gave the stunning response, "my daughter was crying all the time, so I gave her little opium, then she sleeps and I can help my husband in the cultivation of poppy". Other respondents from the same province reported that "in the past we have used the opium capsule for the chest congestion or the respiratory problems of the children and now our men do not let us use the opium capsule because our men say that the continued use of the opium capsule will make them addicted". This shows that they now have awareness of the harmful effects of the drugs.

The respondents from Faryab Province reported that "some women cultivate separate poppy fields for buying the clothes and the jewelries". Some of the respondents said "the cultivation of the poppy is good and has many benefits. It rescues us from the poverty and also there is no need to send our men abroad for work. After the harvest, our men give us money that we spend on the clothes, the jewelries and other needs". With regard to the decision-making process, women responded "our men make the decision to cultivate the opium poppy and we just help them with the weeding and the gum collecting activities".

Poor economic conditions, lack of employment opportunities and devastation of the irrigation infrastructure made the Afghans' living conditions miserable. This led them to seek opportunity for their survival in the cultivation of the poppy crop. The food crops previously grown by the farmers were substituted by the cultivation of poppy because the rate of return on the opium poppy crop was four times higher than that on wheat, the main staple food crop.

192 The opiates economy of Afghanistan

Now, there are 936,000 drug users in Afghanistan.[36] This accounts for 8% of the adult population aged 15–64 years. This is twice the world average. Majority of the addicts are in the central region with 288,000 drug users, followed by the northern region with 204,000 drug users, the southern region with 128,000, the western region 114,000, the eastern region with 107,000, and 95,000 drug users in the northeastern region. During the war with Russia, many Afghan families migrated to Pakistan and Iran as refugees. In Iran, the Afghan refugees were confined to the refugee camps, where they suffered hardships, tension, and pressure for survival. About 40% of the drug users started taking drugs in those refugee camps in Iran under duress. The Afghan refugees in Pakistan, on the contrary, in addition to the refugee camps, were allowed to live anywhere in Pakistan to earn their livelihood. Therefore, the inclination to drug taking in Pakistan's refugee camps was somewhere between 4% and 9%.

There are about 1 million men, women, young male and female, and minor children who are drug users in Afghanistan. More than 50% of the drug users reported that they give opium to their children. About 10% of the drug users were able to get treatment for drugs, while still 700,000 drug users are unable to have access to treatment. This is causing a serious problem for the families, the communities, and the country as a whole.

The menace of drug addiction is rapidly intensifying in Afghanistan. The number of opium users in 2005 was 150,000, which increased to 230,000 in 2009 representing an increase of 53% over a period of just four years. There were 50,000 heroin users in 2005 and this number increased to 120,000 in 2009, registering an increase of 140%. Similarly, the number of users of other opiates reached the level of 360,000 in 2009. This alarming increase in drug use in Afghanistan is creating a lot of social and health problems as well as an increase in crimes and loss of productive assets. Those who inject drugs, or trade sex for drugs, are becoming victims of HIV and other blood-borne diseases.

The men and young males use opium, heroin, and hashish. The young women also use opium, cannabis (hashish), and heroin. The women used opium and painkillers. The children use opium, painkillers, and hashish. The women drug users are the widows and the divorcees. Forty percent of the women drug addicts reported that they started opium use in Iran and 4% in Pakistan. Thirty percent of the drug addicts used heroin, out of which 2% were women. About 630,000 adults (15–64 years old) used hashish and 40% of the women drug addicts used hashish. The financing of the drugs by drug users was through borrowing from family or friends, selling assets, begging, theft, and other crimes. The daily cost for heroin was $2.2, opium $1.6, and other opiates $1.5. The annual cost of drug use in Afghanistan is about $300 million.

How the drug users get addicted is explained by twenty-four-year-old Mohammad Bashir, who was deported from Iran. Bashir said, "I was a good tailor and used to work hard to earn my livelihood. I was so overburdened that I thought that I should use some pain killer to get some relief. I used to either smoke or eat opium. Now I do not know how to get out of this misery".

The London-based Senlis Council,[37] an international drug policy think tank, had asked the Afghan government to implement an opium licensing system for the production of morphine and codeine, the two medicines made from opium. The group suggested that the shortage of painkillers was due to the shortage of opium supply for the manufacturing of these medicines. The group further suggested that until some alternative development takes place, opium licensing was the best solution for overcoming the shortage of painkiller medicines. This policy confused the farmers who were being exhorted to give up cultivation of the poppy crop for the legal crops. The lawmakers in the country's upper house of the parliament discussed this conflicting policy in May 2006. According to a statement by the ministry of narcotics, the lawmakers asked the think-tank group to leave the country immediately as it had only helped the drug traffickers, the enemies of Afghanistan.

In early years of the occupation, the US and its coalition partners ordered forced eradication of the poppy crops. This did not happen in spite of the wasting of hundreds of millions of dollars. During the Obama administration, the policy of forced eradication was abandoned as it did not help the farmers and produced unintended consequences by increasing the number of recruits for insurgency. Now twenty out of the thirty-four provinces are engaged in opium poppy cultivation and these production areas are highly insecure. The eradication of the opium poppy crops by the respective governors of the provinces did not yield sufficient results as it was just around 2% of the total cultivation. The eradication is done either through tractors or through manual uprooting or untimely cutting of the opium poppy crop.

Countries like Afghanistan that grow opium poppy are characterized with the conditions of (1) reduction in growth of the licit economy; (2) increased growth in the illicit economy of poppy production; (3) weak rule of law; (4) increased crimes and violence; and (5) decreased investment in the licit economy leading to poverty and unemployment. In order to reverse the trend of these characteristics, the eradication of poppy cultivation becomes essential. There are two ways that have been used elsewhere for such eradication. These are: (1) forced eradication of opium poppy cultivation by the respective governments; and (2) initiation of alternative development and alternative livelihood programs focused on the need of the opium poppy cultivators.

As forced eradication of opium poppy cultivation has not been successful in Afghanistan, the situation therefore demands that the alternative development and alternative livelihood programs be designed and pursued through the participation of the targeted communities. The success of such alternative development and alternative livelihood programs depends on the improvement of

FIGURE 15.1 Poppy Crop in Afghanistan.

living conditions of the rural communities. Both the alternative development and alternative livelihood programs must, inter alia, focus on: (1) significant and prioritized interventions regarding income-generating activities that not only improve the living conditions of the rural communities through an increase in income and employment, but also build confidence of the communities that would also foster a positive change in their behavior; (2) development of a marketing system through value chain development of the agricultural products and rehabilitation of the infrastructure to provide proper access to the markets; (3) direct participation of the targeted communities in implementation of the interventions; (4) rehabilitation of the productive assets such as improvement of water and irrigation system; (5) protection of the environment through pro-environment measures that ensure that the interventions do not have any negative impact on the environment. This would involve the strengthening of the natural resource base through forestry and watershed management programs. Last but not the least, it would require training of the people through capacity building to enhance their skills and knowledge to become productive assets for their communities and the country as a whole. This scheme would require a long-term vision and financial commitment from international donors.

Notes

1 UNODC, *Afghanistan Opium Survey*, 2015.
2 Ibid.
3 Rashid, *Taliban, Militant Islam, Oil and Fundamentalism in Central Asia*, p. 124.
4 Marsden, *The Taliban, War and Religion in Afghanistan*, p. 144.
5 Ibid., p. 150.
6 UNODC, *Afghanistan Opium Survey*, 2015.
7 UNODC, *World Drug Report*, 2014, p. 117.

8 UNODC, *Afghanistan Opium Survey*, 2015.
9 Ibid.
10 UNODC, *World Drug Report*, 2018.
11 UNODC, *AOTP Update*, 2018.
12 UNODC, *The Opium Economy in Afghanistan: An International Problem*, 2003.
13 UNODC, *Afghanistan Opium Survey*, 2013.
14 UNODC, *The Opium Economy in Afghanistan: An International Problem*, 2003, p. 139.
15 UNODC, *Afghanistan Opium Survey*, 2013.
16 UNODC, *The News Islamabad*, June 26, 2007.
17 Ewans, *Afghanistan: A New History*, pp. 192–193.
18 UNODC, *World Drug Report*, 2005, pp. 39, 41.
19 UNODC, *World Drug Report*, 2005, vol. I and vol. II.
20 UNODC, *Afghanistan Opium Survey*, 2015.
21 UNODC, *Afghanistan Opium Survey*, 2018.
22 UNODC, *World Drug Report*, 2015, p. 39.
23 UNODC, *Transnational Organized Crime in Eastern Africa: A Threat Assessment*, September 2013, p. 23.
24 UNODC, *Afghan Opiates Trafficking through the Southern Route*, 2015.
25 Ibid.
26 US Drug Enforcement Administration (DEA), *Drug Trafficking from Southwest Asia, Drug Intelligence Report*, August 1994.
27 UNODC, *World Drug Report* 2015.
28 Schweich, "Is Afghanistan a Narco State?", 2008.
29 Ibid.
30 Rashid, *Taliban, Militant Islam, Oil and Fundamentalism in Central Asia*, p. 123.
31 Schweich, "Is Afghanistan a Narco State?"
32 UNODC, *Afghanistan Opium Survey*, 2014 and 2015; *World Drug Report*, 2014 and 2015.
33 UNODC, *Afghanistan Opium Survey*, 2018.
34 UNODC, *Afghanistan Opium Survey*, 2014, Socio-economic analysis, p. 17.
35 Ibid.
36 UNODC, *Drug Use in Afghanistan: 2009 Survey*.
37 Rutberg, *Building a New Afghanistan*, p. 192.

Bibliography

Ewans, M., *Afghanistan: A New History*. Curzon Press, Richmond, 2001.

Marsden, P., *The Taliban, War and Religion in Afghanistan*. Vanguard Books, Lahore, 2002.

Rashid, A., *Taliban, Militant Islam, Oil and Fundamentalism in Central Asia*. Yale University Press, USA and I.B. Tauris& Co. Ltd., UK, 2000.

Rotberg, R.I., *Building a New Afghanistan*. World Peace Foundation, Cambridge, MA, 2007.

Schweich, T., "Is Afghanistan a Narco State?", *The New York Times Magazine*, July 27, 2008.

Singh, D.G., *Drugs Production and Trafficking in Afghanistan*. Pentagon Press, New Delhi, 2007.

The News, June 26, 2007, daily newspaper of Pakistan.

United States Drug Enforcement Administration (DEA), *Drug Trafficking from Southwest Asia*. Drug Intelligence Report, August, 1994.

UNODC, *The Opium Economy in Afghanistan: An International Problem*. Vienna, 2003.

UNODC (United Nations Office for Drugs and Crime), *World Drug Report 2005*, Vol. I and Vol. II. United Nations, New York, 2005.

UNODC, *Drug Use in Afghanistan 2009 Survey*, Executive Summary, 2009.

UNODC, *World Drug Report*. United Nations, New York, 2014.

UNODC, *World Drug Report*. United Nations, New York, 2015.

UNODC, Islamic Republic of Afghanistan, Ministry of Counter Narcotics, *Afghanistan Opium Survey*, 2018.

UNODC, *World Drug Report*. United Nations, New York, 2019.

UNODC, *Transnational Organized Crime in Eastern Africa: A Threat Assessment*. Vienna, September, 2013.

UNODC, *Afghan Opiates Trafficking through the Southern Route*. Vienna, 2015.

UNODC, *The Afghan Opium Trade and Africa - A Baseline Assessment*. 2016.

United Nations International Drug Control Programme, Vienna, *Recommended Methods for Testing Opium, Morphine and Heroin*. Manual for use by National Drug Testing Laboratories, 1998.

UNODC, Islamic Republic of Afghanistan, Ministry of Counter Narcotics, *Afghanistan Opium Survey*, 2013.

UNODC, Islamic Republic of Afghanistan, Ministry of Counter Narcotics, *Afghanistan Opium Survey*, 2014.

UNODC, Islamic Republic of Afghanistan, Ministry of Counter Narcotics, *Afghanistan Opium Poppy Survey*, 2014, Socio-economic Analysis.

UNODC, Islamic Republic of Afghanistan, Ministry of Counter Narcotics, *Afghanistan Opium Survey 2015, Cultivation and Production*, 2015.

UNODC, Islamic Republic of Afghanistan, Ministry of Counter Narcotics, *Afghanistan Opium Survey 2015*, Socio-economic Analysis, March, 2016.

UNODC, *AOTP Update, Acetic Anhydride in the Context of Afghanistan Heroin*, Vol. I, 2018.

INDEX

Abdullah bin Hudhafa (carried a letter from Holy Prophet to King Khusro Perwez) 12–13
Acetic anhydride:
  Used as precursor in manufacturing of heroin 184
  Prices of 185, 186
  Smuggling of 185, 190
Achaemenid Empire 5, 160–162, 179
Afghanistan 1, 5, 6, 10–11, 27, 29, 30–31, 40–43, 47, 52–53, 56, 59, 64–67, 69–75, 77, 79–85, 87–97, 99–105, 108–115, 125–126, 128, 133, 139–142, 145, 147–150, 153–155, 157–158, 165, 168, 169, 176, 180–183, 187, 189, 190, 193
  Durrani (Abdali) Dynasty 69–71, 147, 155; Communist regime 118, 119, 122, 124, 132, 133, 138, 152, 156, 176; Amir Dost Mohammad 56, 77, 78, 80–85, 88, 89, 93, 96, 108, 138, 161–162; Amir Shah Shuja 80, 81, 82, 83, 85, 87, 88, 161; Macnaghten, Sir William, British envoy 80–85; Amir Abdur Rahman 89, 92, 93, 94, 95, 96, 97, 99, 103, 112, 151; First Anglo Afghan war 88; Second Anglo Afghan war 90, 161; Third Anglo Afghan War 100; Independence of Afghanistan 90, 92, 99, 101
Akesinos (*see* Chenab River)
Alexander the Great 1–10, 29, 53, 58–60, 149, 151, 160–163

Alexandria (Egypt) 4
Alexandria-Eschate (Samarkand) 6
Amir Temur (Tamerlane) 43, 51–64, 89, 161–163, 172–173, 179
Amu River (*see* Oxus River)
Anatolia 2, 60, 62
Ankara 2, 62, 106, 138
Anushirwan, King of Persia 11, 28
Ardsheer son of Babak, King of Persia 11
Ardsheer son of Sheeruya, King of Persia 12, 14
Aristotle 2
Armenia 11, 18, 27–28, 30, 46–47, 57–58, 172, 187
Asia Minor 2, 10–11, 62
Astis, the governor of Charsada 6
Azarmidokht (daughter of King Khusro Perwez) 12
Azerbaijan 11, 18, 27, 28, 30, 41, 46, 58, 172

Babur (Mohammad Zahir-ud-din) 64–65, 73, 161
Babylon 1, 4, 5, 10, 15, 19, 22
Bactria (*see* Balkh)
Baghdad 4, 13, 15, 17, 46, 56, 58, 61–62
Baghlan 10, 128, 138, 147, 149, 150, 152, 156, 162, 182, 186
Bagram Fort 5, 122, 126, 162
Bahadur Shah Zafar, last Mughal Emperor 67
Bajaur 6, 115, 160
Balkh 1, 5, 6, 10–11, 29, 42, 43, 52–53, 59, 66, 72, 82, 147, 150, 154, 161–162, 168, 181–182

198 Index

Baluchistan 9, 11
Bamian 5, 11, 42, 43, 72, 83, 87, 125, 138, 150, 158
Barikot 6
Barsine, (daughter of King Darius captured by Alexander) 3, 9
Battle of Anbar 15, 17
Battle of Gaugamela 4–5, 160
Battle of Granicus 2
Battle of Issus (Iskenderun) 2–3
Battle of Jalaula 20–21
Battle of Kazima (also known as Battle of Chains) 13–14
Battle of Qadisiyya 17–19, 26
Battle of Ullais (also called Battle of Blood River) 14
Battle of Walaja 14
Bessos (general of Darius' army) 1, 5, 6, 162
Bolan Pass 1, 81, 145–146, 155, 160–162
Borandokht (daughter of King Khusro Perwez) 12
Buddhism 10, 11, 42, 150
Bukhara 11, 30, 43
Bulgaria 2, 62, 185
Byblos (Jubail) 3
Byzantium 2

Canakkale port (Turkey) 2
Charikar (Parwan province of Afghanistan) 6, 84, 87, 92, 162
Charsada (Pakistan) 6
Chenab River 7–8, 59, 71
China 10, 31, 39–41, 43, 46–49, 56, 63, 127, 129–130, 140, 145–146, 148, 184–185, 188
Constantinople (*see* Byzantium)
Ctesiphon (Iraq) 11–15, 17–22
Cyrus, King 1, 9, 160–161, 179

Damascus 3, 46, 56, 60–61
Damghan (Iran) 5
Dardanelles Strait (also called Hellespont Strait) 2
Darius I 1, 5
Darius III (also Darius) 1–6, 9, 160–162, 179

Edirne (city in Turkey) 2
Egypt 1, 3, 4, 11, 46, 48, 56, 60–61, 105–106, 110, 120, 126, 130, 149, 152, 154, 156
Euphrates River 1, 3–4, 13–18, 21

Farghana 11

Gandhara 1, 10, 30, 161
Gaza 3–4, 61

Genghis Khan
Kid as Temujin 34–39
Became and ruled as Genghis Khan 38–47, 49–51, 54–55, 58, 60, 64, 150, 160–163, 179
Ghazni 1, 30, 31, 43, 64, 67, 82, 84, 87, 91, 93, 103, 150, 155, 160
Ghorband Valley 5
Granicus river 2
Greece (Greek) 2, 3, 189
Gulf of Aqaba 4
Gulf of Suez 4, 105

Hellespont Strait (*see* Dardanelles Strait)
Hephaiston (Greek army general) 6
Hephthalites (or White Huns) 11
Herat 1, 5, 11, 29, 42–43, 54–56, 60, 63–64, 69–70, 72–78, 81–82, 88–90, 92–93, 103, 110, 115, 117, 122, 124–126, 132, 137, 138, 140, 145, 147–148, 151, 154–155, 160–161, 163, 182–183, 186
Hindu Kush 5–6, 11, 58, 64, 72, 88, 111, 145, 148, 162
Hormuzan (Persian military general) 19, 21–25, 27
Hydaspes River, *see* Jhelum River
Hyderabad (Pakistan) 9

Indian Caucasus, (*see* Hindu Kush)
Indus River 6–7, 29–30, 43, 46, 59, 88, 145
Indus valley 1, 161
Iran 1, 5, 8–11, 30, 65, 70, 105–106, 112, 114, 117, 119–120, 126, 129, 133, 135–137, 139–140, 145–146, 148, 152, 155–158, 160–163, 169, 179, 185, 187, 188, 192
Iraq 1, 4, 11, 13, 15–17, 21–22, 26–27, 29, 60, 112, 120, 132, 141, 143, 152, 173, 179, 187
Istanbul (*see* Byzantium)

Jhelum River 7, 8, 31, 59, 160

Kabul 5, 10, 30, 59, 64, 65, 69–72, 74–78, 81–87, 89, 91–92, 95–97, 99, 101–115, 117–120, 122, 124–126, 130, 132–133, 135–145, 149–150, 152–158, 161–162, 165, 168, 170–171, 174–177, 180, 182
Kandahar 1, 5, 10, 56, 64–66, 69–70, 72, 74–77, 81–82, 86–93, 96, 100, 103, 107–109, 113, 115–116, 118, 126, 129, 136–138, 142–143, 145 155–156, 161–162, 180, 182–183, 186
Kapisa 5, 10, 152, 182, 184

Index   **199**

Khalid bin al-Walid (Arab warrior) 13, 14, 15, 18
Khawak Pass 5, 59, 162
Khiva 1, 31, 90, 102–103
Khurasan 11–12, 18, 27, 29, 30
Khusro Perwez, king of Persia 11–13
Khyber Pass 6, 76–77, 81–82, 86–87, 90, 95, 100, 160–161, 177
Kirman 8, 9, 11, 21, 29, 30, 69
Kunar Valley 6, 124, 125, 126, 137, 141, 182, 184
Kunduz 5, 11, 52, 128, 136, 143, 147, 152, 162
Kushan Dynasty 10, 11
Khuzistan 11, 22, 23, 25, 27, 30

Lahore 30, 31, 60, 65, 66, 71, 72, 73, 81, 161
Lakhm Dynasty 13
Lapis lazuli 1

Makran 9, 11, 27, 29, 30
Merv 1, 29, 43
Macedonians.1, 2, 3, 4, 5, 6, 7, 8, 9
Memphis (Egypt) 4
Mesopotamia 1, 4
Multan 8, 30, 31, 43, 58, 59, 71, 160
Mundigak (trade center of Lapis Lazuli) 1

Nile River 4
Nishapur (Iran) 29, 42, 43, 72

Oxus River 5, 10, 11, 29, 30, 42, 51, 52, 59, 60, 92, 126, 145, 160, 162, 163, 169, 170

Paiwan Kotal Pass 146, 160, 162
Pakistan 1, 6–11, 27, 29–31, 40–41, 43, 58, 60, 65, 89, 95, 114–117, 120, 126–130, 132–133, 135–140, 142–143, 145–147, 152–157, 160–161, 169, 172, 174–175, 177, 185, 187–188, 192
Palestine 1, 3, 60, 130, 146
Panjshir Valley 5
Parthians 4, 10, 11
Parwan (Afghanistan) 6, 83, 84, 92, 147, 150, 152, 180
Pasargadae (Persian capital built by Cyrus the Great) 9
Persepolis Capital city of Darius) 5, 9, 11, 12, 29
Peshawar 1, 10, 31, 43, 71–73, 75–77, 80, 88–90, 97, 104, 107, 109, 116, 120, 128, 129, 132, 148, 156, 177–178
Persian Gulf 4, 22, 43, 89, 127

Philip-II (King of Macedonia and father of Alexander) 1
Poros (Ruler of the kingdom between Jhelum and Chenab rivers) 7, 8, 160
Port Said (in Sena Peninsula) 4
Princess Shahr Bano (daughter of last Sassanid king, Yazdjurd) 21
Prophet Daniel (died in Susa, Iran) 25
Ptolemy (General in Alexander's army) 7

Ravi River 8, 59
Rhoxane (Alexander marries Rhoxane, the daughter of Oxyartes) 6, 9, 10
Roman Empire 2, 105

Samanid Dynasty 30
Sakas 10
Salahuddin Ayubi (ruler of Egypt) 60
Salang Pass 126, 128, 130, 132, 138, 150, 157, 162
Salman Farsi (a Persian and companion of the Holy Prophet) 20
Samarkand 6, 11, 30, 41, 43, 51, 52, 54, 56, 57, 58, 59, 60, 63, 64, 70, 161, 171, 173
Sassanid Dynasty 11
Sehwan Sharif (Sind, Pakistan) 9
Shiraz (Iran) 5, 9, 29, 57, 60
Sidon port 3
Silk Road 10, 30
Sind (Pakistan) 8, 9, 27, 29, 30, 60, 65, 72, 75, 77, 102
Sistan (Iran) 1, 5, 9, 10, 11, 30, 52, 145
Sultan Mahmud Ghaznavi 30, 56, 87, 146, 160
Surkh Kotal 10
Susa (Iran) 5, 9, 23, 24, 25
Swat Valley (Pakistan) 6
Syr Darya 6
Syria 1, 3, 4, 11, 18, 46, 60, 61, 62, 96, 97, 146

Takht-e-Jamshid (*see* Persepolis)
Tashkent 52, 57–58, 89–90, 92, 103, 138, 172–173
Taxila (Pakistan) 6–7
Tehran (Iran) 11, 28, 133, 140
Tigris River 1, 4, 13, 17, 21
Turkey 1, 2, 4, 42, 46–47, 49, 62, 97, 99, 101, 103, 105–106, 112, 138, 157, 185–188
Turkmenistan 1, 11, 29, 138–140, 145–146, 151, 188
Tyre port 3

200 Index

Ude Gram, (lower Swat valley, Pakistan) 6
Uzbekistan 1, 5, 6, 30, 41, 42, 52, 57, 58, 59, 126, 138, 139, 140, 145, 146, 150, 155, 157, 162, 163, 170, 171, 172, 179, 185, 188

Yazdjurd bin Shahryar (last Sassanid king who lost his empire to Muslims) 21, 12, 17, 18, 21, 23, 29
Yemen 11, 13
Yueh-Chi 10

Printed in the United States
by Baker & Taylor Publisher Services